D1314390

INTRODUCTION TO PROFESSIONAL FOOD SERVICE

written for

The Culinary Institute of America

by

CWO James P. Coffman USN (Ret).
Instructor, Culinary Institute

Eighth Printing

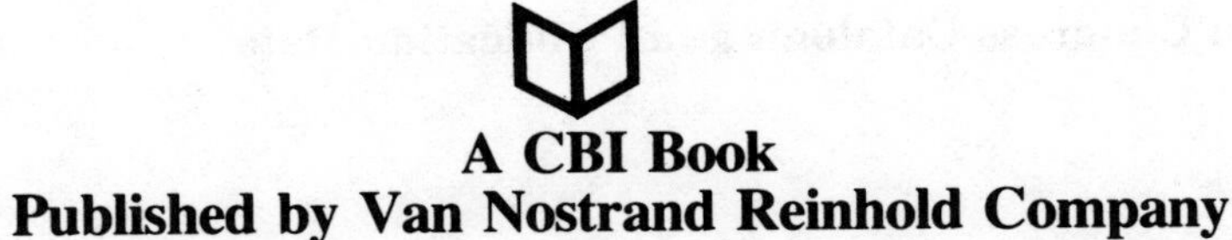

A CBI Book
Published by Van Nostrand Reinhold Company

A CBI Book
(CBI is an imprint of Van Nostrand Reinhold Company Inc.)

Library of Congress Catalog Card Number
ISBN 0-8436-2056-0

Printed in the United States of America

Published by Van Nostrand Reinhold Company Inc.
135 West 50th Street
New York, New York 10020

Van Nostrand Reinhold Company Limited
Molly Millars Lane
Wokingham, Berkshire RG11 2PY, England

Van Nostrand Reinhold
480 La Trobe Street
Melbourne, Victoria 3000, Australia

Macmillan of Canada
Division of Gage Publishing Limited
164 Commander Boulevard
Agincourt, Ontario M1S 3C7, Canada

16 15 14 13 12 11 10 9 8

Library of Congress Cataloging in Publication Data

To my wife MIRIAM

For Her

Patience - While I was working

Encouragement - when I was tired

Help - in correcting and typing practically every page

Understanding - of the many hours of necessary work at home

FOREWORD

There are few professions as important to society or as elevated culturally as the Food Service Profession. The vital importance of food to health and life and the major social significance of dining, and especially public dining, reflect two reasons for the pre-eminence of the food service profession. In addition, if there is proper preparation and service and knowledgeable appreciation, the product and contribution of the food service profession can be one of the most enjoyable of human activities. And this enjoyment can be at the highest aesthetic and cultural level.

But to achieve this status, the Food Service Industry must operate at the highest professional level - which means the most thorough training - and the training must not be merely routine with respect to repetitive tasks, but must achieve real understanding of all aspects of the profession. We Americans admire "know-how", but "know-what" and "know-why" are just as important as know-how if we are to achieve the highest professional standards.

Jacob Rosenthal
Director,
Culinary Institute of America

OPPORTUNITIES IN THE EXPANDING FOOD SERVICE/LODGING MARKET

A comprehensive picture of the size and importance of the food service/lodging industry and the career opportunities it offers was developed in an impressive 1970 survey presented at the National Restaurant Association's 1970 Manpower Conference.

The study emphasizes the importance of this industry to the national economy as it calls attention to the vast number of persons who work in the various kinds of food service/lodging operations.

Nearly 3.4 million people work in food service outlets. This estimate includes active owners--those who work 15 hours or more weekly; the average establishment has nine workers.

Based on annual growth rates of the food service industry, it is estimated that by 1975 the demand for employees will approach four million. In the next decade, the food service industry will require approximately 250,000 additional employees per year. Seventy percent of these new workers are needed to replace those who leave the industry. The remainder are required to fill newly created jobs due to increased demand for meals.

Institutions require more workers per establishment than do public eating places. Colleges and hospitals use more workers than other types of food service operations. Colleges on the average hire 75 persons while hopsitals need 36 persons in their food service operations.

In 1969 women made up about 56 percent of all those employed by public eating and drinking establishments. Part-time personnel formed a sizeable segment--4 out of 10 employees work less than 39 hours per week.

Projected data indicate that food service is available in more than 367,000 establishments throughout the country. Public eating places account for 93 percent of the total number of establishments. States with the largest number of public eating and drinking places are California, New York, Pennsylvania, Illinois, Texas, Ohio, New Jersey, Wisconsin, Michigan and Florida.

The food service industry may have more total outlets and workers than any other single kind of business in the U.S.A. In addition, the food service industry may also have more individual consumer transactions for there are 100 million transactions daily in the nation's food service establishments.

A joint survey of the International Foodservice Manufacturers Assn. and the U.S. Dept. of Agriculture determined that separate eating places alone account for 55 million or over half the total number of transactions. In determining the total number of transactions, directors of the study defined transactions according to this rule: If the same customer was served four times in a single day, he would be counted as four transactions.

The average establishment has 276 such transactions daily. However, institutions have an average of 684 while public eating places have 247. Colleges and hospitals have the largest number of daily transactions, averaging 2636 and 1031 respectively.

In 1969 total sales for public eating and drinking places were $26 billion. Additional food service industry sales were accounted for by other types of establishments serving food away from home including the military services, colleges, elementary and secondary schools, hospitals, drug stores, etc. It requires more than 34 billion pounds of food to satisfy the American public's eating out appetite. Food service equipment purchases total over $700 million annually. This steadily expanding industry is currently building at the rate of $27 billion in new construction; will contract for some $33.5 billion worth of new building by 1975.

Educational opportunities for those who have chosen to prepare for careers in food service/lodging are increasing to match the growing demand for workers. Currently preparation for food service/lodging personnel is being offered by 22 senior colleges, 97 junior and community colleges and 300 vocational and regular high schools. Upon completions of such courses, the student enjoys a wide range of career choices within the industry.

CONCERNING THIS COURSE

Although there are many excellent books available for the food service industry, there are extremely few textbooks. This course is designed to provide fundamental information, in lesson form, for people interested in entering the culinary field. The course objective is to give the trainee a foundation in RELATED food service subjects, as a basis for the study of actual food preparation. Today it is no longer enough just to be proficient in cooking. Only by having a complete, well rounded knowledge can anyone hope to achieve advancement and prestige in the industry.

This course does not pretend to supply the student with ALL the information he needs to know. It would be impractical, if not impossible to assemble all such information into one textbook. If the student achieves the stated "course objective", and acquires a basic foundation, he will be in a position to undertake one or all of the advanced courses, currently being prepared at the Culinary Institute of America, attend the Institute personally, or go out in the field with a good basic knowledge.

CONCERNING THIS TEXT

Each lesson in the textbook covers an important area of food service and is divided into the following sections:

a. Lesson Preview: To help you grasp the overall picture of the lesson, before you start.

b. Text Reading: Provides the information you need to know.

c. Brainteaser: Designed to determine if you understand the lesson. The brainteaser is scored by you, and is for your information.

PROGRESS TESTS will be given at various points in the text and graded by your instructor. Their main purpose is to determine if there are areas where you need more work. By carefully examining your graded Progress Test you can pinpoint problem lessons and spend additional time in those areas.

HOW TO USE THE TEXT

Many students have never been taught HOW to study and learn a subject. Learning a subject is WORK and you should approach it just as though you were being paid to do it. (In a sense you are, in the form of better grades, faster promotion, higher pay, etc.) By observing the following rules you will learn much more, and retain your knowledge longer.

IN CLASS

1. PAY ATTENTION. Listen to what your instructor is saying. Not just part of the time, ALL THE TIME. Get enough rest so you will not be sleepy in

class.

2. TAKE WRITTEN NOTES. By merely listening to someone, a student does not absorb all he needs to know.

3. ASK QUESTIONS about anything you do not understand. When you do not ask questions the instructor assumes you do understand.

AFTER CLASS

1. Read the entire lesson (s) at your normal speed.
2. Start over at the beginning and re-read the lesson slowly.
3. There are several "laws to learning". One of these laws states, "Repetition is a process to learning". You will find that typing or re-copying your notes, after the initial outlining, will be extremely valuable in helping you to understand and retain the knowledge you have acquired.
4. Set up a plan to accomplish a certain amount of study each day. FOLLOW YOUR PLAN.
5. Try to study in a room that is quiet, well ventilated, and has good lighting.
6. If some particular area puzzles you, write it down and ask your instructor at the first opportunity.

TABLE OF CONTENTS

LIST OF ILLUSTRATIONS

LIST OF ILLUSTRATIONS (Continued)

LIST OF ILLUSTRATIONS (Continued)

LIST OF ILLUSTRATIONS (Continued)

LESSON 1

FOOD SERVICE ESTABLISHMENTS AND THEIR ORGANIZATION

LESSON 1 - PREVIEW

This lesson is designed to acquaint the student with exactly what food service consists of, the various kinds of food operations, trends in the business, current and future outlook, and the organization of different types of feeding establishments.

Considerable time should be spent becoming familiar with the organization charts of the different food operations. The student must fully appreciate the fact, ". . . . . . . without organization, there is no organization".

An understanding of the many positions in the food business, and the specific responsibilities of each one, is essential.

When you feel you have mastered the lesson, complete the review quiz (brain-teaser). Be sure to check your answers by looking them up in the text.

WHAT IS FOOD SERVICE?

The origin of the food service industry is lost in antiquity. Inns and way stations existed even before Biblical times. Food stalls existed in fairs and bazaars during medieval times, and earlier. Coffee houses were established in the sixteenth century and the first "restaurant" opened in Paris about 1765. Today there are over 350,000 various types of eating places in the United States, employing over 3,000,000 people, with an annual payroll of over $3,000,000,000.

"The average American spends about $100 per year in restaurants and other commercial eating places. In metropolitan areas, residents eat out much more often than in rural areas and small towns. The New York metropolitan area alone has about 20,000 eating places; the Los Angeles area, over 9,000. Yet some of the Nation's counties have but one or two - or none."

Statistics indicate gross profit averages about 52%. Operating expenses about 44%. "The net profit is around 7 1/2%, of which the owner's salary is over 4% and income tax around 1%. The annual discontinuance rate for all reasons, including bankruptcy and other credit conditions, is over 600 per 10,000 concerns. This is relatively low in comparison with other types of retail businesses."*

Food Service is a hospitality business. As in any business, the prime objective is to make a profit for the owner. In order to accomplish this objective the restaurant industry deals in a service, i.e.: The preparation, sale, and service of quality, palatable food, presented in an attractive manner, with pleasant surroundings, courteous and competent help. To the layman, comparing the price of his steak dinner at a restaurant, with the cost of a steak in a supermarket, it would appear the restaurant business is all profit. As Figure 1-A illustrates, nothing could be further from the truth.

FOOD COST	SALARIES & WAGES	OPERATING EXPENSES	NET PROFIT
30 to 45¢	25 to 30¢	30 to 45¢ Utilities, uniforms, laundry, china, glass, silver, employee relations, insurance, cleaning supplies, printing, advertising, rent, taxes, maintenance, etc.	6 to 8¢

Figure 1–A. How the Restaurant Income Dollar is Spent.

*Courtesy Small Business Administration Bibliography on Restaurants and Catering. (Revised: July 1965)

VARIOUS KINDS OF FOOD SERVICE OPERATIONS

Basically, food service operations break down into two types: 1) SERVICE where the food is brought to the customer; 2) SELF-SERVICE where the customer obtains his own food. Service operations include restaurants, supper clubs, tearooms coffee shops, room service, hospitals (patient feeding), hotel restaurants, home catering, etc. Self-service units include cafeterias, catering buffets, take-out, industrial (in-plant) feeding, institutional feeding (schools, hospitals, military), etc. Many operations are a combination of the two, providing both customer service and self-service. A good example of combined food service is hospital feeding. Sick patients are fed in their rooms. A cafeteria is available for patients and visitors who are ambulatory. In the military services most enlisted men are fed "cafeteria style" and officers are served at tables.

Another way of breaking down food service into broad categories is by restaurant, industrial, institutional, and catering. Although both industrial and institutional generally serve food, "cafeteria style", industrial operations usually sell both meals and/or separate dishes at fixed prices. Institutional operations at colleges sell entire meals at a predetermined price, on a contract basis, over the entire school term. Hospitals charge patients for food on a per diem (daily) basis. Catering businesses charge the customer according to the type of food ordered and the number of people to be served.

TRENDS IN THE BUSINESS

"The strongest trend has been towards eliminating the need for expensive and scarce skilled labor in restaurant kitchens. Pre-processed foods - frozen vegetable and meat dishes, cake and pastry mixes, dehydrated products and individually packaged portions of sugar, condiments, and crackers - have cut labor needs at the service counter and in the kitchen. In addition, these products have facilitated quality and portion controls. The use of more efficient gas and electric cooking and cleaning equipment has helped enhance quality and profits.

"Increased tourist and business travel have helped popularize regional and foreign cookery and have made the public somewhat more critical and selective. Coupled with this trend, the wide acceptance of regional and national restaurant guides and credit card plans has given new incentives for high-quality restaurant operations and has probably materially aided listed establishments". *

From the above paragraphs it would appear that the highly skilled chef is being replaced with a package of pre-processed foods. This is definitely NOT the case. Certain positions most assuredly are being eliminated every day. For example butchers are being hired less and less because of pre-cut and pre-portioned meats. The number of vegetable preparation personnel has been reduced because of prepared, frozen, and dehydrated fruits and vegetables. However, there never has been, nor will there ever be, a replacement for the highly skilled chef. It is our chefs who must take foods brought into the kitchen and through imagination, ability and skill turn them into a pleasurable dining experience.

*Courtesy Small Business Administration Bibliography on Restaurants and Catering. (Revised: July 1965)

WHAT DOES THE FUTURE HOLD?

At this time the future of the restaurant business looks very bright. As the population grows and continues to move out to the suburbs, new restaurants must be activated to meet the demands. Enterprising young men, with "back of the house" experience, coupled with business knowledge, will take advantage of this fertile field and supply the demand.

The latest available statistics indicate that, "The segment of the restaurant business that does catering (has) spiraled upward". In 1963 there were over 9,100 establishments with total sales over $745,000,000 and an annual payroll of about $196,000,000.*

"As practiced today, catering is greatly expanded and diversified. Some of the principal areas in which it is currently a significant activity are - airline feeding; armed services - commissioned and noncommissioned officers' clubs, mess halls; athletic stadiums; banquet service; box lunch; clubs - athletic, beach, city, country, marinas, social, yacht; colleges and universities; commercial restaurants - cafeterias, coffee shops, formal dining, drug store fountains; corrective institutions; department and variety stores; government agencies, buildings, parks; hotels - American and European plan, room service; industrial feeding - including coffee breaks, vending machines, executive dining and employee feeding.

Other principal areas include mental, penal and other institutions, railroad dining car and coach service; sanitariums - including public and private nursing homes; schools - including public, private, and boarding; snack bars, specialty restaurants; steamship lines - lake and ocean; terminals - airport, bus, and railway; and turnpike restaurants."*

FOOD DEPARTMENT ORGANIZATION OF DIFFERENT TYPE OPERATIONS

On the following pages, Organization Charts for various types of food operations are presented. It should be noted that the charts list most positions available but do not imply that any specific operation would use all positions shown. As stated previously, many units today buy pre-portioned meats, thus eliminating the need for a butcher. In still other operations two or more positions are often combined into one job, due to the high cost of labor, size of the unit, or number of customers. Remember, the Organization Chart is tailored to the operation, not the operation to the chart.

LARGE HOTEL FOOD DEPARTMENT. Figure 1-B illustrates an organization of the Food Department in a large hotel. Listed are the various positions, and a brief description of each one.

Chef: In charge of the kitchen. Plans and writes menus. Responsible for the standard and quality of all food prepared. Depending on the size of the operation, may be called, "Executive Chef", "Head Chef", "Chef Steward", "Working Chef".

Sous Chef: Second in command. Responsible for actual kitchen operation and production. Supervision of personnel. Preparation and portioning of all foods.

*Courtesy Small Business Administration Bibliography on Restaurants and Catering. (Revised: July 1965)

Chef Steward: Usually found in a medium size operation. Besides regular chef's duties, the Chef Steward purchases all food supplies.

Working Chef: A position associated with smaller operations. Responsible for the supervision of the entire department. The Working Chef is expected to take over all or part of a particular work station, in addition to his supervisory responsibilities.

Banquet Chef: In charge of all parties for Breakfast, Lunch, Dinner and Buffets.

Second Cook: Prepares stocks, soups and related dishes. Also prepares boiled, stewed, braised, creamed, special ala carte, and chafing dishes.

Soup Cook: Basically the same job as the Second Cook. This position is often combined into one job, depending on the size of the unit.

Broiler Cook: Prepares all broiled foods. May be given responsibility for all roasted foods as well.

Fry Cook: Primarily deep fat frying work. If the organization has no Vegetable Cook on the staff, the Fry Cook may prepare all vegetables.

Vegetable Cook: As the name implies, the Vegetable Cook is responsible for cleaning, pre-preparation, and preparation of all vegetables.

Swing Cook (Roundsman): This position calls for a man who is competent in all phases of food preparation. His job consists of relieving all cooks, on all stations, one day each week, in order that they may have a day off.

Garde Manger: Oversees breading of all meats. Prepares salad dressings, cocktail and other cold sauces required for meat, fish and seafood salads. All cold foods for buffet suppers, including appetizers, canapes, and tea sandwiches.

Pastry Chef: Supervises Pastry Department. Writes dessert menus.

Assistant Pastry Chef: In charge of pastry production, under the Pastry Chef.

Head Baker: Responsible for the production of all breads, rolls, muffins, etc. as required by the menu.

Assistant Baker: Assists the Head Baker in actual production.

Head Butcher: Bones, trims and portions all meats in accordance with the menus.

Fish Butcher: Cleans, fillets and portions all seafoods as required.

Chicken Butcher: Responsible for the cleaning and portioning of all poultry and fowl.

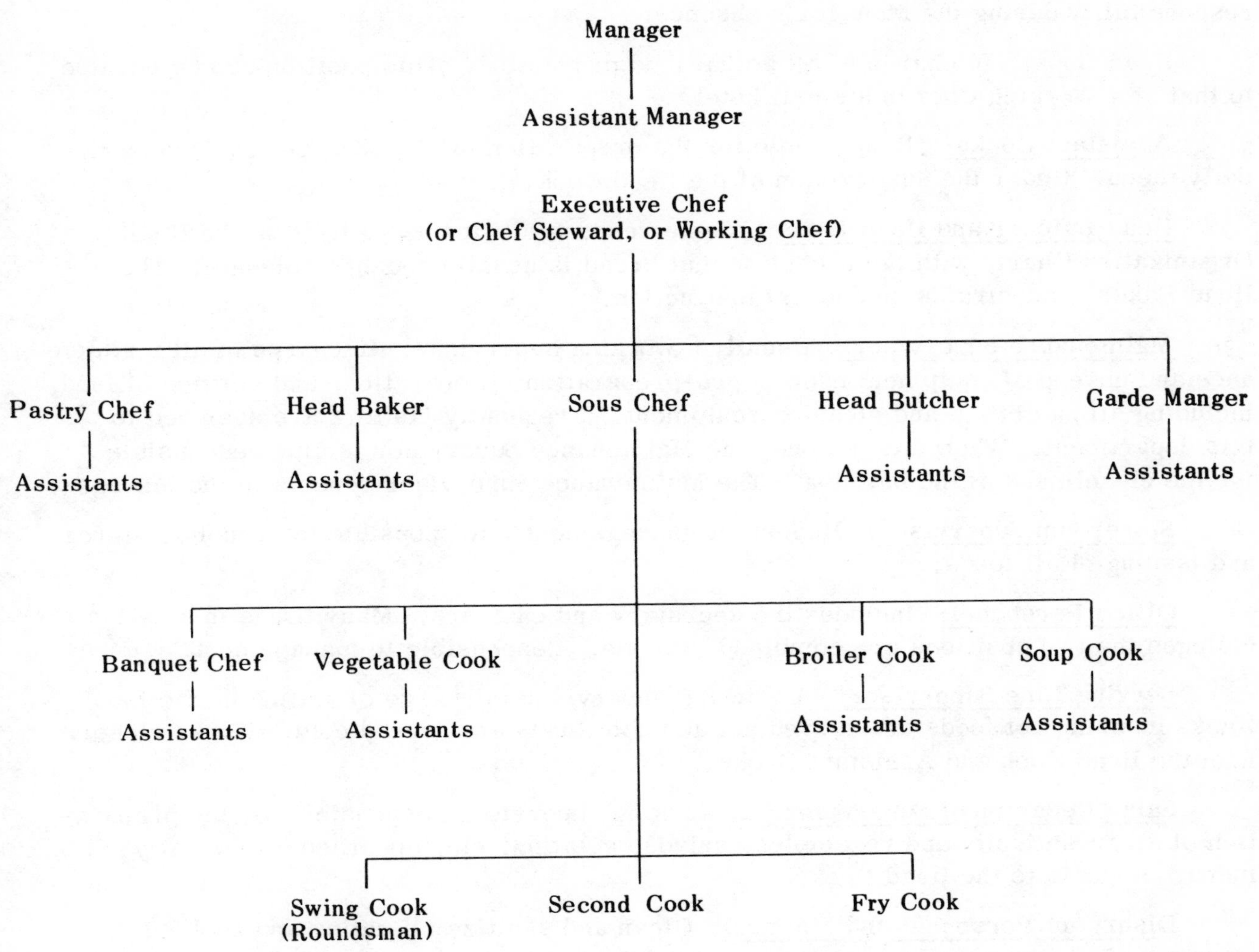

Figure 1-B. Food Department Organization of Large Hotel.

COLLEGE FOOD DEPARTMENT. Listed are position descriptions of the college feeding operation outlined in Figure 1-C.

Food Service Director: A position often established at colleges having more than one cafeteria or feeding unit. In some colleges the Food Service Director has the additional responsibility of Director of Residence Halls. He reports to the Business Manager or President of the college on all matters relating to food costs, personnel requirements, complaints, etc.

Food Manager: Responsible to the Food Service Director for operation of his particular unit. If the college has no central purchasing agent, the Manager may be required to purchase all foods and sundries for his unit. In some cases the senior manager may do all the purchasing for other units as well.

Assistant Food Manager: Assists the Manager in all phases of operation. Frequently writes menus for the Manager's approval. In charge of student help. Assumes responsibility during the Manager's absence.

Head Cook: In charge of all actual food production. This position can be equated to that of a Working Chef in a small hotel.

Assistant Cooks: Responsible for the preparation of all foods as required by the daily menu. Under the supervision of the Head Cook.

Head Butcher and Head Baker: Same responsibilities as outlined in the Hotel Organization Chart, with the exception that bread is usually bought wholesale. The Head Baker concentrates on dessert production.

Maintenance Supervisor: Usually a working supervisor. In charge of all maintenance and upkeep of equipment used in pre-preparation, preparation, and service of food, including all sanitation and cleaning equipment. Frequently janitors are assigned to this department. When this is done, the Maintenance Supervisor is also responsible for the cleanliness of the building. The Maintenance Supervisor reports to the Manager.

Storeroom Supervisor: Reports to management. Responsible for receipt, storage and issuing of all foods.

Office Personnel: Includes the secretary and cashiers. Many times in smaller colleges the two positions are combined into one. Responsible to management.

Serving Line Supervisor: A working supervisor in charge of setting up the food lines, insuring hot foods are served hot and cold foods are served cold. Works closely with the Head Cook and Assistant Cooks.

Salad Department Supervisor: A working supervisor responsible for the preparation of all fresh fruits and vegetables, salads, gelatins, etc. specified on the daily menu. Reports to the Head Cook.

Dishroom Personnel and Sinkman: Clean and sanitize all eating and cooking utensils, Sinkmen usually work for the Head Cook. Dishroom personnel may report to the Serving Line Supervisor.

Student Help: Assigned to various phases of the operation, except the actual preparation of food. Responsible to the permanently employed help at the station to which they are assigned.

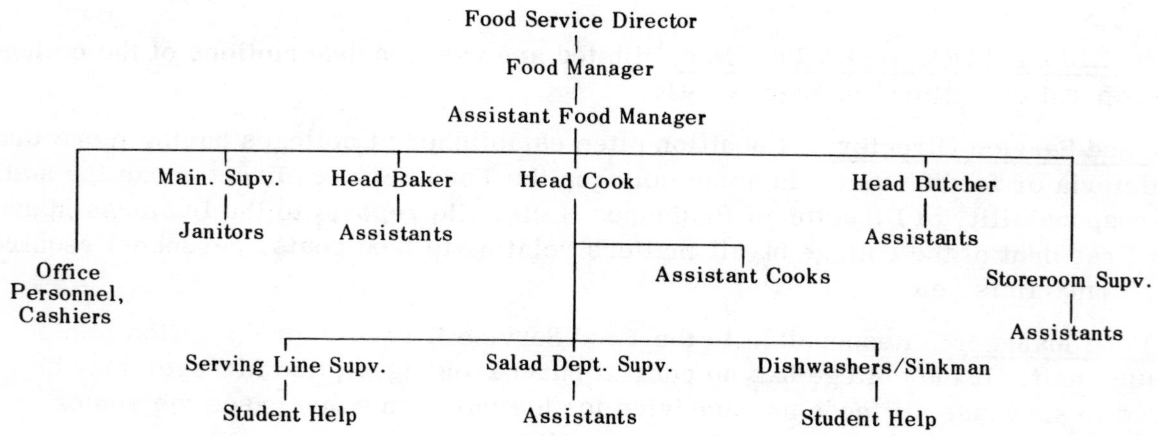

Figure 1-C. Organization Chart for College Feeding Operation.

HOSPITAL FOOD DEPARTMENT. Hospital feeding has its own set of problems not normally associated with other food operations. Special diet patients require highly skilled personnel with special training and knowledge. Some patients must have their food portioned out in grams. Figure 1-D illustrates the Food Department Organization of a hospital.

Description of positions peculiar to hospital food departments are listed below.

Director of Dietetics: Overall responsibility for the department. Includes policy making, long and short range planning, departmental organization, and direction.

Administrative Dietitian: Organizes, plans, and directs food-service programs, applying principles of nutrition and management to menu planning and food preparation and service and instructs individuals and groups in application of principles of nutrition. Develops standards of sanitation and for selecting, inspecting, and purchasing food, equipment, and supplies. Supervises selection and training of nonprofessional food-service personnel. Prepares reports of financial management, safety practices, and program efficiency. Evaluates physical layout and equipment, employee utilization, and work procedures, and coordinates dietary services with those of other departments to increase effectiveness of program.*

Therapeutic Dietitian: Plans and directs preparation and service of diets prescribed by PHYSICIAN. Consults medical, nursing, and social service staffs concerning problems affecting patients' food habits and needs. Formulates menus for therapeutic diets based on indicated physiologic and psychologic needs of patients and integrates them with basic institutional menus. Inspects meals served for conformance to prescribed diets and standards of palatability and appearance. Instructs patients and their families on the requirements and importance of their modified diets, and on how to plan and prepare the food. May engage in research. May teach nutrition and diet therapy to DIETETIC INTERNS, medical and nursing staff, and students.*

*Courtesy The American Dietetic Association, Chicago, Illinois

A GUIDE FOR THE ORGANIZATION OF THE DEPARTMENT OF DIETETICS IN A HOSPITAL (100 to 350 beds)

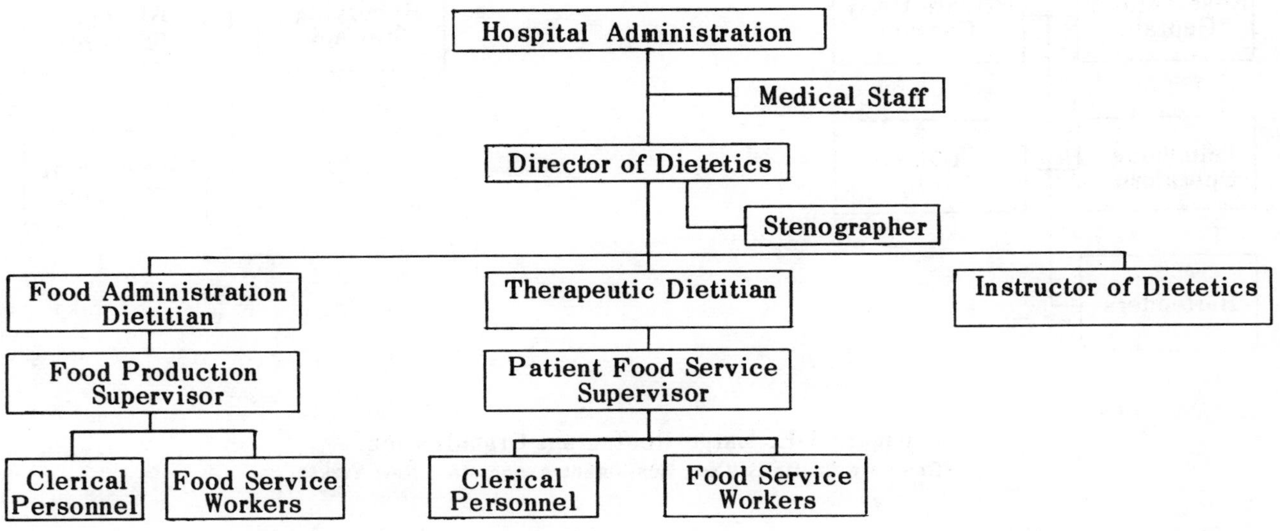

Figure 1-D. Hospital Food Department Organization
(Courtesy American Dietetic Association)

LARGE RESTAURANT ORGANIZATION. Figure 1-E shows a large restaurant organization. The chart below is for a restaurant developing a volume of about $4,000,000 annually, with an average luncheon check of $10 and an average dinner check of $15.

The student will note the block entitled, "Supporting Services". A central office supplies the Director with staff services in: Recruitment, employment, training, legal, purchasing, public relations, advertising, group sales promotion, product research and development, engineering, design, etc.

All cooks and other kitchen workers, exclusive of the dishwashers, report directly to the Executive Chef. Waiters and busboys report directly to their respective dining room managers. All cashiers report directly to the Head Cashier.

The Food and Beverage Controller has the responsibility of providing and maintaining all control systems for food and beverages. Any cost or control problems are referred to him for assistance and guidance. (This never relieves the Manager of his responsibility for overall control of the operation.) In accomplishing the objectives of his job, the Food and Beverage Controller provides help to the Chef, Head Bartender, Purchasing Agent, Receiving Clerk, and any other personnel that require it.

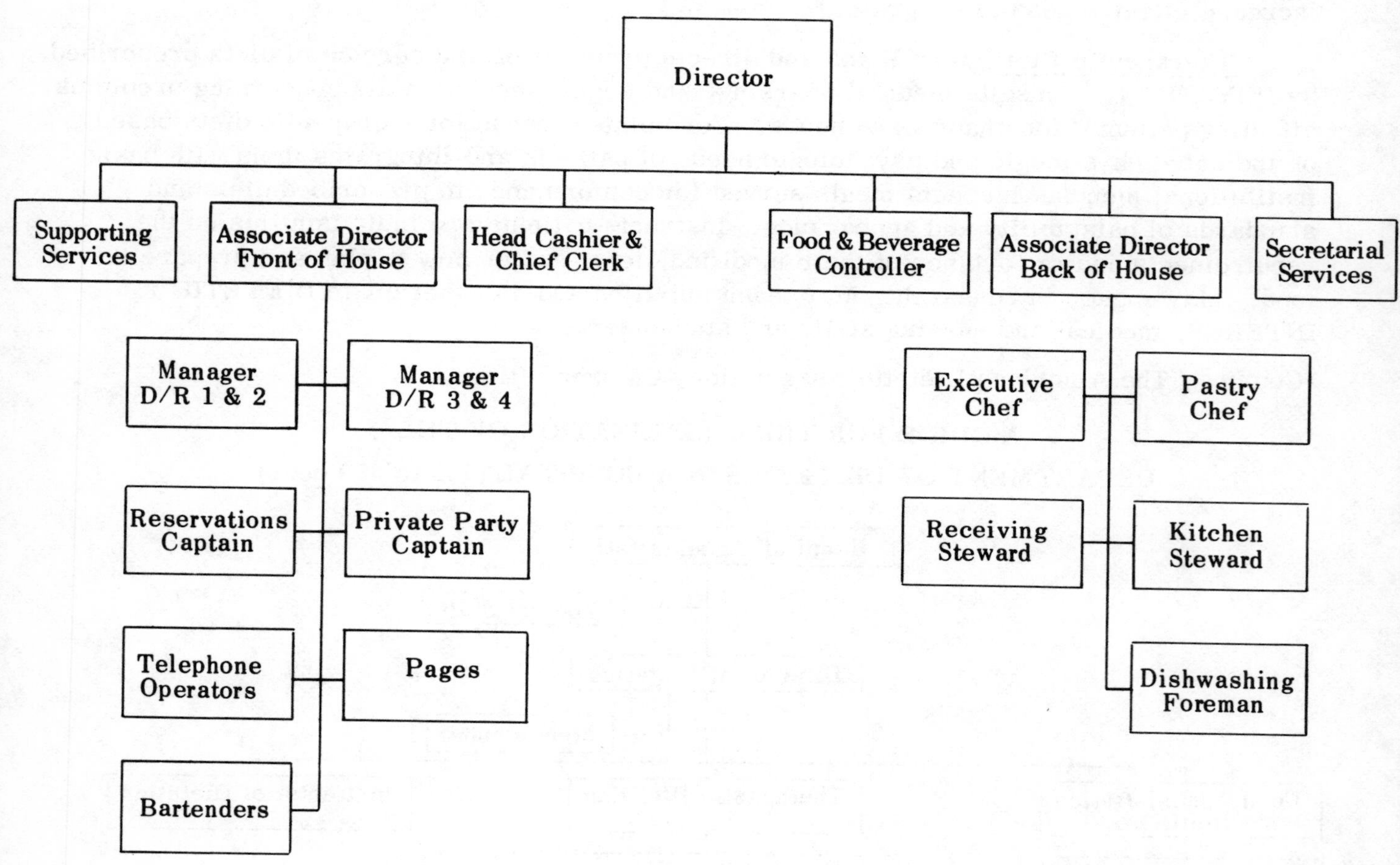

Figure 1-E. Large Restaurant Organization.
(Courtesy Austin B. Cox, Restaurant Associates, New York)

SMALL RESTAURANT ORGANIZATION. Figure 1-F below, shows the organization for a smaller size restaurant, with an estimated gross income of $250,000 annually. It is doubtful if an operation of this size would be able to afford a Baker, even though the position is shown on the chart. Purchasing, receiving, storing, and issuing of food would probably be under the supervision of the Manager, utilizing the services of the Dishwashers or Pot Washers, in their spare time.

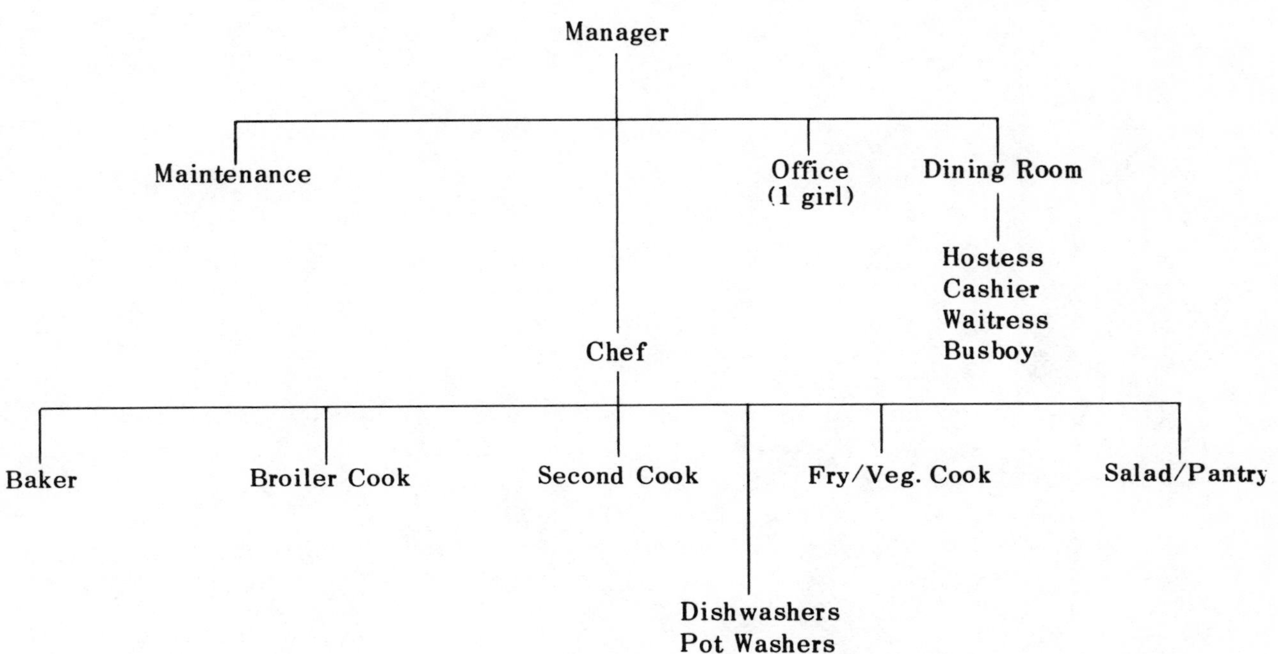

Figure 1-F. Small Restaurant Organization.

WHY HAVE AN ORGANIZATION CHART?

In this lesson the student has seen five organization charts, representing different sizes and types of food establishments. The importance of organization charts cannot be overemphasized. The key word is "organization". Without good organization a successful business is almost impossible to attain. An organization chart shows exactly who is responsible for doing what. It prevents duplication of effort by graphically illustrating what each employee is expected to do. In addition, with a well planned chart, every employee knows, or should know, exactly to whom he is expected to report. Employees have a right to know where they fit into a company. A good chart will answer that question for them.

LESSON I - BRAINTEASER

After you are certain you understand the material in this lesson, answer the questions below. When you have completed the brainteaser, check your answers in the text.

Use the following scale to evaluate your understanding of this lesson:

10 Correct---Outstanding
9 Correct---Excellent
8 Correct---Good
7 Correct---Fair
6 Or Under
Correct---Restudy the Lesson.

1) Current statistics indicate the average NET PROFIT in the food industry is:

a. 5 1/2%
b. 6 1/2%
c. 7 1/2%
d. 8 1/2%
e. 9 1/2%

2) Approximately how many food establishments fail annually, for all reasons?

a. Over 400
b. Over 500
c. Over 600
d. Over 700
e. Over 800

3) Food Service is a ____________________ business. The prime objective is to
(one word)

__________________________________.
(three words)

4) Basically, food service is broken down into two types: ______________________ and

____________________________.

5) Operations should be tailored to fit the Organization Chart. True ______ False ______.

6) Depending on the size of the operation, the Chef may be called:

a. c.
b. d.

7) Describe the duties of a "Swing Cook" (Roundsman).

8) In college feeding the person who would normally have charge of <u>student</u> help is the:

a. Manager
b. Assistant Manager
c. Head Cook
d. Food Service Director
e. Maintenance Supervisor

9) In hospital feeding, the Food Administration Dietitian works for the Food Production Supervisor. True ______ False ______.

10) On the chart below draw lines to match the positions in Column A with the type of food service establishment where they would normally work (Column B).

A	B
Therapeutic Dietitian	Catering Operation
Executive Chef	Small Restaurant
Head Cook	Hospital
Pastry Chef	Large Restaurant
Controller	College
Vegetable/Fry Cook	Hotel
	Tearoom

Note: Certain positions in Column A may logically work in more than one of the businesses listed in Column B.

LESSON 2

SANITATION AND SAFETY PRECAUTIONS OF PERSONNEL AND EQUIPMENT

LESSON 2 PREVIEW

ALL personnel in the food industry must be acutely aware of the necessity for maintaining the highest sanitation standards in equipment, working areas, and personal sanitation. In this lesson the student learns WHAT he should keep clean, WHY he must maintain the sanitation standards and WHEN (how often) certain types of equipment should be cleaned.

Important personal and equipment safety precautions are listed. LEARN THEM WELL! This knowledge could very well save you, or a friend, from a serious accident.

Memorize the classes of fires and how to combat them. Fire classifications presented in this lesson are used by Fire Departments all over the Nation.

A knife is a chef's "third hand". As you study the section on knives you may recall some accident, or near accident, that occurred through careless knife handling. Knives are an excellent tool AND a dangerous weapon. Treat them with the respect they deserve.

PERSONAL SANITATION

The importance of personal sanitation and hygiene cannot be overemphasized. The professional food service employee must eat, sleep and live sanitation. It is not enough merely to know and understand the various facets of sanitation and hygiene. ALL workers must make it their own responsibility to maintain the highest personal standards of cleanliness, keep their work areas clean and sanitary, and encourage fellow workers to adhere to a standard of excellence in these respects. In other occupations a little dirt on the floor or workbench usually means nothing more than a change of clothing. In the food industry it can mean illness for customers, loss of business, financial ruin.

All employees must be clean and neat at all times. This includes clean clothes, fingernails clean and short, hair neatly trimmed and reasonably short. Women employees must wear hair nets or hats. Men must wear hats. Hands should be washed with soap and water as often as necessary, AND ALWAYS AFTER VISITING TOILET FACILITIES. It is extremely important that persons with communicable diseases, boils, infected wounds, sores on the skin, respiratory ailments (colds, etc.) do not work in food preparation areas.

Foods should never be touched with the hands unless absolutely necessary. When possible use tongs, ladles, forks, spoons, etc. When handling utensils such as silverware, glasses, cups or other items that may come into contact with a customer's mouth, touch only the base of the item.

Always turn your head away from food prior to coughing, sneezing, or blowing your nose. Be sure you wash your hands immediately afterward.

Nearly all cities have regulations prohibiting smoking in food preparation areas.

All food handlers must learn to keep their hands away from their face while on duty. This applies especially to the nose, mouth, hair, and eyes.

PERSONAL SAFETY PRECAUTIONS

No normal person would intentionally cause himself or someone else an accident. Yet every day these same people UNINTENTIONALLY do cause accidents by thoughtlessness, carelessness, or even just "playing around" in the kitchen. The phrase, "accidents are costly" is true. They are costly in pain, suffering, permanent injury, and death. In addition, they are costly in time and money that must be spent to hire and train new personnel to fill the vacancy left after an accident. Every member of the industry must constantly be alert to protect himself and his co-workers against accidents. The following rules will help prevent accidents.

1. Never use a hose to wash down machines with electric motors. There is always the danger of electrical shock.

2. When cleaning machines, always pull the master switch first, especially if the floor is wet.

3. If you see something spilled on the floor stop and clean it up, even if you do not work at that particular station. You may save someone from a serious fall.

4. Enter swinging doors slowly and carefully, until you are positive there is no one trying to enter from the other side.

5. Be sure all walk-in refrigerators have <u>inside</u> door releases, in good working order.

7. Never put your hands in moving machines such as mixers, vegetable peelers, dicers, choppers, cutters, etc. Always stop the machine first.

7. Always make sure the floor you are standing on is clean, free of grease, and dry. If not, stop what you are doing and clean it up immediately.

8. In order for a fire to start, there must be three elements; heat, oxygen, and a combustible material. If any one of the three is missing, there will be no fire. Fires are divided into three classifications. Learning and remembering each of the three classes will help you combat a fire correctly.

Class "A": Rubbish, Wood, Paper, etc. Use water to extinguish.
Class "B": Oil. Use foam to extinguish.
Class "C": Electrical. Use CO_2 to extinguish.

9. Keep canopies and exhaust screens over ranges and ovens clean. It is particularly important to clean them after extensive grilling. When grease accumulates in these areas a definite fire hazard is created.

10. Always throw waste paper and rubbish in the proper containers. Make sure containers are carried out of the kitchen when full and replaced with clean empty containers.

11. Never allow anything burnable to pile up near electric motors, ranges, ovens, under stairways, etc.

12. When you accept a position with a company, learn the location of all fire extinguishers and exits as soon as possible. Find out the telephone number of the local fire department. You may save someone's life.

EQUIPMENT SANITATION AND SAFETY

Food production and service equipment saves many man-hours of work. Such equipment can help an establishment produce high quality products, uniform in size, more economically. It relieves employees of hours of tedious hand production. Equipment, improperly used, can also cause: loss of fingers and hands, blindness, food poisoning, and costly repairs. Whether you receive help or headaches from your equipment depends in part on how much you know about its safe operation; and keeping it sanitary.

<u>Refrigerators:</u> Clean at least once a week, and always after defrosting. Scrub shelves and racks with baking soda and hot water to remove odors. (Use about 2 tablespoons of soda to 1 gallon of water.) Defrost refrigerators when the ice on the coils becomes about 1/2 inch thick. When possible issue foods from the freezer to the various departments on a once-a-day basis, to cut the compressor workload. Never use an ice pick, or other sharp instrument, to remove ice from the coils. Sharp instruments may damage or puncture the coils, resulting in food contamination or expensive repair bills.

<u>Grills:</u> After use, let cool and scrape down. Clean with a pumice stone; wash with a damp cloth and dry. Never throw cold water on a hot grill because of the danger of warping. After cleaning, grease lightly with salad oil or unsalted shortening. If your restaurant uses electric grills, pull the main switch when not in use.

<u>Electric Mixers:</u> Wash attachments and bowls with hot soapy water. Rinse well

with clean hot water. When operating mixer, do not fill bowls over half full, unless using splash cover. Never put your hands, or anything else, in the bowl while the machine is running. Stop the paddle before scraping down sides. Always start machine in low speed to prevent spillage and possible burns. (See Figures 2-A, 2-B, 2-C.)

Figure 2–A. Four Speed All Purpose Mixer, 80 Quart Capacity.
(Courtesy Hobart Manufacturing Company, Troy, Ohio)

Oil Dropper, Bowl Splash Cover

To make mayonnaise, the Oil Dropper (above) is used to discharge the oil into the mix at a proper rate of flow. The Splash Cover is desirable in some mixing operations, and can be furnished for various sizes of mixer bowls.

Figure 2-B. Oil Dropper and Splash Cover.
(Courtesy Hobart Manufacturing Company, Troy, Ohio)

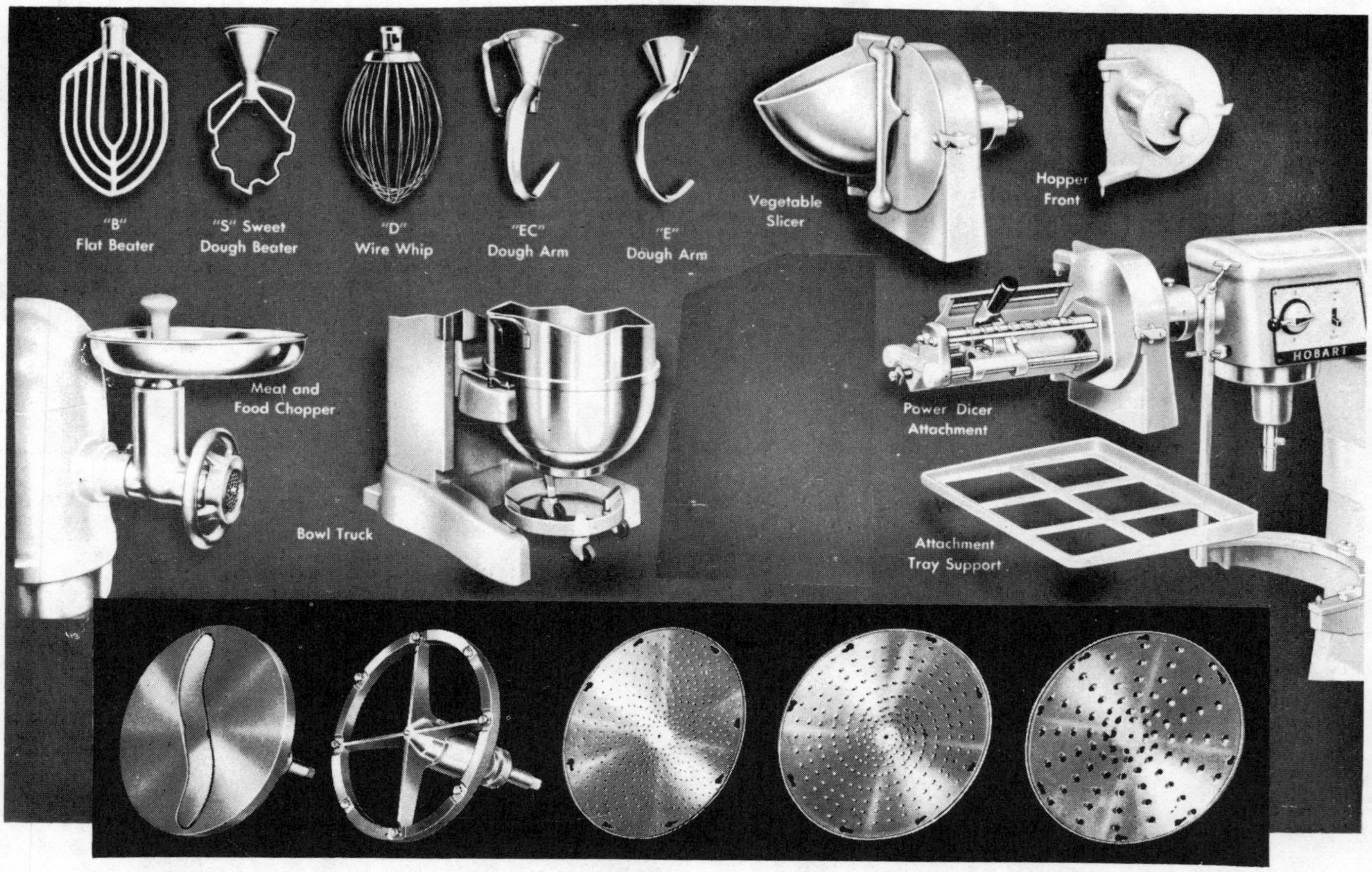

Adjustable Slicer Plate $\frac{5}{8}$" to very thin — **Plate Holder and Drive Shaft Assembly** — **Grater Plate** — **$\frac{3}{32}$" Shredder Plate** — **$\frac{5}{16}$" Shredder Plate**, $\frac{3}{16}$" and ½" Plates not shown

Figure 2-C. Mixer Attachments.
(Courtesy Hobart Manufacturing Company, Troy, Ohio)

Coffee Urns: The Coffee Brewing Center of the Pan American Coffee Bureau, 120 Wall Street, New York, recommends the following procedures:

Cleaning and Care of Urns:

1. Always rinse urn immediately after each use.
2. Add small quantity of hot water, brush sides and rinse with hot water until it runs clean. Urn is now ready for next batch.
3. At end of each day clean and brush urn several times, then rinse thoroughly with hot water.
4. Remove clean-out cap at end of coffee faucet (or take apart faucets which have no caps) and scrub pipe leading to center of urn. Clean urn gauge glass with brush and urn cleaner. Rinse!
5. Scrub the faucet, then rinse it thoroughly with hot water.
6. Place a gallon or more of fresh water in urn until next use.
7. Remove cover and clean. Replace cover, and leave partly open.
8. ALWAYS REMEMBER TO EMPTY, AND RINSE THE URN WITH BOILING WATER BEFORE USING AGAIN.

Semi-Weekly Cleaning Procedure:

1. Be sure outer jacket is 3/4 full of water.
2. Turn on heat and fill urn liner 3/4 full of water; use only urn cleaning compounds, following manufacturer's directions; mix thoroughly and let stand about 30 minutes.
3. Clean gauge glasses, faucet pipe, plugs, etc. using long thin brush. Use urn cleaning solution for scrubbing. Take faucet valve apart and clean thoroughly. Clean all tubes well.
4. Scrub inside of urn and inside of cover with long handled brush. Be sure to clean "lug nut" in base of urn liner.
5. Rinse inside of urn three or four times with hot water - scrubbing each time. Also rinse parts well. Repeat until all traces of foreign odor and cleaning solution are removed.
6. Leave a gallon or more of fresh water in urn with cover partly open until next use. If cold water is used, allow urn to cool to prevent cracking liner.
7. Urn baskets may be cleaned by immersing in urn cleaner solution and scrubbing with a stiff brush. Rinse thoroughly and let dry. Sprayheads should be checked to see that all holes are open. If any are clogged, remove sprayhead and use stiff wire to open.
8. Don't use soap, scouring powders, or abrasives to clean coffee brewing equipment. (See Figures 2-D and 2-E.)

Figure 2–D. Urn–O–Matic Coffee Urn.
(Courtesy Continental Coffee Company)

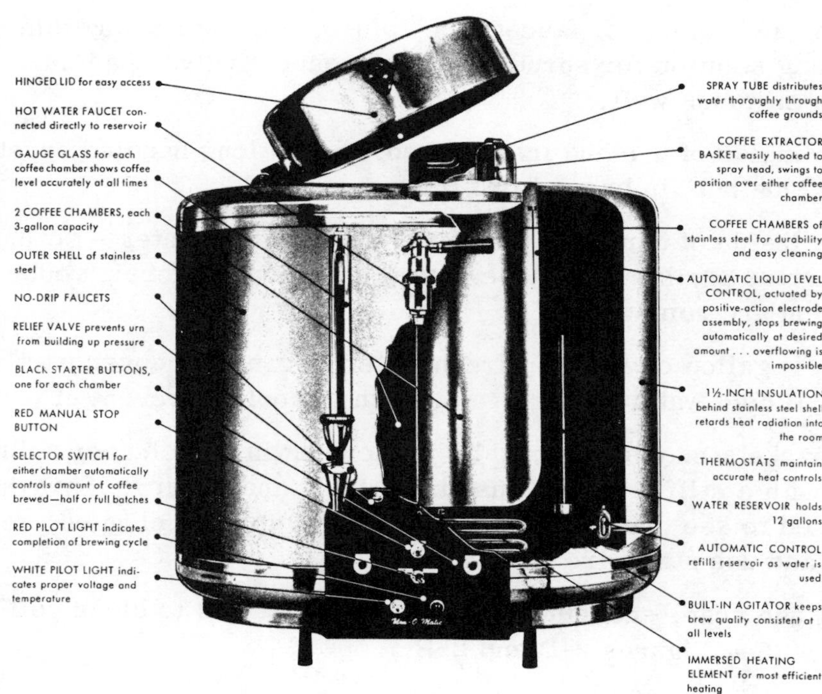
HINGED LID for easy access
HOT WATER FAUCET connected directly to reservoir
GAUGE GLASS for each coffee chamber shows coffee level accurately at all times
2 COFFEE CHAMBERS, each 3-gallon capacity
OUTER SHELL of stainless steel
NO-DRIP FAUCETS
RELIEF VALVE prevents urn from building up pressure
BLACK STARTER BUTTONS, one for each chamber
RED MANUAL STOP BUTTON
SELECTOR SWITCH for either chamber automatically controls amount of coffee brewed—half or full batches
RED PILOT LIGHT indicates completion of brewing cycle
WHITE PILOT LIGHT indicates proper voltage and temperature
SPRAY TUBE distributes water thoroughly through coffee grounds
COFFEE EXTRACTOR BASKET easily hooked to spray head, swings to position over either coffee chamber
COFFEE CHAMBERS of stainless steel for durability and easy cleaning
AUTOMATIC LIQUID LEVEL CONTROL, actuated by positive-action electrode assembly, stops brewing automatically at desired amount . . . overflowing is impossible
1½-INCH INSULATION behind stainless steel shell retards heat radiation into the room
THERMOSTATS maintain accurate heat controls
WATER RESERVOIR holds 12 gallons
AUTOMATIC CONTROL refills reservoir as water is used
BUILT-IN AGITATOR keeps brew quality consistent at all levels
IMMERSED HEATING ELEMENT for most efficient heating

Figure 2–E. Urn–O–Matic Coffee Urn.
(Courtesy Continental Coffee Company)

Deep Fat Fryers: Frying temperatures should run 380° F. or lower, depending on the type of food to be fried. Higher frying temperatures cause a breakdown and burning of grease, as well as an unsatisfactory product. Baskets should be filled no more than 1/2 full (unless specified higher by the manufacturer) to prevent bubbling over. Hot grease and water are explosive. Be sure foods that have been in water are thoroughly drained prior to immersion in grease. To clean a fryer, drain the grease, clean with boiling water and a stiff brush. Rinse with clear water and dry.

In recent years a new type of pressure fryer has appeared on the market. The pressure is developed from the natural moisture in foods. A lid on the fryer traps the moisture and uses it as steam. To clean a pressure fryer, close drain valve, fill pot to fat line with a mild solution of water and detergent. Add 1/2 cup of deep fat fryer cleaner and bring solution to a boil. Scrub the pot with a stiff brush. Drain and refill with water, adding 1/2 cup of white vinegar to neutralize the alkaline left by the cleaning compound. Bring to a boil, drain, rinse with hot, clear water. Dry pot and elements thoroughly. Never turn the unit on when empty or the coils will be damaged. (See Figures 2-F and 2-G.)

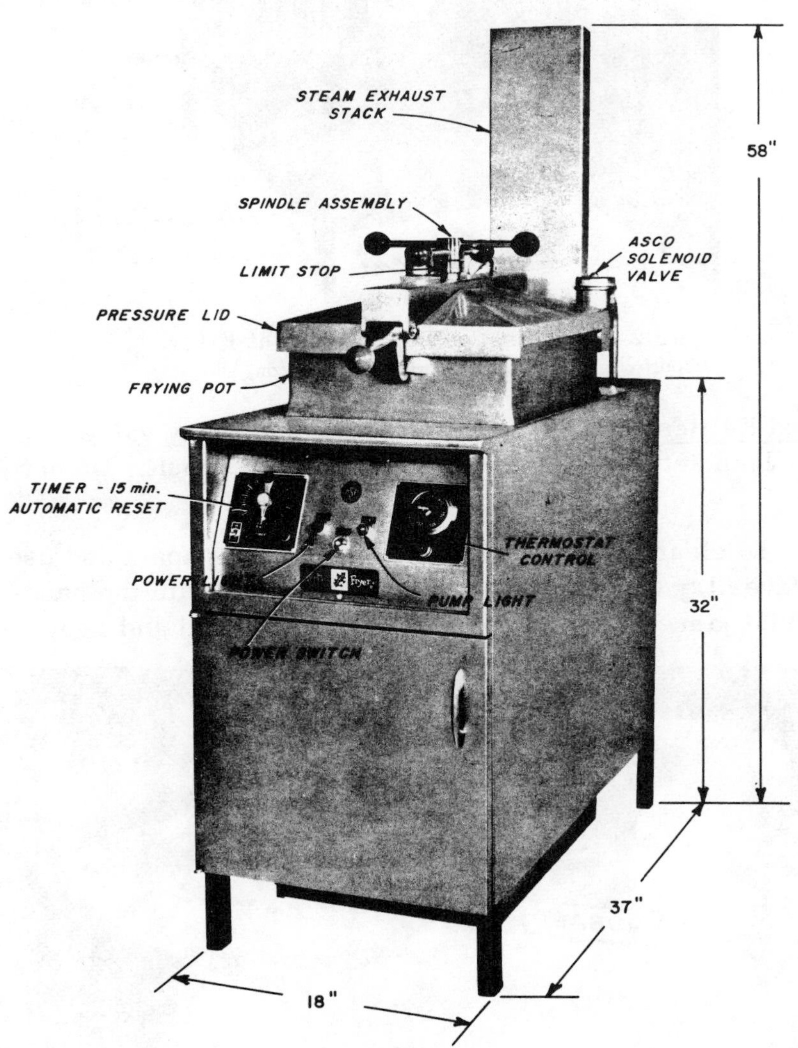

Figure 2–F. Pressure Type Deep Fat Fryer.
(Courtesy Henny Penny Corporation, Eaton, Ohio)

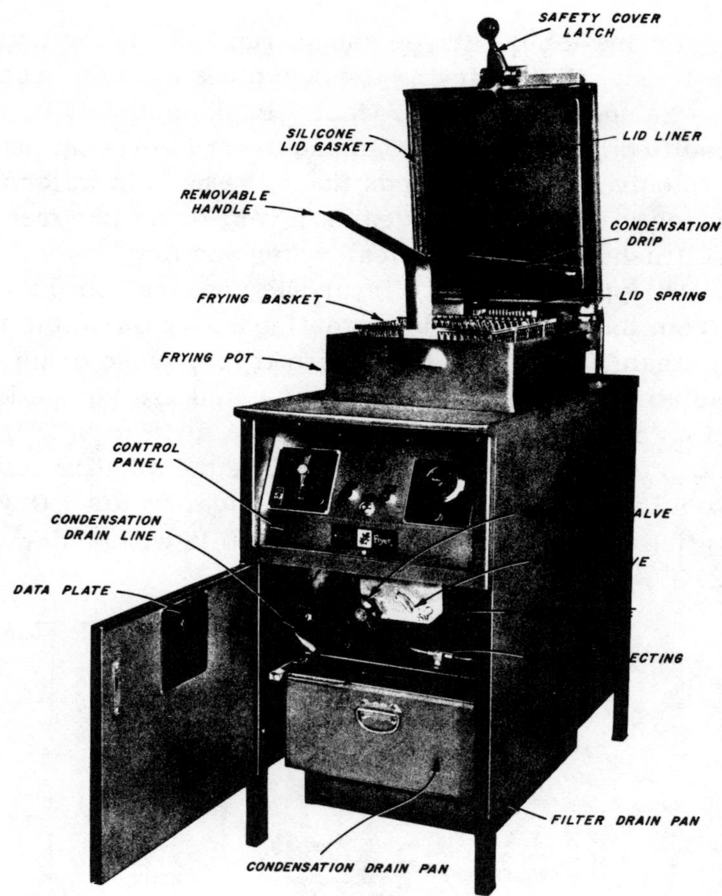

Figure 2–G. Pressure Type Deep Fat Fryer.
(Courtesy Henny Penny Corporation, Eaton, Ohio)

Steam Jacketed Kettles: Check to be sure that the safety valve is open before turning on steam. Clean kettles with hot water and a stiff brush. Do not use soda, soap or lye for cleaning.

Food Cutter: To clean a food cutter take the machine apart and use hot soapy water and a stiff brush. Never try to force food into cutter blades with the hands, or anything else. If the food should jam, stop the machine, open the guard and remove. (See Figure 2-H.)

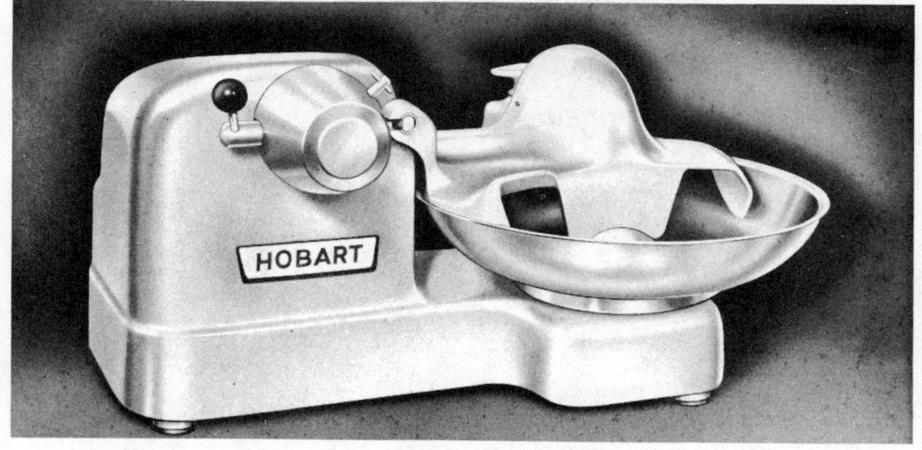

Figure 2–H. Food Cutter.
(Courtesy Hobart Manufacturing Company, Troy, Ohio)

Vegetable (Potato) Peelers: To clean a vegetable peeler, remove the bottom wheel and the strainer. Take to sink and scrub with hot water and a stiff brush. Use the same materials for the inside of the machine. Rinse thoroughly with clear, hot water. Never put hands in the machine, while it is in motion.

Steamers: Make sure the steam is off and the pressure gauge reads "O" prior to opening doors. Remove racks and wash separately in the sink, with hot soapy water. Wash the remainder of the machine and rinse. Drying is not necessary.

Meat Block: Meat Blocks should be cleaned with a scraper and a wire brush after each use. Use a special cutting board when cleaning or cutting hot meats, fish, liver, poultry. Never thaw meat on the block because blood seeps down into the wood. Place a special cutting board on top of the block when using a meat cleaver, to prevent unnecessary damage.

Meat and Vegetable Chopper: Start the motor, then feed meat or foods into grinder. Never use anything but a stomper to push foods into worm. Keep each size grinding plate with its own cutting blade so each blade and plate will groove in together. To clean the chopper, remove the head from the machine, dismantle and wash in hot soapy water. Rinse and let air dry. When possible dry the plate and blade on a hot grill, or in the oven. (See Figure 2-I.)

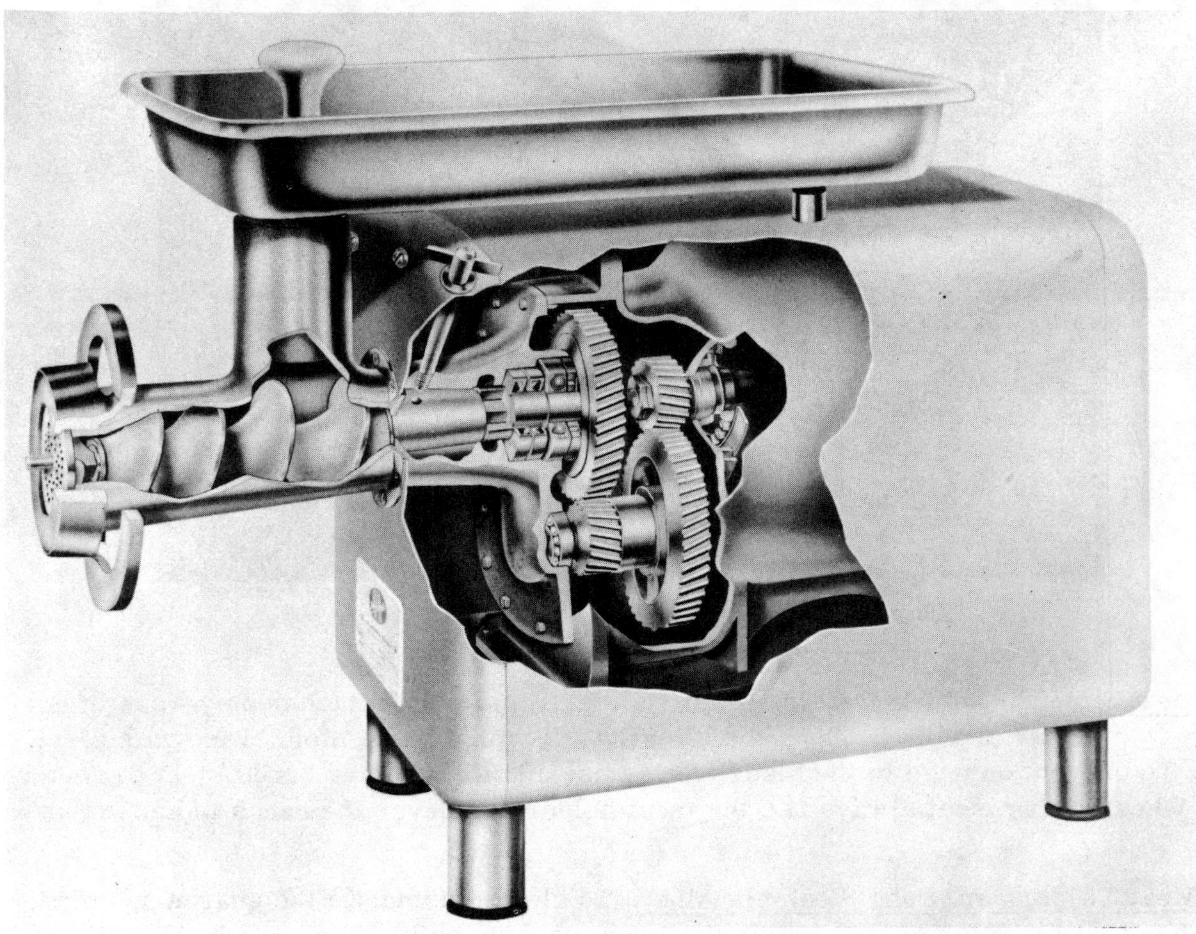

Figure 2–I. Large Capacity Meat Chopper.
(Courtesy Hobart Manufacturing Company, Troy, Ohio)

Meat Saw: When installing a blade on a meat saw, it should be tightened just enough to prevent slippage. Too much tension causes blades to break faster. Be sure the meat is always placed firmly against the sliding tray. Never try to force meat through the saw. Before cleaning a meat saw throw the master switch to "off". Wash with hot soapy water, rinse and dry. (See Figure 2-J.)

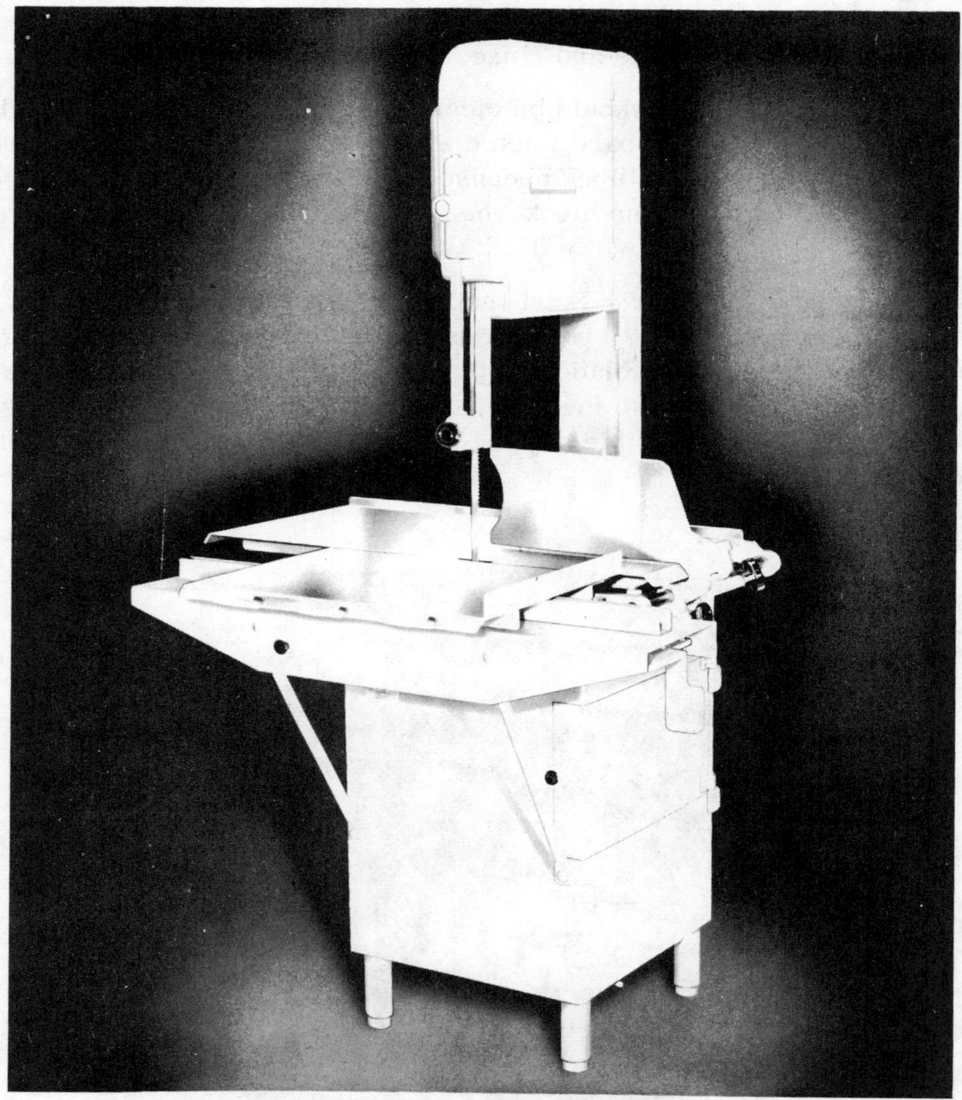

Figure 2–J. High Speed, Heavy Duty Meat Saw.
(Courtesy Hobart Manufacturing Company, Troy, Ohio)

Meat Slicer: Before cleaning a meat slicer remove all attachments, wash in hot soapy water, rinse and dry. Clean the slicer itself with a damp cloth, wipe with a dry cloth. To prevent damage to the blade, never use a knife or other hard object to remove food. When slicing meat always use the meat holder and never the hands to keep meat in place.

Meat Tenderizer (Cube Steak Machine): To clean, dismantle the guards and blades. Wash in hot soapy water, rinse and dry. Clean machine with a damp cloth. Should food become stuck in the machine, shut off switch, remove the guards; if necessary, remove blades. (See Figures 2-K, 2-L.)

Figure 2–K. Tenderizer.
(Courtesy Hobart Manufacturing Company, Troy, Ohio)

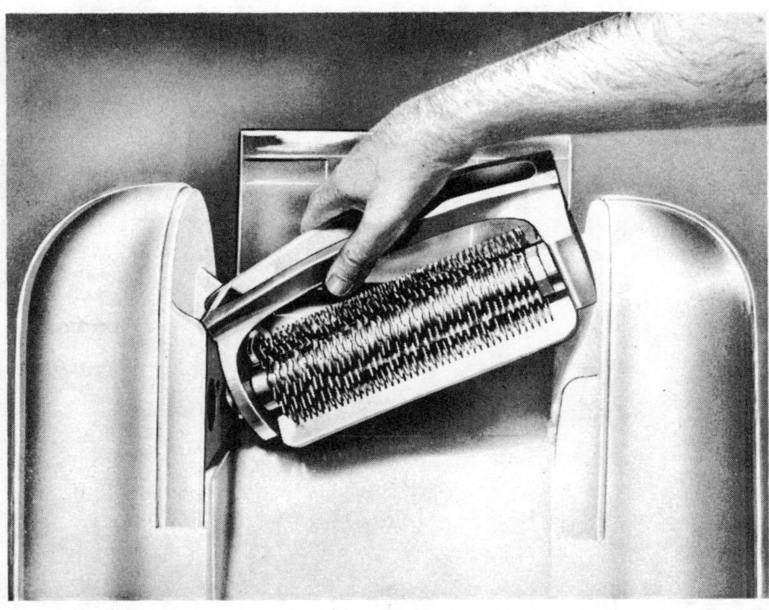

Figure 2–L. Removing Blades from Tenderizer.
(Courtesy Hobart Manufacturing Company, Troy, Ohio)

<u>Dishwashing Machines</u>: Often called one of the most important pieces of equipment in a food establishment, dishwashers are manufactured in many sizes and models. In order to properly clean and sanitize dishes, and other utensils, wash water must be 120° - 140° F. Rinse water temperature must be 180° F. Supervisors must constantly be alert to insure these temperatures are maintained. All dishroom personnel must be trained to stop machines and call the supervisor should a drop in temperature occur. (See Figures 2-M, 2-N, 2-O.)

Figure 2–M. Single Tank Dishwasher.
(Courtesy Hobart Manufacturing Company, Troy, Ohio)

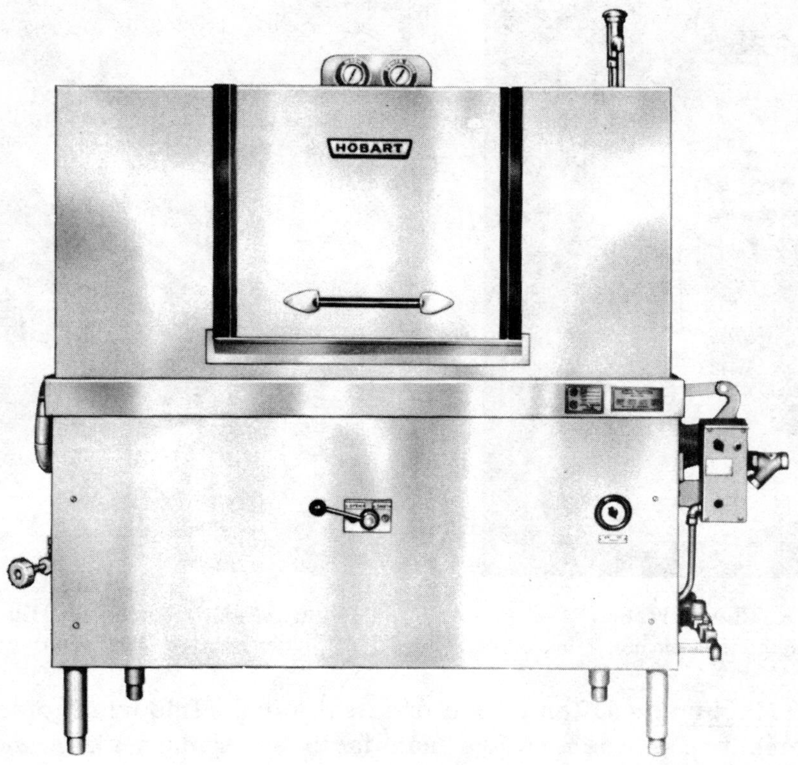

Figure 2–N. Double Tank Dishwasher.
(Courtesy Hobart Manufacturing Company, Troy, Ohio)

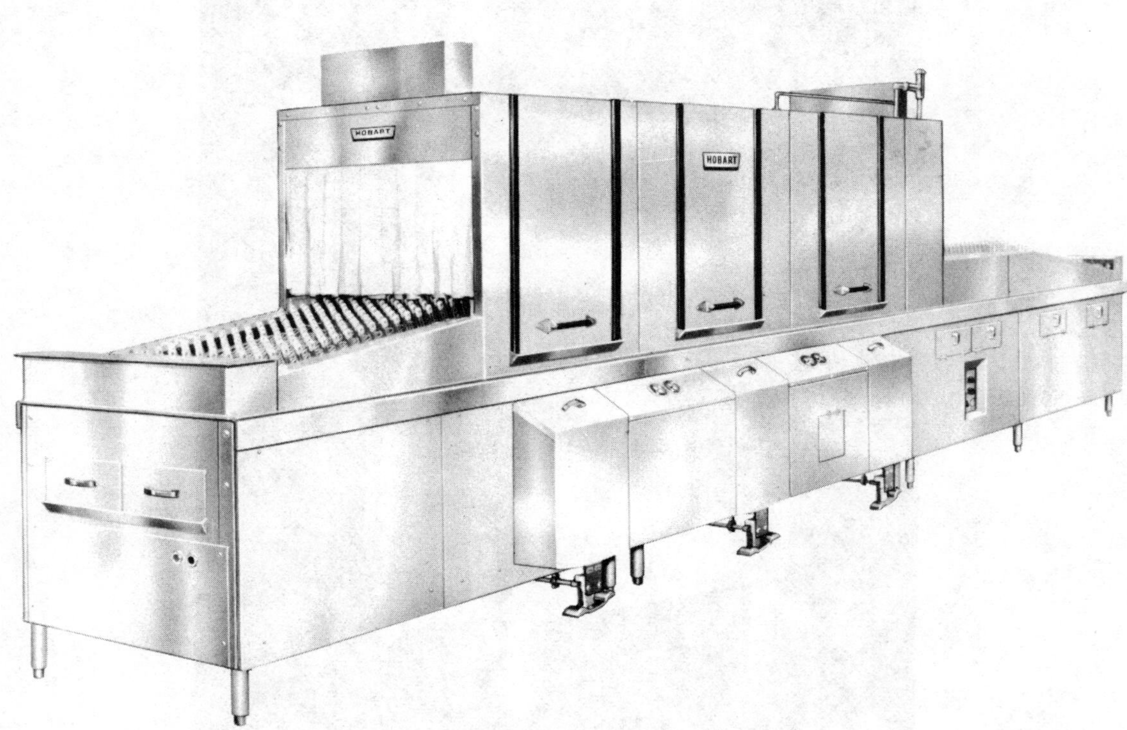

Figure 2–O. 22 Foot Flight-Type Fully Automatic Continuous Racking Dishwasher.
(Courtesy Hobart Manufacturing Company, Troy, Ohio)

At the end of each day, the following cleaning procedure is recommended for dishwashing machines:

1. Turn off the pump and conveyor (or belt).
2. Drain water from tank(s). BE SURE HEAT IS OFF FIRST, to prevent burning tank or bursting tank seams.
3. Clean, wash and rinse spray arms by removing caps, and scrubbing interior with brush. Use table knife or other utensil to clean water slots. Replace spray arms.
4. Clean the dish tables leading to and away from the machine. Rinse and dry.
5. Remove and clean all scrap trays. Place clean trays on rinse tables to air dry.
6. Open drain valve and drain machine. Remove any garbage or foreign matter from tank.
7. Scrub machine interior with hot water and detergent. Flush well with hot rinse water.
8. Remove and clean pump inlet strainer. Place on rinse table with scrap trays to air dry.
9. Remove curtains, if applicable, and scrub thoroughly with detergent solution. Rinse well, use cold water for final rinse. Hang up to dry.
10. Clean exterior of machine. Wipe dry.
11. Leave access doors open so machine will air out overnight.

Knives and Cleavers: All knives must be kept sharp. A dull knife is always more dangerous than a sharp knife because it requires more pressure to use. This increases the danger of slippage, and generally a more severe cut. Never let tools or knives with wooden handles soak in water. As the handles dry there is shrinking and separation providing a perfect place for bacteria to hide. All personnel must be trained never to put knives in a sink full of soapy water. The next person to reach into the sink could receive a serious cut Never throw knives loosely in a drawer. A suitable knife rack should be made or procured. Throwing knives in a drawer not only damages the blade, but in addition creates a hazard when looking for knives. Never carry a knife when carrying something else. This presents a dangerous situation for you and anyone near you. All our lives we automatically grab for a falling object. The smart food handler soon learns to reverse this habit, when he sees a knife fall. NEVER REACH FOR A FALLING KNIFE!

Use meat cleavers as little as possible. Cleavers cause bones to break-up, driving particles into the surrounding meat.

LESSON 2 - BRAINTEASER

After you are certain you understand the material in this lesson, answer the questions below. When you have completed the brainteaser, check your answers in the text.

Use the following scale to evaluate your understanding of this lesson:

10 Correct---Outstanding
9 Correct---Excellent
8 Correct---Good
7 Correct---Fair
6 Or Under
Correct ---Restudy the lesson.

1) Food service employees should wash their hands with soap and water as often as necessary, and always after ______ ______ ______

2) Name the three elements necessary for a fire to start.

a) b) c)

3) Refrigerators should be cleaned at least:

a. Once a day
b. Once a week
c. Once a month
d. When convenient
e. After every inventory

4) The Coffee Brewing Center recommends urn cleaning compounds be left standing in the urn for about:

a. 10 minutes
b. 15 minutes
c. 30 minutes
d. 45 minutes
e. One hour

5) According to the lesson, what are the three things that should NOT be used to clean coffee brewing equipment?

a) b) c)

6) What is the highest recommended temperature for deep fat frying of foods?

a. 340°F.
b. 360°F.
c. 380°F.
d. 400°F.
e. 420°F.

7) A vegetable (potato) peeler should be cleaned with hot soapy water and a stiff brush.

True ______ False ______.

8) Certain types of meats may be thawed on the meat block. True _______ False _______

9) Describe the procedure for cleaning a meat slicer.

10) Draw a line to match up the safety or sanitary precaution in Column A with the statement it applies to in Column B.

Column A	Column B
Turn head when coughing or sneezing	Machines with electric motors
Touch only the base or handle	Class A Fire
Insure pressure gauge reads "O" before opening door	Steam Jacketed Kettles
Never use a hose to wash down	Class B Fire
Use CO_2 to extinguish	Steamers
Use WATER to extinguish	Class C Fire
	Eating Utensils
	Wash hands afterwards

LESSON 3

FOOD POISONING

LESSON 3 - PREVIEW

This lesson provides the student with an insight into the various types of food poisonings, and related food borne illnesses. Only by having a thorough understanding of the cause, effect and prevention of food poisonings can the food worker protect customers against needless pain and suffering, preserve his own job and health, and help guard his employer from loss of business, adverse publicity, and legal damage suits.

In Lesson 2 you learned something about the sanitation requirements for kitchen equipment and food handlers. In other classes, and "on the job training", you will be exposed to much more information about sanitation in the kitchen and the surrounding areas.

Poor sanitation practices can contribute significantly to an outbreak of food poisoning. For example, a restaurant without proper window screens invites flies (and their many diseases) into the establishment. If we wanted to apply a mathematical formula we could say that PS + 2L = FP (POOR SANITATION plus LACK of knowledge, or LACK of interest, equals FOOD POISONING.)

Some managers are "too busy" to worry about a little dirt or spillage. They will tell you it is impossible to work without it, and they have more important things to think about. Most food experts agree there will be dirt and spillage when working with food. There is nothing wrong with this PROVIDED it is promptly and frequently cleaned up.

Unfortunately, in some establishments, a little more spillage accumulates on top of the last spillage, or a little spillage in one area is joined by some in another area. In a very short length of time, the only steady customers left are bacteria, insects, and rodents. (See Figure 3-A.)

The Rat

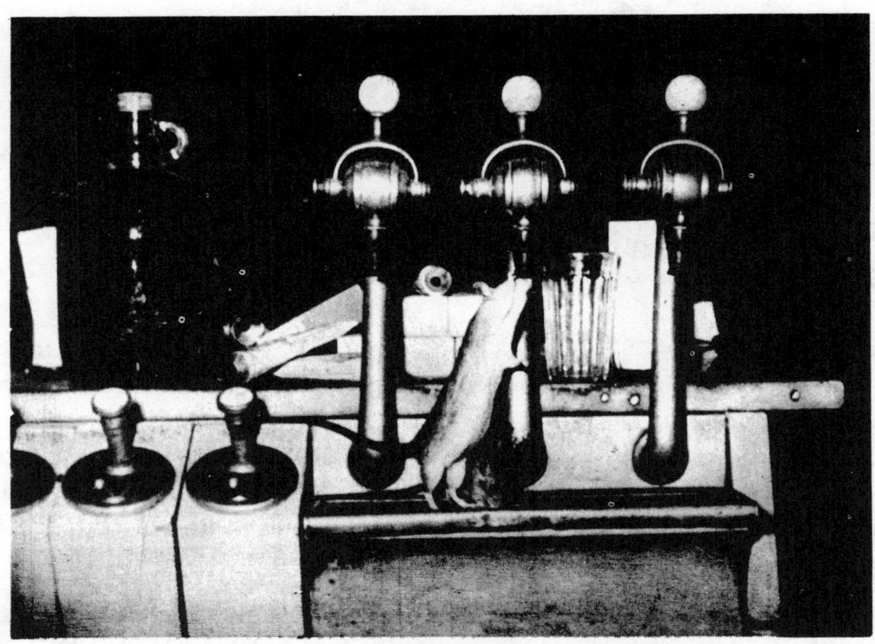

AFTER HOURS!

Figure 3–A. An Uninvited Customer.
(Courtesy Utah State Department of Health, Food Service Sanitation Manual)

A few years ago, anyone getting sick from food was said to have, "Ptomaine" (pronounced, toe-main) poisoning. Chemists soon found that this term was inaccurate. Today, food poisoning is generally broken down into three categories: a) BACTERIAL - caused by live harmful bacteria, or toxins produced by the multiplication of harmful bacteria; b) CHEMICAL - caused by the introduction of poisons into foods, such as insect sprays and powders, fruit and vegetable sprays, and the reaction of certain types of food to certain metals; c) POISONOUS PLANTS AND ANIMALS caused by eating certain species of mushrooms, fish, etc.

BACTERIAL FOOD POISONING

Most all cases of food poisoning today result from the multiplication of bacteria. Some strains of bacteria, so far as we know, are neither helpful nor harmful to humans. Others are very useful to us. A very small percentage are detrimental to human health.

Staphylococcus (or "Staph") Food Poisoning. Staphylococcus is one of the most common types of food poisoning. Unfortunately for humans, Staph Bacteria are toxin producing. The bacteria themselves are easily destroyed by heat but the toxins they produce are not. These toxins can withstand temperatures near boiling for some time.

Staphylococci are practically everywhere. (See Figure 3-B.) Man is probably the greatest carrier because boils, infected cuts, sores on the skin, nasal drip and mucus in the throat, all make a nice home for these bacteria.

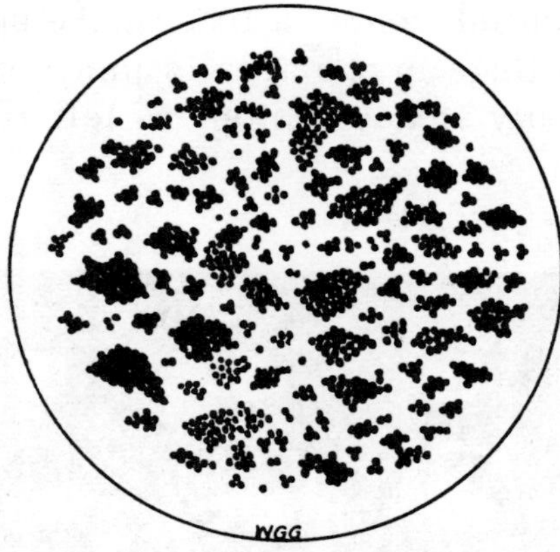

Figure 3-B. Staphylococcus Bacteria.
(Courtesy Utah State Department of Health, Food Sanitation Manual)

Foods containing Staph do NOT change appearance and have the same taste and smell as uncontaminated foods. Symptoms include vomiting, diarrhea, nausea, and headaches. They usually appear within four hours after ingestion. Foods most likely to develop Staphylococcus poisoning are poultry, ham (and other meats), cream- and custard-filled pastries, milk and milk products, warmed over foods. (Students should be cautioned that there are many other foods susceptible to Staph poisoning. The above list contains only the more common dangerous foods.)

Salmonella Food Poisoning. Another of the more frequently occurring food poisons is Salmonella. It is caused by eating food contaminated with living bacteria. Symptoms appear up to 24 hours after ingestion and consist of chills, headaches, cramps, vomiting, diarrhea, and fever. People have been disabled and off-work from 1 to 2 weeks with this type of poisoning. Because Salmonella grow and multiply in the intestinal tract of humans and animals, many outbreaks start with infected animals. Another way of spreading Salmonella is through faulty food preparation and processing. One of the most common sources of this type of food poisoning is roast turkey. Other sources include, but are not limited to, eggs, poultry, milk, milk products, and food handlers.

Streptococcus Food Poisoning. In the past few years this particular food poison has not presented much of a problem to food experts. The reasons for this are not clear. It may be that more intelligent food handling has eliminated the threat. Perhaps doctors after finding one type of bacteria, in a specific food poisoning case, do not look for any other types. Whatever the reason for its decline, we do know that Streptococcus is the mildest of the bacterial poisonings. Symptoms include nausea and sometimes vomiting and diarrhea. They appear within a few hours after ingestion and usually disappear within 24 hours, of their own accord. The primary source of Streptococcus poisoning is dairy products. Secondary sources include meats, poultry, and cream-filled desserts. (See Figure 3-C.)

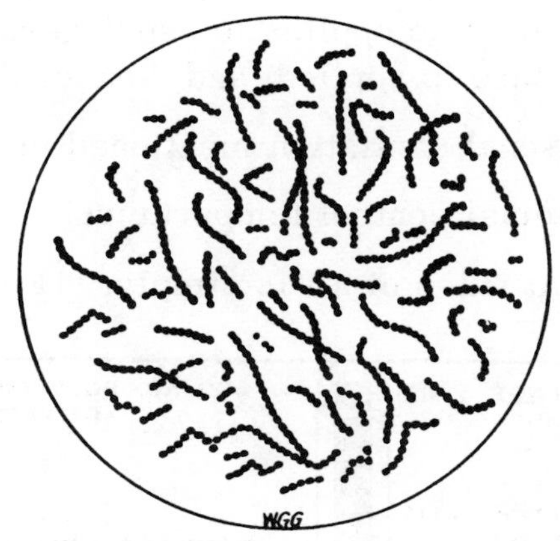

Figure 3-C. Streptococcus Bacteria.
(Courtesy Utah State Department of Health, Food Sanitation Manual)

Botulism Food Poisoning. It is imperative for students to understand that while Staphylococcus and Salmonella make people very ill, they very rarely cause death. With Botulism poisoning the opposite situation prevails. Botulism is a killer! About 1 in 3 persons infected with Botulism survive, and they must receive a serum within a very short time after ingestion.

Botulism Bacteria are found in the soil, practically everywhere. Their resistance to heat and cold is remarkable. In addition, they can and do live and grow without air. Because air is not necessary to their survival, Botulism are able to produce their deadly toxic substance in canned foods.

Fortunately in the United States, today's highly efficient canning and food processing procedures keep this specific food poisoning a rarity. This is not always true of other countries. Recently some imported Tuna was found to contain Botulism toxin.

Symptoms of Botulism food poisoning are extreme weakness, dryness of the mucus membranes, difficulty in swallowing and breathing, and finally death from respiratory paralysis. These symptoms will generally appear 12 to 36 hours after eating contaminated food. One way in which Botulism Bacteria announce their presence to food preparation personnel is by causing one or both ends of a can to bulge out. NEVER serve food from a bulging can!

Prevention of Bacterial Food Poisoning. Protecting your customers from bacterial food poisoning does not require a medical degree. All that is necessary is a little common sense and adherance to the following rules:

a. Never hold food over 2 hours after preparation unless it is refrigerated to 40° F. or below, or heated to 140° F. or above.

b. When refrigerating leftovers, place them in shallow pans not over 4 inches deep, so the cold can penetrate to the center of the food. (Remember, refrigeration will stop bacteria from reproducing, or producing toxins, but it will NOT eliminate the toxins already formed.)

c. Use ONLY government inspected meats and poultry.

d. Never allow personnel with colds, boils, infections or other illnesses to work in the food preparation areas.

e. When opening cans check both ends for bulges. If the ends bulge out destroy the contents immediately. This also applies to "springers" (cans with ends that "spring back" when pressure is applied) and "leakers".

f. Follow the rules for personal sanitation mentioned in Lesson 2.

g. Learn and apply the bacterial control temperatures. (See Figure 3-D.)

h. One of the most important rules of all is simply: "IF IN DOUBT, THROW IT OUT"!

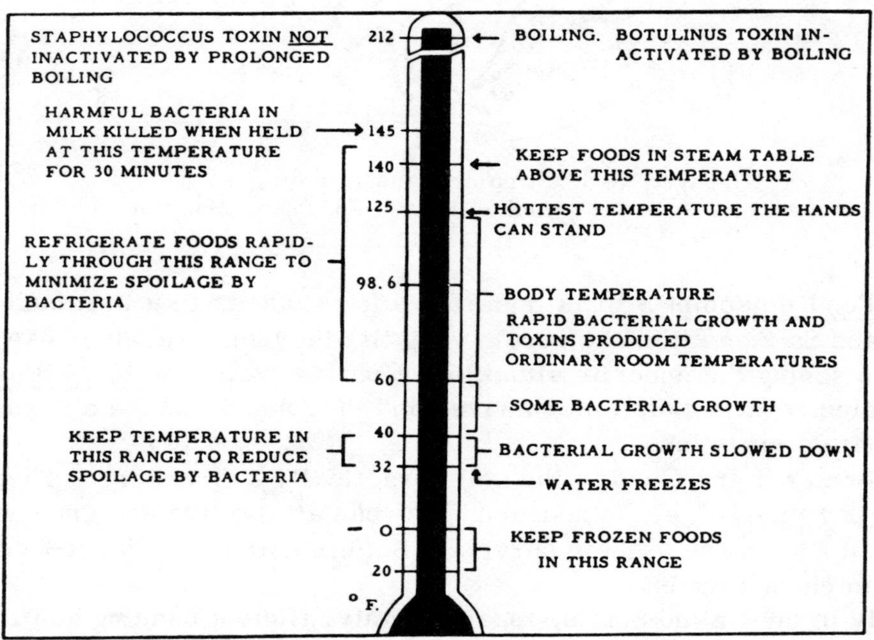

Figure 3-D. Temperature in Bacteria Control.
(Courtesy Utah State Department of Health, Food Sanitation Manual)

A Word of Caution. Because the symptoms of bacterial food poisoning are very similar to symptoms associated with certain types of Asian Flu, the Food Manager should make every effort to have an analysis done when outbreaks of illness occur. More than one Food Manager has been erroneously charged with the food poisoning of customers actually infected with flu virus.

CHEMICAL FOOD POISONING

Occasionally foods are contaminated by chemical poisons. Although not as common as bacterial poisoning, it is none-the-less serious to the victim and the Food Manager involved.

Cadmium Food Poisoning. This poisoning is caused by acid type foods and drinks standing in cadmium plated utensils. Symptoms of nausea, vomiting and diarrhea may appear within 1/2 hour after ingestion. Dangerous foods include cold drinks and food with high acidity such as lemonade, tomatoes, fruit punch, etc. Refrigerator ice-cube trays that are cadmium plated are very hazardous.

Lead Poisoning. Foods sprayed with insecticides containing lead, or foods coming into contact with lead pipes, may develop lead poisoning. Pans that are lead soldered may also cause contamination. Because lead is a cumulative poison, the body will store small doses over a period of time. If the source is not withdrawn, a critical situation develops.

Arsenic Poisoning. Although arsenic food poisoning occurs only rarely, enough cases have been reported to make a brief discussion worthwhile. Like lead poisoning, arsenic is cumulative, and therefore dangerous. Rat poisons and fruit sprays have been known to contain arsenic. Symptoms start within a very few minutes after eating contaminated food and include vomiting, diarrhea, and a painful urge to evacuate the bowels or bladder.

Fluoride Poisoning. One of the many poisons used to kill cockroaches is a white powder called, "Sodium Fluoride". Since baking powder is also white there is a danger of confusing the two. Always play safe. Never allow any type of poison to be stored in food preparation areas.

POISONOUS PLANTS AND ANIMALS

Mushrooms. A favorite food and garnish of many gourmets, mushrooms can also provide your last meal on earth. Although most of the 5000 plus species are edible, many are not. Symptoms may occur within a few minutes to a few hours after ingestion and include anything from a mildly upset stomach to certain death. Never take chances. Buy mushrooms from approved vendors only.

Rhubarb Leaves. Some people are allergic to the leaves of Rhubarb. To be safe, cook only the edible portion of the stalks.

Poisonous Fish. When purchased from quality sources, the hazard of poisonous fish is practically non-existent. However, the student should be aware that eating certain types of fish could result in violent illness and death. A good rule to follow is, never eat fish that blow themselves up like a balloon, such as Swellfish, Puffer, Porcupine, etc. The cooking of these fish will NOT destroy their poison potential.

OTHER FOOD ILLNESSES

Diarrhea and Dysentery. Frequently among students there is a misunderstanding concerning the difference between diarrhea and dysentery. The following definitions should clear up any confusion.

Diarrhea: A frequent discharge from the intestines characterized by a loose and fluid evacuation.

Dysentery: A disease of the large intestine with gripping pains and a discharge of mucus and blood. Severe diarrhea with the associated continual desire to evacuate the bowels.

Both Diarrhea and Dysentery can be spread by impure water or food that has become contaminated. The best preventative is to maintain the highest personal sanitation standards and strict sanitation in all food preparation and related spaces.

Trichinosis. A disease resulting from consuming Trichina Worms that have survived in undercooked meat, usually pork. The worms incubation period is about 9 days. Symptoms often resemble other diseases and have been diagnosed as heart disease, rheumatic fever, etc. To prevent Trichinosis, ALWAYS serve pork well done. (Well done pork is gray in color.) A thermometer into the center of the meat should read 150°F.

Pork Tapeworm. Caused by eating undercooked pork or Pork Tapeworm eggs. Symptoms are similar to Trichinosis. Tapeworm eggs can be carried on human hands so it is imperative that food workers observe the rules concerning hand washing.

Beef Tapeworm. This illness can be introduced into the body from infected beef. To be safe, use only government inspected beef. If for some reason you are not using USDA inspected beef, NEVER serve it rare.

THE UNINVITED CUSTOMERS

Every food operation is susceptible to four types of uninvited customers. Each one of the four will be happy to sample your food if he can. When it comes time for the check they will leave germs, disease and filth as payment. These four are the FLY, the COCKROACH, the RODENT, and the DIRTY FOOD HANDLER.

The Housefly. If there are any clean flies in the world, no one has ever found them. The female fly lays her eggs in any type of filth. She is particularly fond of manure, garbage, human waste, decomposing matter, sewers, city dumps, etc. The eggs remain in filth as they advance from the Larva to Pupa and finally fly. In other words, the fly comes into the world covered with germs, and they maintain those germs until their life cycle is completed. When flies come in contact with food the result is immediate contamination. (See Figure 3-E.)

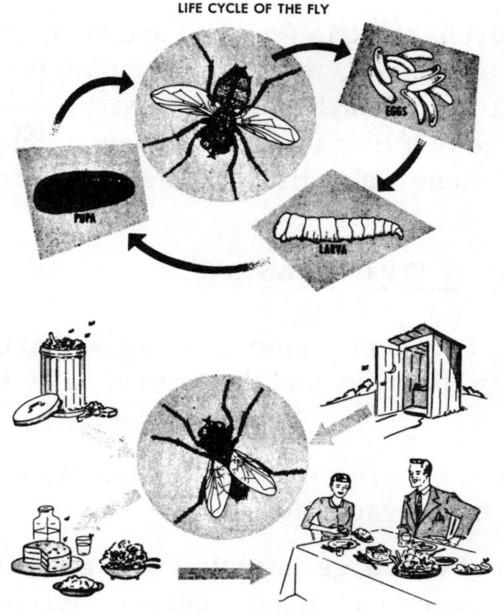

Figure 3–E. How Flies Spread Germs.
(Courtesy Utah State Department of Health, Food Service Sanitation Manual)

Applying the rules below will help you win the everlasting battle against flies.

a. Spray when necessary, being careful not to contaminate food. (Pyrethrum may be used in vaporizer type sprayers for all flying insects.)

b. Keep refuse cans clean and covered.

c. Screen in all garbage and can storage areas.

d. Be sure window and door screens have no holes, and are properly installed.

The Cockroach. In some ways the roach is harder to combat than the fly. For one thing, roaches do not like light, so they patronize the restaurant after everyone has gone home. A second problem is the powerful insecticides needed to eliminate them. (Roaches build up an immunity to insecticides and new ones must be developed.) Sprays harmful to roaches are also harmful to humans. For this reason extreme care must be taken when spraying in or around food preparation areas. Most all roach sprays are residual (will leave a residue), which creates another problem. In addition, roaches can be eliminated one week and brought right back in the next week, in the same cardboard boxes with the canned goods. Despite the problems involved in extermination, it is well worth your time. Roaches, like flies, breed and live in filth.

The Rat. Rats and other rodents carry many diseases. In order to survive they need two things: a) Food; b) A home. Eliminate these two comforts and the rat will move on. If they are found, use traps and poisons. Always place poisons near or on the floor to prevent possible spillage into foods.

The Dirty Food Handler. Food handlers that do not have the highest standards of personal cleanliness, or cannot be trained to acquire them, or personnel that will not or do not handle food and utensils properly, should seek other fields of employment. No employee in the industry can be allowed to decide for himself which particular rules, regarding sanitation and hygiene, he chooses to follow. ALL the rules must be followed. It is a responsibility of management to enforce all sanitation and personal hygiene regulations, and to take whatever measures are necessary to protect the health of customers, and the integrity of the business.

A FINAL WORD

Always remember that in the majority of reported food poisoning outbreaks, the food was good up to and including preparation. Contamination occurred between preparation and serving. Limit the time between preparation and serving to 2 hours. As stated earlier in the lesson, if food must be held longer than 2 hours, refrigerate to 40°F. or below, or heat to 140°F. or above.

LESSON 3 - BRAINTEASER

After you are certain you understand the material in this lesson, answer the questions below. When you have completed the brainteaser, check your answers in the text. Use the following scale to evaluate your comprehension of this lesson:

10 Correct---Outstanding
9 Correct---Excellent
8 Correct---Good
7 Correct---Fair
6 Or Under
Correct---Restudy the lesson.

1) Food poisoning is generally broken down into three categories: ________________,

________________, ________________.

2) Which one of the BACTERIAL poisonings is most dangerous to humans?

________________.

3) Define the term, "toxin produced".

4) Cans that are swollen or blown indicate which type of poisoning?

a. Staphylococcus
b. Salmonella
c. Botulism
d. Chemical
e. None of the above

5) Many experts consider roast turkey to be the greatest source of which type of poisoning?

a. Staphylococcus
b. Salmonella
c. Botulism
d. Chemical
e. None of the above

6) The maximum holding time for food, <u>without</u> heat or refrigeration, between preparation and serving is:

a. 1 hour
b. 2 hours
c. 3 hours
d. 4 hours
e. Makes no difference

7) Describe the correct procedure for refrigerating leftovers.

8) Explain why cockroaches are more difficult to eliminate than most other insects.

9) Pork, to be well done, should have an internal temperature of: ____________ ^{o}F.

10) Explain the phrase, "cumulative poison".

LESSON 4

NUTRITION

LESSON 4 - PREVIEW

For personnel in the food service industry, the study of nutrition is more than a need, it is a responsibility. Good health does not come to a person automatically, it is a combination of many factors. Perhaps the most important factor is a balanced diet of properly prepared foods. It is with the "proper preparation of foods" that the food service worker assumes his responsibility. In order to achieve proper preparation, he must first understand the fundamentals of nutrition. For example, he must know the difference between water soluble and fat soluble vitamins, and the effect of various cooking methods on each type.

Nutrition is a lengthy and complicated subject. In this lesson only the basic elements are presented such as calories, fats, carbohydrates, proteins, certain water soluble and fat soluble vitamins, and minerals. For students interested in further study, there are many excellent books available.

NUTRITION

What is Nutrition? The word, "nutrition" means, ".... processes by which an animal or plant takes in and utilizes food substances". The word "nutrient" is defined as a nourishing substance. In plain words, if a person eats properly prepared foods, in the right quantities, his body will absorb the required nutrients, and he will have accomplished much towards maintaining good health.

Responsibility of Food Service Personnel. When a man decides to join the food industry, he takes on the responsibility of acquiring a knowledge of nutrition. How much he will know depends a great deal on the specific area of the food industry he chooses. Obviously, a restaurant manager or chef will not require the detailed knowledge of nutrition that would be necessary for a hospital food manager.

In a restaurant the customer has the right to choose any food, or foods, that appeal to his palate. If a guest decides to eat a luncheon consisting of french fried potatoes, macaroni salad and potato chips, it is not the manager's place to point out the starchiness of the diet.

At a hospital, and to a degree in other institutional feeding operations, the customer's choice is relatively limited. An operation of this type makes a complete study and comprehension of nutrition mandatory.

The school lunch program manager or chef who is not cognizant of the Basic Four Food Groups, and the daily intake required from each group, may not give his "captive customers" the nutrients they require and need. This is not to be construed as meaning that the hotel food manager, or chef, does not need a basic knowledge of nutrition. Even though hotel and restaurant customers have freedom of selection, supervisory personnel still have a moral obligation to prepare each dish as nutritiously as possible. If managers and chefs are not aware that water soluble vitamins dissolve in water used to cook vegetables, they could erroneously permit that water to be wasted down the drain, instead of using it in soups, sauces and gravies.

Advantages of Good Nutrition. The nutritional needs of the body depend on various factors which will be discussed later in the lesson, under "calories". All other things being equal, a person with a proper intake of nutrients will be: a) Mentally alert; b) In good physical health; c) Display good resistance to infections; d) Ambitious in work and play; e) Optimistic about life.

Hunger. Nutritionally speaking we are concerned with two types of hunger. The first one is referred to as "hollow". Hollow hunger is an empty feeling in the stomach. When we miss a meal our stomach feels empty. With hollow hunger, any food will bring relief, a candy bar, a piece of fruit, etc. The second type of hunger is "hidden". A person with hidden hunger may not feel hungry but there is actually a nutritional deficiency in the body. Depending on the amount of deficiency, hidden hunger may show up as poor eyesight, bleeding gums, swollen feet, decayed teeth, skin disease, or many other illnesses.

Milligrams, Grams, Kilograms. Almost all vitamins, minerals, carbohydrates, fat, and protein are measured in MILLIGRAMS, (abbreviated "mg"), or GRAMS (abbrievated "gm"). Vitamins A and D are measured in INTERNATIONAL UNITS (abbreviated "IU"). In the United States, vitamins A and D are referred to in USP (United States Pharmacopoeia). The following table illustrates milligram, gram and kilogram equivalencies.

1 milligram (mg) = 0.001 grams, or .0154 grains

1 gram (gm) = 15.432 grains, or .0022046 pound

1 kilogram (kg) = 1000 grams, or 2.2046 pounds

For students interested in comparison, one (1) ounce equals 480 grains, or 28.3495 grams.

CALORIES, FATS, CARBOHYDRATES AND PROTEINS

Calories. Today everyone is "calorie conscious". People in all walks of life are becoming increasingly concerned about the number of calories they take into their bodies. No doubt the reason behind all this concern is the publicity given to the effects of being overweight on the heart, muscles, and other parts of the body.

It is not necessary for all food service personnel to know the physiological and specific fuel factors of the calorie, or the method of measuring them. What a culinary student should know is that a calorie is, ".... a unit for measuring the energy value of food". In terms of heat, 1 calorie is the amount of heat required to raise 1 kilogram of water $1^{\circ}C$. A third way of expressing a calorie is; 1 calorie equals 3.968 BTU (British Thermal Units). For example, we know 1 tbsp. of granulated sugar contains 50 calories. This means when the sugar is used in the body it will release 198.4 BTU's of energy to be used for work, sports or other things.

In nutrition, when we refer to calories we always mean, "Kilocalories". Kilocalories are also called, "large" or "great" calories. They are 1000 times as large as the small calories used in physics.

The number of calories required by a given individual depends on many factors such as climate, basic metabolism, type of work, sex, age, state of health, size of the person, etc. Because of the multitude of items influencing caloric intake, it is difficult to assess the daily number of required calories. For an average size man, 25 years old, weighing about 180 pounds, a daily intake of approximately 3300 calories should be sufficient. We are assuming, of course, our average man lives in a normal climate (not extremely hot or cold), and does not engage in unusually heavy physical activity. A woman under the same conditions, weighing about 125 pounds, would need about 2000 calories per day.

Fats. Fats are a necessary element of the diet. They provide the body with fuel for energy and warmth, help the body use fat-soluble vitamins, protect nerves and support internal organs. In addition, they supply food for the body in the absence of nourishment because the body will literally feed on itself. Fats take longer to digest which helps to prevent an empty feeling in the stomach.

Visible sources of fats are meats (ie: bacon, etc.), oils, shortening, lards, butter, and margarine. Invisible sources include meats, poultry, fish, dairy products, baked goods, nuts, fruits, and vegetables.

Carbohydrates. As the name implies, carbohydrates are a composition of carbon, hydrogen, and oxygen. All sugars and starches are classified as carbohydrates. Although they do supply some vitamins, minerals and protein in the diet, (depending on the specific type of food eaten), their main purpose is to furnish energy to the body. Excessive amounts of carbohydrates in the diet will result in excess fat. Sources are candy, desserts, starches (rice, macaroni, etc.), soft drinks, ice cream and other similar foods.

Proteins. The organic substance known as protein is so important to humans, life could not exist without it. Proteins are the body builders. They build and repair body cells, as well as perform many other vital functions necessary to health.

There are three classifications of proteins, "complete", "partially complete", and "incomplete". This breakdown is based on the ability of the proteins to keep the body alive and growing. Complete proteins contain all the amino acids* required for body maintenance and normal growth. Partially complete proteins will normally keep a person alive but do not contain enough amino acids to permit normal growth. Incomplete proteins are so lacking in essential amino acids they will not permit life or growth. (See Figure 4-A.)

This rat ate foods that furnished good quality protein, but not enough. It weighs only 70 grams.

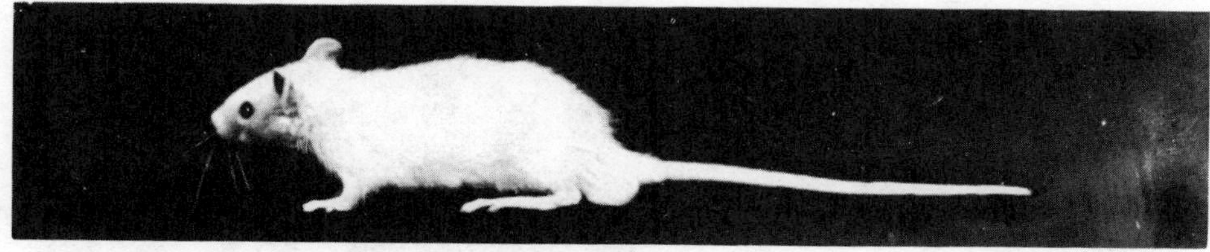

This rat ate foods that furnished plenty of protein, but not the right combination to give good quality. It weighs only 65 grams.

This rat had plenty of good quality protein from a variety of foods. It has good fur, well-shaped body, and weighs 193 grams.

Figure 4–A. Adequate and Inadequate Supply of Proteins.
(Courtesy United States Department of Agriculture)

Sources of complete proteins are meat, fish, poultry, milk, cheese, ice cream, and eggs. All other foods are said to be incomplete protein foods. When serving incomplete proteins, it is necessary to supplement them with complete proteins. For example, spaghetti is an incomplete protein and should be served with meat balls or meat sauce.

*Amino acids are nitrogen containing acids, some of which are the building blocks of proteins.

VITAMINS

General Information. Vitamins are organic compounds that perform various useful functions in the body. Often they are referred to as "disease fighters" because they help guard against infection. This is not to imply they are a cure-all, but in some instances the severity of the infection is greatly reduced if the diet is adequately supplied with the required vitamins. Vitamins are broken down into two general classifications: a) Water soluble (B and C); b) Fat soluble (A, D, E, K). In general, fat soluble vitamins can be stored in the body. Water soluble vitamins are usually passed from the body daily.

Fat Soluble Vitamins

Vitamin A is necessary for good skeletal growth, normal teeth formation, and the ability to see in dim light ("night vision"). It also provides some protection of the mucus membranes of the nose, mouth and eyes. Although easily destroyed by air and light, vitamin A has excellent body storage capabilities. The adult MDR (minimum daily requirement)* is 5000 IU. Sources include fish liver oils, milk, butter, fortified margarine, cheese, egg yolk, liver, dark green leafy vegetables, and yellow fruits and vegetables. (See Figure 4-B.)

This rat had no vitamin A. Note the infected eye, rough fur, and sick appearance. It weighs only 56 grams.

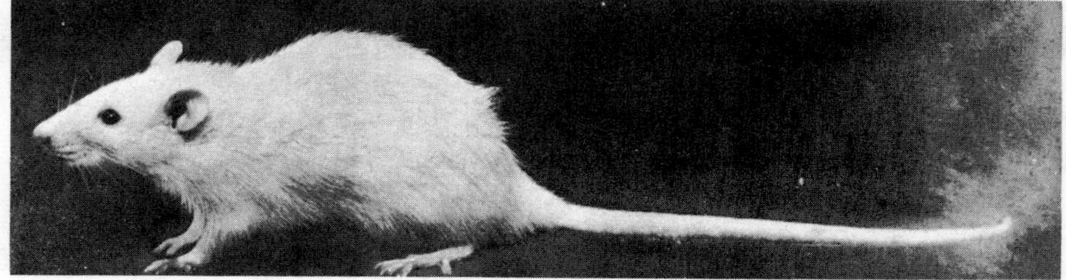

This rat had plenty of vitamin A. It has bright eyes, sleek fur, and appears alert and vigorous. It weighs 123 grams.

Figure 4–B. Adequate and Inadequate Supply of Vitamin A.
(Courtesy United States Department of Agriculture)

*ALL minimum daily requirements are based on the average man concept explained in the "calories" section.

Vitamin D is often spoken of as the "sunshine" vitamin because a few hours of sunlight apparently supplies daily requirements. It is measured in IU and can be stored in the body. The male adult MDR has not been established. Vitamin D is useful in helping the body utilize calcium and phosphorus. It also plays a big role in the prevention of rickets. Primary sources are sunlight, fish liver oils, and fortified foods. (See Figure 4-C, 4-D.)

This rat had no vitamin D. Its poorly shaped body and bowlegs are typical signs of rickets.

This rat had plenty of vitamin D. It has grown to normal size and its bones are strong and straight.

Figure 4–C. Adequate and Inadequate Supply of Vitamin D.
(Courtesy United States Department of Agriculture)

Figure 4–D. Vitamin D Deficiency. A cow with bowed front legs and enlarged joints, due to advanced rickets. Note her apparently normal calf.
(Courtesy United States Department of Agriculture)

Vitamin E can be stored in the body in small amounts. It is measured in milligrams and the adult MDR is unknown to date. All the functions of vitamin E in the body are not certain at this time, but it does provide some protection to the red blood cells. Vitamin E can be found in the oils of wheat germ, soy bean, corn, etc. Eggs and meats furnish small amounts.

Vitamin K is usually measured in micrograms. The body will store limited amounts. At the present time the adult MDR is not firmly established. Vitamin K has been found to be very useful as a blood coagulant. Sources include green leafy vegetables and pork liver.

Water Soluble Vitamins

The Vitamin B Complex contains several vitamins. In this course we will only be concerned with three; Thiamine (B-1), Riboflavin (B-2), and Niacin.

Thiamine (B-1) can be stored in the body only a short time and must be replaced daily. The adult MDR is 1.2 mg. Among other things, thiamine helps maintain normal appetite, muscle tone of the gastrointestinal tract, and a healthy nervous system. Thiamine is found in lean pork (an excellent source), liver (and other organ meats), brewers yeast, wheat germ, whole grain and enriched cereals and breads, legumes and milk. (See Figure 4-E.)

This rat, 24 weeks old, had practically no thiamine. It has lost the ability to coordinate its muscles.

The same rat 24 hours later, after receiving a food rich in thiamine. It has already recovered.

Figure 4–E. Thiamine Deficiency and Recovery.
(Courtesy United States Department of Agriculture)

Riboflavin (B-2) has limited body storage. The adult MDR is about 2 mg. daily. Some of the functions of riboflavin are maintaining general health and well being keeping the eyes from being light sensitive and easily tired, and helping to convert food to energy. Milk, liver, organ meats, eggs, green leafy vegetables, dried yeast and enriched foods, all provide riboflavin in the diet. (See Figure 4-F.)

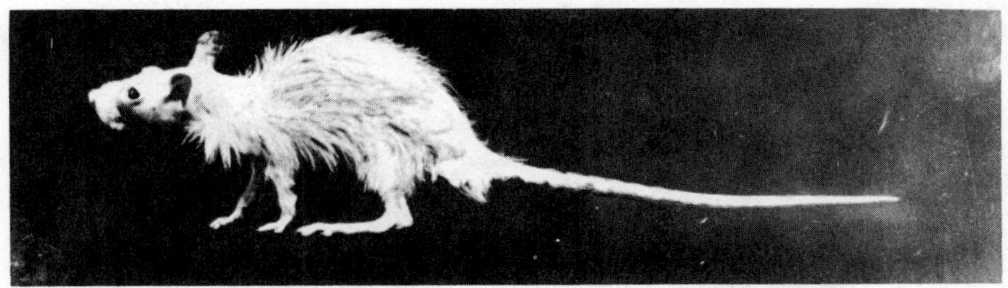

This rat, 28 weeks old, had no riboflavin. It soon became sick, and lost hair, especially about the head. It weighs only 63 grams.

The same rat 6 weeks later, after receiving food rich in riboflavin. It has recovered its fine fur and now weighs 169 grams.

Figure 4–F. Riboflavin Deficiency and Recovery.
(Courtesy United States Department of Agriculture)

Niacin, as is true of all water soluble vitamins, does not store well in the body. The adult MDR of 10 to 15 mg should be replaced daily. Niacin has been found valuable in the prevention of pellagra (a disease of the skin). It works well with other B vitamins to give energy to the body. The diet is supplied with Niacin by lean meats, fish, poultry, enriched and whole grain cereals and breads, legumes, nuts, and brewers yeast. (See Figure 4-G.)

Figure 4-G. These two pigs are litter mates. Both were fed identical diets except the larger one received an adequate supply of niacin and the smaller one did not.
(Courtesy United States Department of Agriculture)

Vitamin C (Ascorbic Acid) is more easily destroyed than any other vitamin. It is sensitive to light, heat, and alkalies. The adult male MDR of about 70 mg should be replaced in the body daily. Vitamin C is noted for its ability to prevent scurvy, * help hold body cells together, and provide good bones and teeth. Citrus fruits, tomatoes, fresh strawberries, cantaloupe and potatoes (cooked with the skins on) are all good sources. (See Figure 4-H.)

This guinea pig had no ascorbic acid and developed scurvy. Note crouched position due to sore joints.

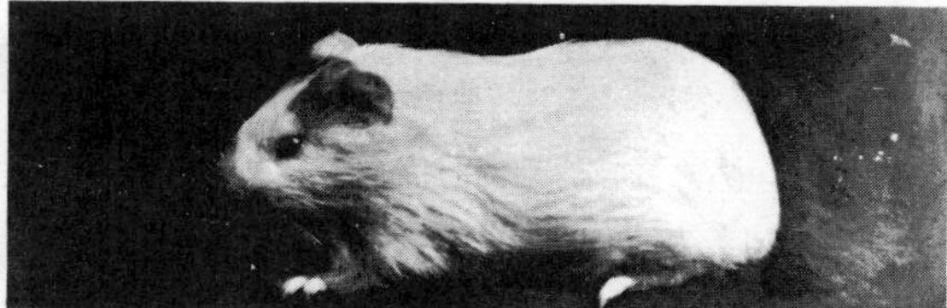

This guinea pig had plenty of ascorbic acid. It is healthy and alert; its fur is sleek and fine.

Figure 4–H. Adequate and Inadequate Supply of Vitamin C.
(Courtesy United States Department of Agriculture)

* A disease characterized by swollen and bleeding gums, and livid spots on the skin.

Minerals

Calcium is necessary for good bones, teeth, and heart action. It has been found useful in blood coagulation. In addition, calcium is believed to provide energy to the body and increase body size. Over one third of the adult MDR (about 1 gm) can be obtained from 1 cup of fresh or non-fat drymilk. Cheese and dairy products (except butter) are additional sources. (See Figure 4-I.)

This rat did not have enough calcium. Note the short, stubby body, due poorly formed bones. It weighs 91 grams.

This rat had plenty of calcium. It has reached full size, and its bones are well-formed. It weighs 219 grams.

Figure 4–I. Adequate and Inadequate Supply of Calcium.
(Courtesy United States Department of Agriculture)

Phosphorus is supplied in the diet by milk, cheese, egg yolk, meat, fish, and fowl. The adult MDR is about 1 gm. Phosphorus works with other minerals to provide good bones and teeth, normal blood, and energy.

Iron helps the blood carry oxygen from the lungs to the cells. A person suffering from an iron deficiency (adult MDR 8 to 10 mg) will develop anemia. Liver is the best source. Other organ meats, lean meats, shellfish, and egg yolk also provide iron in the diet. (See Figure 4-J.)

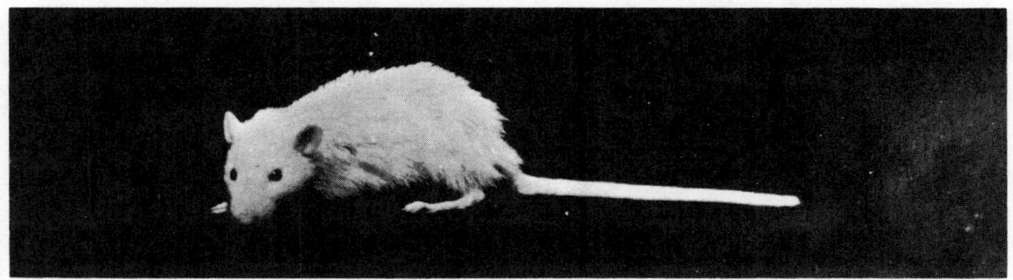

This rat did not have enough iron. It has pale ears and tail. Eight months old, it weighs only 109 grams.

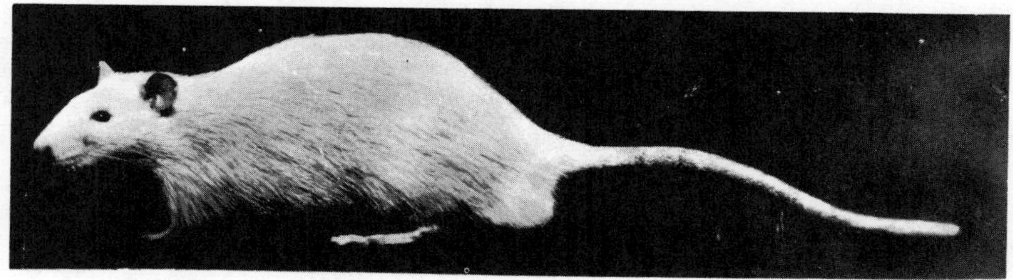

This rat had plenty of iron. Its fur is sleek and its blood has three times as much red coloring as the rat above. Though only 5½ months old, it weighs 325 grams.

Figure 4–J. Adequate and Inadequate Supply of Iron.
(Courtesy United States Department of Agriculture)

Iodine is an essential nutrient in the human diet. It has a direct bearing on the amount of thyroid hormone produced by the thyroid gland. When iodine is ingested in insufficient quantities, or completely omitted from the diet, the thyroid gland enlarges, causing a "simple" or "endemic goiter". Fortunately, this is not a problem in the United States today because of the nationwide preventative measures in force. Although the exact MDR for iodine is not yet established, most nutritional experts agree that, "150 to 300 mcg is ample". People who consume seafood on a regular basis will probably have a sufficient intake of iodine. However, the safest way of insuring that the correct amount is ingested is through the use of iodized salt.

Recommended Daily Dietary Allowances

The recommended daily dietary allowances, as specified by the National Academy of Sciences, National Research Council, are shown in Figure 4-K.

A WORD OF CAUTION

It can readily be seen from the information in this lesson only a very tiny amount of nutrients is required in the daily diet. When studying nutrition, the student frequently begins to "diagnose himself". For example, many students, as they become aware of the symptoms of certain vitamin deficiencies, become absolutely sure they have the same problem, and taking vitamins will cure them. THIS IS A DANGEROUS PRACTICE. Heavy doses of some vitamins can be harmful. A medical doctor is the only one qualified to determine if a person's diet should be supplemented with additional vitamins, or other nutrients.

Food and Nutrition Board, National Academy of Sciences—National Research Council

Recommended Daily Dietary Allowances[1], Revised 1963

· Designed for the maintenance of good nutrition of practically all healthy persons in the U.S.A.

(Allowances are intended for persons normally active in a temperate climate)

	Age[2] Years from to	Weight kg. (lbs.)	Height cm. (in.)	Calories[3]	Protein gm.	Calcium gm.	Iron mg.	Vitamin A Value I U	Thia-mine mg.	Ribo-flavin mg.	Niacin Equiv.[4] mg.	Ascorbic Acid mg.	Vitamin D I U
Men.....	18-35	70 (154)	175 (69)	2,900	70	0.8	10	5,000*	1.2	1.7	19	70	
	35-55	70 (154)	175 (69)	2,600	70	0.8	10	5,000	1.0	1.6	17	70	
	55-75	70 (154)	175 (69)	2,200	70	0.8	10	5,000	0.9	1.3	15	70	
Women...	18-35	58 (128)	163 (64)	2,100	58	0.8	15	5,000	0.8	1.3	14	70	
	35-55	58 (128)	163 (64)	1,900	58	0.8	15	5,000	0.8	1.2	13	70	
	55-75	58 (128)	163 (64)	1,600	58	0.8	10	5,000	0.8	1.2	13	70	
	Pregnant (2nd and 3rd trimester)			+ 200	+20	+0.5	+5	+1,000	+0.2	+0.3	+3	+30	400
	Lactating			+1,000	+40	+0.5	+5	+3,000	+0.4	+0.6	+7	+30	400
Infants[5]..	0- 1	8 (18)		kg.x115 ± 15	kg.x2.5 ± 0.5	0.7	kg.x1.0	1,500	0.4	0.6	6	30	400
Children..	1- 3	13 (29)	87 (34)	1,300	32	0.8	8	2,000	0.5	0.8	9	40	400
	3- 6	18 (40)	107 (42)	1,600	40	0.8	10	2,500	0.6	1.0	11	50	400
	6- 9	24 (53)	124 (49)	2,100	52	0.8	12	3,500	0.8	1.3	14	60	400
Boys.....	9-12	33 (72)	140 (55)	2,400	60	1.1	15	4,500	1.0	1.4	16	70	400
	12-15	45 (98)	156 (61)	3,000	75	1.4	15	5,000	1.2	1.8	20	80	400
	15-18	61 (134)	172 (68)	3,400	85	1.4	15	5,000	1.4	2.0	22	80	400
Girls.....	9-12	33 (72)	140 (55)	2,200	55	1.1	15	4,500	0.9	1.3	15	80	400
	12-15	47 (103)	158 (62)	2,500	62	1.3	15	5,000	1.0	1.5	17	80	400
	15-18	53 (117)	163 (64)	2,300	58	1.3	15	5,000	0.9	1.3	15	70	400

[1] The allowance levels are intended to cover individual variations among most normal persons as they live in the United States under usual environmental stresses. The recommended allowances can be attained with a variety of common foods, providing other nutrients for which human requirements have been less well defined. See text for more detailed discussion of allowances and of nutrients not tabulated.

[2] Entries on lines for age range 18-35 years represent the 25-year age. All other entries represent allowances for the midpoint of the specified age periods, i.e., line for children 1-3 is for age 2 years (24 months); 3-6 is for age 4 ½ years (54 months), etc.

[3] Tables 1 and 2 and figures 1 and 2 in text show calorie adjustments for weight and age.

[4] Niacin equivalents include dietary sources of the preformed vitamin and the precursor, tryptophan. 60 mg tryptophan represents 1 mg niacin.

[5] The calorie and protein allowances per kg for infants are considered to decrease progressively from birth. Allowances for calcium, thiamine, riboflavin, and niacin increase proportionately with calories to the maximum values shown.

* 1,000 I U from preformed Vitamin A and 4,000 I.U. from beta-carotene.

Figure 4-K. Recommended Daily Dietary Allowances.

(Courtesy NAS-NRC Pub. 1146, Recommended Dietary Allowances, Sixth Revision 1963)

FOR THOSE INTERESTED IN SPECIFIC NUTRIENTS

A food value chart is convenient for those who wish to check for individual nutrients.

Run through the following simplified chart and look for the stars to find what percent of the total daily requirement of various nutrients is furnished in an average serving of food. All foods are not high in all nutrients. To illustrate, one would not expect

NUTRITIVE VALUES OF AVERAGE SIZE

Food	Size of Serving	Calories	Vitamin A	Vitamin B1 Thiamine	Vitamin B2 Riboflavin	Niacin	Vitamin C Ascorbic Acid	Protein	Minerals Calcium	Minerals Iron
CANNED FRUITS										
Apple sauce, sweetened	½ cup	88	—	◆	◆	—	◆	—	—	◆◆
Apple sauce, unsweetened	½ cup	47	—	◆	◆	—	◆	—	—	◆◆
Apricots, syrup	4 med. size halves, 2T syrup	95	◆◆◆◆	◆	◆	◆	◆◆	◆	◆	◆◆
Blackberries, syrup	½ cup	86	◆◆	◆	◆	◆	◆◆	◆	◆	◆◆
Blueberries, syrup	½ cup	113	—	◆	◆	◆	◆◆◆	—	◆	◆◆
Cherries, red sour, pitted	½ cup	55	◆◆◆	◆	◆	◆	◆◆	◆	◆	◆◆
Cherries, sweet, syrup	½ cup	114	—	◆	—	—	◆◆	◆	◆	◆◆
Cranberry sauce, sweetened	¼ cup	115	—	◆	◆	—	◆◆	—	—	◆
Figs, syrup	3 figs, 2T syrup	136	◆	◆	◆	◆	◆	◆	◆◆	◆◆
Fruit cocktail, syrup	½ cup	81	◆◆	—	—	◆	◆◆	—	◆	◆◆
Grapefruit sections, syrup	½ cup	80	—	◆	◆	◆	◆◆◆◆	—	◆	◆◆
Olives, ripe	3 large	24	—	—	◆	—	—	—	◆	◆
Peaches, cling, syrup	2 med. halves, 2T syrup	84	◆◆◆	—	◆	◆◆	◆◆	—	—	◆◆
Peaches, Freestone, syrup	2 med. halves, 2T syrup	88	◆◆	—	◆	◆◆	◆◆	—	—	◆◆
Pears, syrup	2 med. halves, 2T syrup	78	—	—	◆	◆	◆◆	—	◆	◆
Pineapple, sliced, syrup	2 small or 1 lg. slice, 2T syrup	93	◆	◆◆	◆	◆	◆◆◆	—	◆◆	◆◆
Purple plums, syrup	3 plums, 2T syrup	91	◆◆◆◆	◆	◆	◆	◆◆	—	◆	◆◆◆
CANNED JUICES, NECTARS										
Apple juice	1 cup	124	◆	◆◆	◆◆	—	◆◆	—	◆	◆◆◆
Apricot nectar	1 cup	134	◆◆◆◆	◆	◆	◆◆	◆◆	◆	◆	◆◆
Grape juice	1 cup	160	—	◆◆	◆◆	◆	—	◆	◆◆	◆◆
Grapefruit juice	1 cup	106	—	◆◆	◆	◆	◆◆◆◆	◆	◆◆	◆◆
Grapefruit & Orange juice	1 cup	120	◆	◆◆	◆	◆◆	◆◆◆◆	◆	◆◆	◆◆
Lemon juice	1 T	5	—	—	—	—	◆◆	—	—	—
	½ cup	36	—	◆◆	—	—	◆◆◆◆	—	◆	◆
Orange juice	1 cup	112	◆◆	◆◆◆	◆◆	◆◆	◆◆◆◆	◆◆	◆◆	◆◆
Peach nectar	1 cup	104	◆◆◆	◆	◆	◆◆	◆◆	◆	◆	◆◆
Pear nectar	1 cup	110	—	◆	◆	◆	◆◆	—	◆	◆◆◆
Pineapple juice	1 cup	122	◆◆	◆◆◆	◆	◆	◆◆◆◆	◆	◆◆	◆◆◆
Prune juice	1 cup	170	—	◆◆	◆◆◆	◆◆	◆◆	◆◆	◆◆	◆◆◆◆
Tangerine juice	1 cup	98	◆◆◆	◆◆◆	◆◆	◆◆	◆◆◆◆	◆◆	◆◆	◆◆
Tomato juice	1 cup	50	◆◆◆◆	◆◆	◆◆	◆◆	◆◆◆◆	◆◆	◆	◆◆◆
Vegetable juice cocktail	1 cup	40	◆◆◆◆	◆◆◆	◆◆	◆◆◆	◆◆◆◆	◆◆	◆◆	◆◆◆
SOUPS (as served)										
Beef broth, bouillon and consomme	¾ cup	26	—	◆◆	◆	◆◆	—	◆◆	◆	◆◆
Bean with bacon or pork	¾ cup	134	◆◆◆	◆◆	◆	◆◆	—	◆◆	◆	◆◆
Chicken noodle	¾ cup	53	◆	◆◆	◆	◆	◆◆◆	◆◆	◆	◆◆
Mushroom, cream of	¾ cup	111	◆	◆◆	◆◆	◆◆	—	◆◆	◆◆	—
Tomato	¾ cup	72	◆◆◆	◆◆	—	◆◆	—	◆◆	◆	—
Vegetable	¾ cup	63	◆◆◆◆	◆◆◆	◆◆	◆◆	◆	◆◆	◆◆	◆◆
Vegetable beef	¾ cup	65	◆◆◆◆	◆◆	—	◆◆	—	◆◆	◆	—

Figure 4–L. Nutritive Value of Canned Foods.

to find meat, fish and poultry high in Vitamin C which is supplied in vegetables and fruits. And while the amount of niacin supplied by vegetables and fruits helps make up the daily requirement one turns to meat, fish, poultry, enriched bread and cereal for the larger portion of this nutrient. This again illustrates the need for variety in our daily foods. In addition to the foods individually listed in this chart many other canned foods make major nutritional contributions to infant, youth and adult diets.

LEGEND: ◆ 1% to 2.5% of recommended daily dietary allowance
◆◆ 2.5% to 10% of recommended daily dietary allowance
◆◆◆ 10% to 25% of recommended daily dietary allowance
◆◆◆◆ 25% or above recommended daily dietary allowance

SERVINGS OF CANNED FOODS

Food	Size of Serving	Calories	Vitamin A	Vitamin B1 Thiamine	Vitamin B2 Riboflavin	Niacin	Vitamin C Ascorbic Acid	Protein	Minerals Calcium	Minerals Iron
CANNED VEGETABLES										
Asparagus, green	6 med. spears	20	◆◆◆	◆◆	◆◆	◆◆	◆◆◆	◆◆	◆◆	◆◆◆
Asparagus, white	6 med. spears	21	◆	◆◆	◆◆	◆◆	◆◆◆	◆◆	◆	◆◆◆
Beans, baked w/pork and molasses	½ cup	154	—	◆◆	◆◆	◆◆	◆◆	◆◆◆	◆◆	◆◆◆◆
Beans, w/pork, tomato sauce	½ cup	140	◆	◆◆	◆◆	◆◆	◆◆	◆◆◆	◆◆	◆◆◆
Beans, green	½ cup	20	◆◆	◆◆	◆◆	◆	◆◆	◆	◆◆	◆◆◆
Beans, lima green	½ cup	81	◆◆	◆◆	◆◆	◆◆	◆◆◆	◆◆	◆◆	◆◆◆
Beans, red kidney	½ cup	108	—	◆◆	◆◆	◆◆	—	◆◆	◆◆	◆◆◆
Beans, wax	½ cup	20	◆	◆◆	◆◆	◆	◆◆	◆	◆◆	◆◆◆
Beets	½ cup	38	—	—	◆	—	◆◆	◆	◆	◆◆
Carrots	½ cup	29	◆◆◆◆	◆	◆	◆	◆◆	◆	◆◆	◆◆
Corn, cream style, white	½ cup	91	—	◆	◆◆	◆◆	◆◆	◆◆	—	◆◆
Corn, cream style, yellow	½ cup	92	◆◆	◆◆	◆◆	◆◆	◆◆	◆◆	—	◆◆
Corn, whole kernel, white	½ cup	70	—	◆	◆◆	◆◆	◆◆	◆◆	—	◆◆
Corn, whole kernel, yellow	½ cup	75	◆◆	◆	◆◆	◆◆	◆◆	◆◆	—	◆◆
Mushrooms	⅓ cup	17	—	◆	◆◆◆	◆◆	—	◆	—	◆◆
Peas, Alaska	½ cup	69	◆◆◆	◆◆	◆◆	◆◆	◆◆◆	◆◆	◆◆	◆◆◆
Peas, sweet	½ cup	60	◆◆◆	◆◆	◆◆	◆◆	◆◆◆	◆◆	◆◆	◆◆◆
Peppers, sweet	1 med.	11	◆◆◆◆	—	◆	◆	◆◆◆◆	—	—	◆◆
Pimientos	1 med.	8	◆◆◆	—	◆	◆	◆◆◆◆	—	—	◆◆
Potatoes, white	3-4 very small	96	—	◆◆	◆◆	◆◆	◆◆◆	◆◆	◆	◆◆◆
Pumpkin	½ cup	34	◆◆◆◆	◆	◆◆	◆◆	—	◆	◆◆	◆◆
Sauerkraut	½ cup	21	◆	◆◆	◆◆	—	◆◆◆	◆◆	◆◆	◆◆
Spinach	½ cup	22	◆◆◆◆	◆	◆◆	◆	◆◆◆	◆◆	◆◆◆	◆◆◆
Sweet potatoes	½ cup	123	◆◆◆◆	◆◆	◆◆	◆◆	◆◆◆◆	◆◆	◆◆	◆◆
Tomatoes	½ cup	21	◆◆◆	◆◆	◆	◆◆	◆◆◆◆	◆	◆◆	◆◆
Turnip greens	½ cup	16	◆◆◆◆	◆	◆◆	◆◆	◆◆◆◆	◆	◆◆◆	◆◆◆◆
CANNED FISH & SEAFOOD										
Clams	½ cup	37	◆	◆◆	◆◆	◆◆	—	◆◆	◆◆	◆◆◆◆
Crab meat	½ cup	83	—	◆◆	◆◆	◆◆◆	—	◆◆◆	◆◆	◆◆
Lobster	½ cup	75	—	◆	◆◆	◆◆	—	◆◆◆	◆◆	◆◆
Mackerel	½ cup	192	◆◆	◆◆	◆◆◆	◆◆◆◆	—	◆◆◆◆	◆◆◆	◆◆◆
Salmon, pink	½ cup	188	◆	◆	◆◆	◆◆◆◆	—	◆◆◆◆	◆◆◆	◆◆◆
Salmon, red	½ cup	188	◆◆	◆	◆◆	◆◆◆◆	—	◆◆◆◆	◆◆◆	◆◆◆
Sardines in oil	5 med. or 7 small	168	◆◆	—	◆◆	◆◆◆	—	◆◆◆	◆◆◆◆	◆◆◆
Sardines (Pilchards) in tomato sauce	1½ large	227	—	—	◆◆◆	◆◆◆◆	—	◆◆◆◆	◆◆◆◆	◆◆◆◆
Shrimp	10-12 med.	46	—	—	◆	◆◆	—	◆◆◆	◆◆	◆◆◆
Tuna in oil, drained solids	½ cup	170	◆	◆◆	◆◆	◆◆◆◆	—	◆◆◆◆	◆	◆◆◆
CANNED MEAT & POULTRY										
Beef, corned	3 oz.	192	—	◆	◆◆◆	◆◆◆	—	◆◆◆◆	◆	◆◆◆◆
Beef, corned, hash	½ cup	163	—	◆	◆◆	◆◆◆	—	◆◆◆	◆◆	◆◆◆
Beef gravy	¼ cup	30	—	—	◆	◆◆	—	◆◆	—	◆◆
Beef, roast	3 oz.	202	—	◆	◆◆◆	◆◆◆	—	◆◆◆◆	◆	◆◆◆
Beef stew	¾ cup	158	◆◆◆◆	◆◆	◆◆	◆◆◆	◆◆	◆◆◆	◆◆	◆◆◆
Chicken, boned	3 oz.	151	—	—	◆◆	◆◆◆	—	◆◆◆	◆	◆◆◆
Chicken stew	¾ cup	162	◆◆◆◆	◆◆	◆◆	◆◆◆	—	◆◆◆	◆◆	◆◆
Chili con carne	½ cup	167	—	◆◆	◆◆	◆◆	—	◆◆◆	◆◆	◆◆◆
Luncheon meat (pork)	2 slices, 1¾" x ⅜" x 3½"	260	—	◆◆	◆◆	◆◆◆	—	◆◆◆	◆	◆◆◆
Macaroni/cheese sauce	⅔ cup	179	◆◆	◆◆	◆◆◆	◆◆	—	◆◆◆	◆◆◆	◆◆◆
Spaghetti/tomato sauce	⅔ cup	143	◆◆◆	◆◆◆	◆◆◆	◆◆◆	◆◆◆	◆◆	◆◆	◆◆◆
Vienna sausage	4-5	127	—	◆	◆◆	◆◆	—	◆◆◆	—	◆◆◆

(Courtesy National Canners Assn. ,Washington, D. C.)

LESSON 4 - BRAINTEASER

After you are certain you understand the material in this lesson, answer the questions below. When you have completed the brainteaser, check your answers in the text.

Use the following scale to evaluate your understanding of this lesson:

10 Correct---Outstanding
9 Correct---Excellent
8 Correct---Good
7 Correct---Fair
6 Or Under
Correct---Restudy the Lesson.

1) Describe the two types of hunger.

2) One calorie equals how many BTU's? __________.

3) Providing the body with FUEL and WARMTH is a function of __________________.

4) Define an Amino Acid.

5) Explain the difference between "complete", "partially complete" and "incomplete" proteins.

6) Ascorbic Acid is also called, ____________________. It prevents a disease called, ____________________.

7) Which vitamin is called the "sunshine vitamin"? What are the sources of this vitamin?

8) Before an operation, a patient would very likely be given large doses of vitamin ____________________, to help coagulate the blood faster.

9) Name the two sources of IODINE. Which one of the two is the best source?

10) A person who had trouble adjusting his vision to changes in the intensity of light would very likely be suffering from a deficiency of ____________________________.

LESSON 5

PURCHASING AND RECEIVING OF FOODS

LESSON 5 - PREVIEW

In this lesson the student is introduced to the basic principles of purchasing and receiving foods. All necessary forms are explained, such as the: Market Quote Sheet, Food Specifications, Purchase Orders, Meat Tags, Request for Credit Memo, Receiving Clerk's Daily Report, and Distribution Sheets. Learning and understanding these forms will do much towards providing an understanding of the fundamentals of cost control, so vitally necessary to a food establishment's survival.

PURCHASING AND RECEIVING OF FOODS

In order to be proficient in the food industry, a working knowledge of the purchasing and receiving of foods is essential. If there is a breakdown in purchasing procedures or in proper receiving techniques, the profit is either eliminated or drastically reduced. The very foundation of cost control starts with this area. Because it is impossible for the manager or executive chef to be everywhere at once, personnel chosen for the responsibility of supervising the purchasing or receiving departments must be selected with extreme care. It does not take great imagination to visualize the fate of the business if the Purchasing Agent or Receiving Clerk is dishonest.

FOOD PURCHASING

Regardless of the craftmanship of the chef, or the ability of the maitre d', no dish can be acceptable if the original product is of poor quality. The method of purchasing, the ability of the purchasing agent, the use of specifications and correct forms are all a part of efficient purchasing procedures.

Market Quotation Sheet. There are many methods of purchasing foods. Probably the most common is "Open Market Buying". The purchaser receives quotations from various purveyors (two or more quotations should be obtained on every item) and records them on a Market Quotation Sheet. (See Figure 5-A.)

The lowest quotation on each item is circled, to indicate from which purveyor the merchandise is to be procured. Many times the lowest price is NOT the best price. The purchaser must consider other factors such as quality, yield, delivery charges, quantity required to obtain the quoted price, etc. In addition, the vendor must be given some consideration. For example, suppose a restaurant requires 1 lug of tomatoes and 1 crate of lettuce. Vendor A quotes low on tomatoes and high on lettuce. Vendor B quotes high on tomatoes and low on lettuce. If the difference in price is a few cents per pound, it would be better to have one vendor deliver both items, rather than each vendor deliver one item. Not only does this make it easier and more economical for one vendor, it also eliminates the necessity of two different deliveries, and the processing and paying of two different invoices. Handling time is also decreased because the two crates can be taken to storage in one trip.

The Purchasing Agent. There are no two purchasing agents alike. Some are highly qualified, possessing the required knowledge and skill, while others are not. A good purchasing agent must have the highest standards of personal integrity. He does not accept gifts from, or show partiality to, any purveyor. He must have a good working knowledge of the sources of various foods, their good and bad quality characteristics, correct storage procedures, the storage time and temperatures of various foods, yield testing, food preparation, and food specifications. His personality must be of such caliber he can work with management, chefs, vendors, and delivery men. He must be a sharp businessman and buyer but never a cheat. From the qualifications required, it can readily be seen the position of purchasing agent is not easily filled. Even if the manager or executive chef must take on the added workload of purchasing until a suitable man can be found, it is much better to wait for the right man, than to hire a poorly qualified or dishonest one.

Food Specifications. In order to provide uniformity and cost control of foods it is necessary to set up standardized purchasing specifications. A specification is nothing more than a list showing the exact description of the item desired in relation to quality, size, grade, count, or other pertinent information. (See Figure 5-B.)

CULINARY INSTITUTE OF AMERICA
STEWARD'S DAILY MARKET QUOTATION SHEET
MEATS, POULTRY, SEAFOOD

Date May 12, 1966

ITEM	Specification	Purchase	ABC	USMP	PC	
BEEF						
CHUCK, square cut, bone in						
CHUCK, square cut, clod in, bnls.						
RIBS, primal	CHOICE Spec # 117.1	120#	.63	(.60)	.62	
FOREQUARTER						
ROUND, straight (R/S on)						
ROUND						
FULL LOIN, trimmed 10"						
SHORT LOIN						
SHELL (strip) bone in						
SIRLOIN END, bone in						
TOP BUTT						
TENDERLOIN, long						
TENDERLOIN, short						
FLANK STEAK, steer, trimmed						
STRIP STEAKS	CHOICE Spec. # 113.2	200 ea.	2.71	(2.66)	2.69	
BRISKET, fresh, deckel off						
BRISKET, corned, deckel off						
BRISKET, corned, deckel off						
OXTAIL, steer						
LIVER, steer						
VEAL						
CARCASS						
CHUCK, dbl., square cut						
HOTEL RACK						
LEGS, pair						
LOIN						
CALVES LIVER						
SWEET BREADS						
TRIPE						

ITEM	Specification	Purchase				
LAMB						
CARCASS						
FORESADDLE						
HOTEL RACK						
SHOULDER, dbl.						
CHUCK, dbl.						
HINDSADDLE, long						
LEGS, pair						
LOIN, dbl.						
LAMB BACK						
PORK						
HAM, fresh						
SHOULDER, bone in						
PORK LOIN, fresh						
BUTT						
TENDERS						
SPARE RIBS						
PROVISIONS						
HAM, RTE, bone in						
HAM, pullman						
HAM, pearshaped						
HOCKS, smoked						
BACON, hotel, sliced						
CANAD. BACON, dom.						
SAUSAGE, link						
SAUSAGE, bulk						
SAUSAGE, roll						
SALT PORK						
FRANKFURTER						
BEEF TONGUES, smoked						

ITEM	Specification	Purchase			
POULTRY					
BROILERS					
ROASTERS					
CORNISH GAME HEN					
FOWL					
DUCKS, L.I.					
TURKEY					
GOOSE					
SEAFOOD					

Figure 5-A. Market Quotation Sheet.

White - Steward's Copy
Yellow - Dean's Copy (to be submitted daily after placing orders)

113.2 SIRLOIN STRIP STEAKS

U.S. Choice. 14 ounces, boneless. 8 inch length, 1/4 inch fat covering. Allowable variation: 1/4 ounce. No end or vein steaks. Quote by ounce or individual steak. Age of strip from which steaks are cut: 3 to 4 weeks. Pack 20 steaks to box, individually wrapped in plastic wrap.

117.1 BEEF RIBS

U.S. Choice. Oven prepared. Weight: 18 pounds to 23 pounds each. Remove back strap, blade bone, and blade bone cartilage. Heavy fat covering not permitted. Cut from 7 bone rib. Aged 7 to 21 days from date of slaughter. Wrapped in plastic. Must be air-tight.

300.1 MILK, HOMOGENIZED

Not less than 3.5% Butterfat. Bacterial Coli-Count less than 5. SPC less than 25,000. Deliver in 5 gal. Norris Dispensers.

Figure 5-B. Standard Purchasing Specifications.

Specifications are usually set up by management, based on menu requirements. As with all other control forms, they are good only if used. Everyone connected with purchasing and receiving should have his own copy. This includes the Manager, Purchasing Agent, Receiving Clerk, all dealers supplying the establishment, and anyone else with a "need to know".

In order to remain effective, occasional revision, or new specifications, may be necessary. For example, at certain times of the year lobsters may become so high priced that buying them is not compatible with the pricing policies or clientele of the restaurant. In this case the menu might be changed to lobster tails, requiring new specifications. Large Grade A Eggs may run several cents a dozen higher than Medium Grade A Eggs. If the medium eggs are close in size to the large eggs, a revision of specifications to medium eggs would be intelligent.

One of the most important functions of a specification is to insure that the purchaser is getting price quotes from all vendors, on the same identical item. Assuming all vendors have a copy of the specifications, the purchasing agent would call each one and ask for a quotation on an item, "....in accordance with our specification number______________." Normally, suppliers will quote prices within a few cents per pound of each other. Any price extremely high or low should be questioned, to insure that both the purchaser and the vendor are using the same specification, and talking about the same item.

Purchase Orders. Some operations use purchase orders for all purchases. The decision of whether or not to use purchase orders when buying food should be based on available personnel (for typing and filing), size of the operation, and amount of control needed or desired. Whenever possible, purchase orders should be used because they provide additional control over purchasing and receiving.

Although the same form is used, purchase orders are divided into two types, "open delivery" and "regular" or one delivery. An open delivery purchase order can be set up for any length of time, but normally does not exceed one month. It is used for items required on a daily or weekly basis, such as bread, milk, ice cream, etc. If the open delivery purchase order is intended for one month, the Delivery Date Block would be filled in like this:

July 1-31, 1966. If an operation were receiving the same item once a week, all month the Delivery Date Block would read: July 5, 11, 18, 25, 1966. Open Delivery orders should be kept to a minimum because they involve several delivery slips, for the one order. This creates additional problems in handling slips, lost and misplaced slips, bookkeeping, etc. (See Figure 5-C.) From a control standpoint, the regular, or one delivery, purchase order is better because there is only one delivery slip and one delivery of merchandise. The pre-printed purchase order form should be designed to fit a standard size window envelope, to eliminate typing of the vendor's name and address on regular envelopes.

Explanation of Purchase Order Columns. The first three lines are used for the name, address, city, state, and zip code of the purveyor.

Delivery Date (s): Filled in as required for regular or open delivery purchase orders.

Delivery Instructions: The specific building, section, or address where delivery is desired.

For Office Use Only: For operations maintaining separate cost accounts.

Terms: Record applicable discount, or other terms as specified by the vendor.

Authorizing Signature: Signature of the person authorized to approve purchase orders.

Serial, Model, or Specification Number: On purchase orders for equipment insert the serial, model, or catalog number. On purchase orders for food use the specification number.

Item: An accurate, complete description of the item desired. If a specification number is used, the description may be shortened since the specification itself gives complete details.

Quantity Ordered: Type in the quantity needed, and the correct unit of sale such as 50 lbs., 25 doz., 4 gal., etc.

Quantity Received: Write or type the exact quantity received. When using open delivery purchase orders, all delivery slips for the period must be added and the total quantity received recorded.

Unit Price: Record the dollar and/or cents figure per unit.

Extension: Multiply the number of units received times the unit price and enter total.

Sub Total: Add the figures in the Extension Column and enter the total amount.

Less Discount: Enter the amount of discount (if any) in red ink.

Purchase Order Total: Subtract discount from Sub Total Column. Enter new total.

Shipment Received and Verified by: The signature, in ink, of the person actually receiving the merchandise. (See Figure 5-D.)

Shipment Received and Verified by (Purchase Request Originator): Some establishments, when purchasing equipment and certain other items, require a Purchase Order Request, as authorization to prepare a Purchase Order. If a Purchase Order Request is required, this section would be signed by the originator of the request. This would relieve the actual receiver from responsibility for the merchandise. This section would not be used on food purchase orders. (See Figure 5-E.)

Culinary Institute of America

PURCHASE ORDER

No. 1124

TO PURVEYOR: OUR PURCHASE ORDER NUMBER (ABOVE) MUST BE SHOWN ON ALL YOUR INVOICES AND PACKAGES.

HAPPY COW DAIRY COMPANY
(NAME OF PURVEYOR)

123 Milk Can Lane
(ADDRESS OF PURVEYOR)

New Haven, Connecticut 06511
(PURVEYOR'S CITY AND STATE)

DELIVERY DATE (S): May 1 - 31, 1966

DELIVERY INSTRUCTIONS: Deliver fresh Mon. thru Fri. no later than 6 A.M. to storeroom receiving area.

TERMS: 1% 10 - Net 30 days

AUTHORIZING SIGNATURE

FOR OFFICE USE ONLY:

CHARGE TO (ACCOUNT):	TOTAL TO DATE:	BALANCE:

SERIAL, MODEL, OR CIR SPEC. NUMBER	ITEM	QUANTITY ORDERED	QUANTITY RECEIVED	UNIT PRICE	EXTENSION
300.1	Milk Fresh Homo., 5 gal. Norris	2100 Gal	2250 gal	$1.04	$2340.00

Date Received for payment: 6/4/66

Prices, Extensions and Total Verified by: RC

Date Paid: 6/10/66

Check Number: 2643

Bursar's Initials: W.G.H.

SUB TOTAL: $ 2340.00

LESS DISCOUNT: $ 23.40

PURCHASE ORDER TOTAL: $ 2316.60

SHIPMENT RECEIVED AND VERIFIED BY:

CULINARY INSTITUTE REPRESENTATIVE — 5/31/66 (DATE)

SHIPMENT RECEIVED AND VERIFIED BY:

PURCHASE REQUEST ORIGINATOR — (DATE)

Figure 5–C. Open Delivery Purchase Order.

Culinary Institute of America

PURCHASE ORDER

No. 1140

TO PURVEYOR: OUR PURCHASE ORDER NUMBER (ABOVE) MUST BE SHOWN ON ALL YOUR INVOICES AND PACKAGES.

TO

UNHAPPY STEER MEAT PACKING COMPANY
(NAME OF PURVEYOR)

456 Cutup Drive
(ADDRESS OF PURVEYOR)

New Haven, Connecticut 06511
(PURVEYOR'S CITY AND STATE)

DELIVERY DATE (S): May 16, 1966

DELIVERY INSTRUCTIONS: Deliver prior to 3 P.M. to storeroom receiving.

TERMS: Net 30 days

AUTHORIZING SIGNATURE

FOR OFFICE USE ONLY:		
CHARGE TO (ACCOUNT):	TOTAL TO DATE:	BALANCE:

SERIAL, MODEL, OR CIR SPEC. NUMBER	ITEM	QUANTITY ORDERED	QUANTITY RECEIVED	UNIT PRICE	EXTENSION
113.2	Sirloin Strip Steaks, Pre-Fab 14 oz	200 ea.	200 ea	$2.66	$532.00
117.1	Choice Ribs (6)	120 lb.	131 lb.	.60	78.60

Date Received for payment: 5/18/66
Prices, Extensions and Total Verified by: M.S.C.
Date Paid: 6/1/66
Check Number: 3066
Bursar's Initials: W.G.H

SUB TOTAL: $ 610.60

LESS DISCOUNT: $ —

PURCHASE ORDER TOTAL: $ 610.60

SHIPMENT RECEIVED AND VERIFIED BY:		SHIPMENT RECEIVED AND VERIFIED BY:	
	5/16/66		
CULINARY INSTITUTE REPRESENTATIVE	(DATE)	PURCHASE REQUEST ORIGINATOR	(DATE)

Figure 5–D. Regular Purchase Order.

Culinary Institute of America

PURCHASE ORDER

No. 4071

RUSTY EQUIPMENT COMPANY
(NAME OF PURVEYOR)

789 Loose Bolt Avenue
(ADDRESS OF PURVEYOR)

Chicago, Illinois 80416
(PURVEYOR'S CITY AND STATE)

TO PURVEYOR: OUR PURCHASE ORDER NUMBER (ABOVE) MUST BE SHOWN ON ALL YOUR INVOICES AND PACKAGES.

DELIVERY DATE (S): June 15, 1966

DELIVERY INSTRUCTIONS: Deliver to Maintenance Dept. Supervisor, Taft Hall, Angell Campus

TERMS: 2% 10 - Net 30 days

Folsom
AUTHORIZING SIGNATURE

FOR OFFICE USE ONLY:		
CHARGE TO (ACCOUNT):	TOTAL TO DATE:	BALANCE:

SERIAL, MODEL, OR CIR SPEC. NUMBER	ITEM	QUANTITY ORDERED	QUANTITY RECEIVED	UNIT PRICE	EXTENSION
3031	Fast Cook Radiant Broiler S-60	1 ea.	1 ea.	$512.50	$512.50
	Date Received for payment: 6/19/66				
	Prices, Extensions and Total Verified by: J.M.C.				
	Date Paid 6/25/66				
	Check Number 4073				
	Bursar's Initials W. G. N.				

Tel/Con 5/10/66 CIA Folsom & REC Johnson

SUB TOTAL: $512.50

LESS DISCOUNT: $ 10.25

PURCHASE ORDER TOTAL: $502.25

SHIPMENT RECEIVED AND VERIFIED BY: W. T. Doore 6-15-66
CULINARY INSTITUTE REPRESENTATIVE (DATE)

SHIPMENT RECEIVED AND VERIFIED BY: J. P. Coffman 6/16/66
PURCHASE REQUEST ORIGINATOR (DATE)

Figure 5–E. Equipment Purchase Order.

FOOD RECEIVING

The Purchasing Agents' ability to buy top quality merchandise will be of no value unless the Receiving Clerk makes sure he is actually receiving the right merchandise, with the right quality, and in the right quantity. In order to accomplish this task the Receiving Clerk must have a working knowledge of food specifications, as set up by his employer.

Each time food is received it must be checked, weighed, or counted, as applicable. This means opening cases, weighing or counting each item as necessary to verify contents, regardless of the truck drivers still waiting. All merchandise must be checked against the Market Quote Sheet, (and purchase order, if used) to insure the merchandise was actually ordered, and that the quantity and prices agree.

In order for the Receiving Clerk to do his job properly, receiving areas must have the proper equipment. This includes accurate scales, hand or motorized trucks, wire cutters, marking pencils, etc.

Meat Tags. Meat Tags (See Figure 5-F.) should be used to tag all large cuts of incoming meats for the following reasons:

a. To show the name of the purveyor, should a question of quality or quantity arise.
b. Prevent re-weighing when issuing. (Provided entire unit is used.)
c. Provide a check on the accuracy of the Receiving Clerk.
d. Help assure accurate stock rotation.
e. Speed inventory taking.
f. Facilitate ordering. (Bottom half sent to Purchasing Agent when item is issued.)

CULINARY INSTITUTE

MEAT TAG

No. ____________

Date: ______________

Dealer: ____

Cut of meat: __________________ Wt.: __________

Unit Price: $ __________ Extension: $ __________

- -

No. ____________

Date: ______________

Dealer: ____

Cut of Meat: __________________ Wt.: __________

Unit Price: $ __________ Extension: $ __________

Figure 5-F. Meat Tag.

Request for Credit Memo. After merchandise has been delivered, and signed for by the Receiving Clerk, it is company property. Should an error be discovered, a request for a credit memorandum must be made out. The original copy is sent to the vendor. The duplicate copy is given to the accounting department. The triplicate is retained by the Receiving Clerk. Some operations may require a copy for the Purchasing Agent. (See Figure 5-G.)

Culinary Institute of America

REQUEST FOR CREDIT MEMO

UNHAPPY STEER MEAT PACKING COMPANY

Nº 0491

ress: 456 Cutup Drive

, State: New Haven, Connecticut Zip Code: 06511 DATE May 16, 1966

GENTLEMEN: Please send us Credit Memo for the following:

VOICE NO.	ITEM	QUANTITY	UNIT of SALE	UNIT PRICE	EXTENSION
98765	BEEF RIB (1)	23	lbs.	$ .60	$13.80
				TOTAL	$13.80

EASON:

Not to our specifications. Not choice meat.

By [signature]

Title Steward

Figure 5-G. Request for Credit Memo.

Dealers' Invoices and Invoice Stamps. An invoice is a statement from the vendor listing the merchandise delivered together with the quantity, price extension and total money value. A dealer's invoice should accompany every delivery because it simplifies accounting, provides a cross-check on quantity and prices, and facilitates bill paying. Occasionally establishments use "blind receiving" to check on the efficiency of the Receiving Clerk. In this case the invoice is forwarded by mail, rather than with the order.

The Receiving Clerk counts the merchandise and records the exact amount received on the Receiving Clerk's daily report. When the invoice is received, the two figures are compared for accuracy.

Every invoice should be stamped with an "invoice stamp", containing the information shown below:

Received By: ______________________

Date Received: ______________________

Prices Checked By: ______________________

Calculations Checked By: ______________

Receiving Sheet Reference: ______________

Approved for Payment By: ______________

Date Paid: ______________________

Check Number: ______________________

Receiving Clerk's Daily Report. Many operations use a Receiving Clerk's Daily Report to show all food purchases, and their distribution, for each day. In addition, the report provides valuable usage data on purchasing such as dollar distribution, price index, and amount spent for different categories.

Explanation of Daily Report Columns.

There is no heading over the first column. It is often used to record invoice numbers.

Quantity. The exact amount, by individual item, received that day.

Unit. The unit of the item, such as pounds, dozens, gallons, etc.

Description. The company from which the material was received is written on one line; subsequent lines show the actual items received. Descriptions should be as complete as possible.

✓ Column. Used to indicate that the current perishable item price has been taken from the report and entered in the Perishable Price Book.

Unit Price. The specific unit price as shown on the Market Quote Sheet, the dealer's invoice, and the purchase order, if used.

Amount. The extension derived by multiplying the quantity received times the unit price.

Total Amount. The TOTAL AMOUNT of each individual invoice.

Food Direct. The dollar amount of purchases ".......that bypass the storeroom and go directly to the using department."

Food Stores. The dollar amount of purchases taken into the storeroom for stock.

Sundries. The dollar amount of items used in a food department, or establishment, other than food. (Example: Cleaning Supplies.)

The student's attention is invited to the fact that all three Purchase Journal Distribution Columns, (Food Direct, Food Stores, and Sundries), must balance with the Total Amount Column. (See Figure 5-H.)

NO. 1366

RECEIVING CLERK'S DAILY REPORT

DATE May 16, 1966

Invoice #	QUAN.	UNIT	DESCRIPTION	√	UNIT PRICE	AMOUNT	TOTAL AMOUNT	PURCHASE JOURNAL DISTRIBUTION: FOOD DIRECT	FOOD STORES	SUNDRIES
			Unhappy Steer Packing Co.							
A-98765	200	ea.	Strip Steaks 14 oz		2.66	532—				
	131	lbs.	Ribs, Choice (6)		.60	78 60	610 60		610 60	
			Happy Cow Dairy							
74-310 H	20	lbs	Cottage Cheese 4/5		.21	4 20	4 20		4 20	
			Bent Can Wholesalers							
AM 54981	2	cs.	"A" Brand (R.L.) Calif. Tom. Puree 106 S.G. 6/10		7.50	15—	15—		15—	
			Over-Ripe Produce Co.							
OR 7361	5	Bags	Potatoes, Irish Calif #1	√	6.25	31 25	31 25		31 25	
			Antique Restaurant Supply							
7841350	1	cs	Napkins, Dinner 17x15 1/2000		7—	7—	7—			7—
			Smellie Bros. Fish Co. Inc.							
SBF 3004-10	1	Bu	Clams, Cherrystone		18—	18—	18—	18—		
			Unhappy Steer Meat Packing Co. CREDIT MEMO # 491							
A-98765	23	lbs	Rib, Choice (Not to Spec.)		.60	(13 80)	(13 80)		(13 80)	
			TOTALS				672 25	18—	647 25	7—

Note: This form does not necessarily reflect a full days purchase. It is designed to acquaint the student with the various entries and illustrate how they are posted.

SIGNATURE

Figure 5–H. Receiving Clerk's Daily Report.

Receiving Clerk's Daily Reports are made out in duplicate. One copy is sent to the accounting department and one copy is retained by the Receiving Clerk, for his personal file.

Food Distribution Sheets. There are many types of Food Distribution Sheets, and various ways to use them. A small establishment may find it more advantageous to use only a Distribution Sheet and not bother with the Steward's Daily Report. Large operations may utilize both the Receiving Clerk's Daily Report and a Distribution Sheet.

By comparing column headings of the two forms (Figures 5-H and 5-I), you can readily see both records have a place in helping to achieve excellent cost control.

The Receiving Clerk's Daily Report shows receipts by day, company, amount, unit price, and total. It also breaks down the purchase dollar amount into food direct, food stores, and sundries.

The Distribution Sheet, when used in the Receiving Department, illustrates the day, company, and exact dollar purchase by item. This latter figure can be extremely useful. For example, suppose the customer count and wholesale prices over the past two months remained relatively stable, but the food costs went up 3%. By comparing total dollars spent for each category, the manager may find meat purchase dollars have increased, over last month. This could mean pilferage, waste, improper preparation, or excessive portion sizes. While this information could be obtained from the Receiving Clerk's Daily Report, it would be considerably more difficult.

The Distribution Sheet in Figure 5-I would be used by the Receiving Department. The Distribution Sheet shown in Figure 5-J can be used by any department within the operation, to illustrate daily departmental food and sundries costs.

Explanation of Columns:

Column 1: The date of the entries.

Column 2: The name of the vendor supplying the merchandise.

Columns 3 to 12: Specific breakdown by item. Notice the sheet shows no Dairy or Cheese Columns. These items would be entered under "Milk and Cream".

Column 13: Food Direct is used for purchases that by-pass the storeroom and are sent directly to the using department.

Column 14: The total amount of each invoice, from each company.

Column 15: The dollar value of sundries purchased or used, depending on whether the Distribution Sheet is "receiving" or "departmental".

Column 16: Computed by adding columns 14 and 15.

Notice on the Receiving Department Distribution Sheet (Figure 5-I) how the erroneous entry in Column 6 was handled. Nearly all companies require records be kept in ink. ALL errors should have one line drawn through them and initialed. This allows the auditors, and everyone else, to see specifically what error was made, and how it was corrected.

RECEIVING DEPARTMENT

DISTRIBUTION SHEET

No. 136 — 16 May 1966

1 DATE	2 BOUGHT OF	3 MEATS	4 GAME AND POULTRY	5 FISH	6 VEGE-TABLES	7 FRUITS	8 BUTTER	9 EGGS	10 MILK AND CREAM	11 GROCERIES	12 ICE CREAM	13 FOOD DIRECT	14 TOTAL	15 SUNDRIES	16 GRAND TOTAL
	Brought Forward	4910 72	330 41	78 50	361 10	220 08	178 —	122 90	275 80	898 60	164 20	43 80	7584 11	45 50	7629 61
	Unhappy Steer Packing Co.	610 60											610 60		
	Happy Cow Dairy Co								4 20				4 20		
	Bent Can Wholesalers									15 —			15 —		
5/16	Over Ripe Produce Co.				31 25 ~~30 25~~ JPC								31 25		
	Antique Restaurant Supply													7 —	
	Smellie Bros Fish Co.											18 —	18 —		
	Unhappy Steer Packing Co. Credit Memo # 386	(13 80)											(13 80)		
	TOTAL TODAY	596 80			31 25				4 20	15 —		18 —	665 25	7 —	672 25
	TOTAL TO DATE	5507 52	330 41	78 50	392 35	220 08	178 —	122 90	280 —	913 60	164 20	61 80	8249 36	52 50	8301 86

Figure 5-I. Receiving Distribution Sheet.

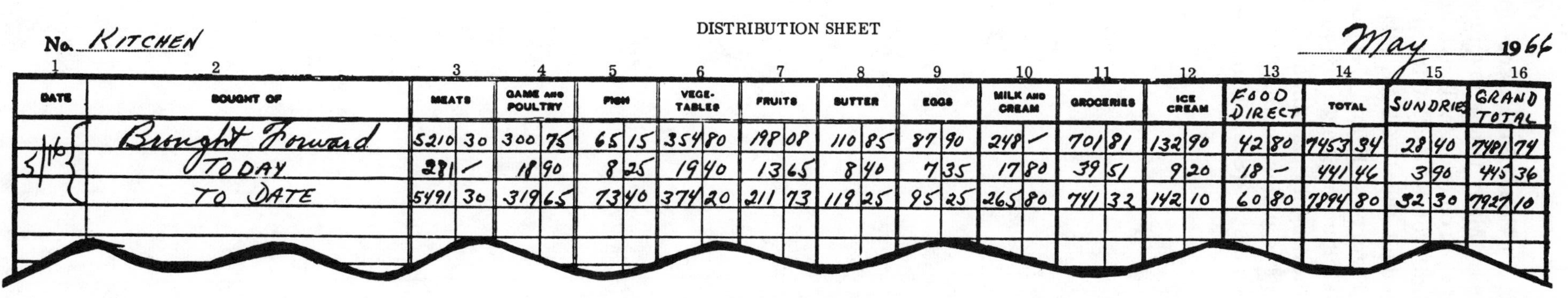

DISTRIBUTION SHEET

No. KITCHEN — May 1966

1 DATE	2 BOUGHT OF	3 MEATS	4 GAME AND POULTRY	5 FISH	6 VEGE-TABLES	7 FRUITS	8 BUTTER	9 EGGS	10 MILK AND CREAM	11 GROCERIES	12 ICE CREAM	13 FOOD DIRECT	14 TOTAL	15 SUNDRIES	16 GRAND TOTAL
5/16	Brought Forward	5210 30	300 75	65 15	354 80	198 08	110 85	87 90	248 —	701 81	132 90	42 80	7453 34	28 40	7481 74
	TODAY	281 —	18 90	8 25	19 40	13 65	8 40	7 35	17 80	39 51	9 20	18 —	441 46	3 90	445 36
	TO DATE	5491 30	319 65	73 40	374 20	211 73	119 25	95 25	265 80	741 32	142 10	60 80	7894 80	32 30	7927 10

Figure 5-J. Kitchen Distribution Sheet.

Direct Food Purchases do not allow the same control as regular storeroom purchases. Many times invoices are held up, or lost, by the department receiving the direct purchases. Always keep direct purchases to an absolute minimum.

The "Total Today-GRAND TOTAL", on the Receiving Distribution Sheet, must exactly equal the "TOTAL AMOUNT" column on the Receiving Clerk's Daily Report. Look at Figures 5-H and 5-I to verify this.

Distribution Sheets explained above are relatively easy to understand. If the student thoroughly masters the principles of these simple forms, he will have little or no trouble understanding the more complicated Distribution Sheet explained in another course. (See Figure 5-K.)

Culinary Institute of America, Inc.

DISTRIBUTION OF FOOD COST

UNIT__________ PERIOD: FROM________ TO________

	MEAT	FISH	POULTRY	FRUIT AND VEGETABLES	DAIRY PRODUCTS	BAKERY PRODUCTS	OTHER FOODS	LIQUORS	TOTAL
Carried Forward									
COST TODAY									
TO DATE LAST WEEK									
TO DATE TODAY									

RECONCILIATION

(a) Total issues ________

(b) Distributed cost ________

Difference ________

NOTE: (a) should equal (b)

NON-EDIBLE KITCHEN SUPPLIES	
Today	
To date last week	
To date today	

Figure 5-K. Distribution Sheet.

LESSON 5 - BRAINTEASER

After you are certain you understand the material in this lesson, answer the questions below. When you have completed the brainteaser, check your answers in the text. Use the following scale to evaluate your comprehension of this lesson:

10 Correct --- Outstanding
9 Correct --- Excellent
8 Correct --- Good
7 Correct --- Fair
6 or Under
Correct --- Restudy the Lesson

1) The most common method of purchasing is ________________ ________________

____

2) A SPECIFICATION shows the exact description of the item desired as to ______________,

______________, ______________, ______________, or other pertinent information.

3) Describe the difference between an "open" and "regular" purchase order.

4) Name at least four reasons why MEAT TAGS should be used.

5) A CREDIT MEMORANDUM is made out in the original and ______________ copies.

Explain the distribution of each copy.

6) List the reasons why an INVOICE STAMP should be used.

7) Explain the reason for the CHECK (✓) COLUMN on the Receiving Clerk's Daily Report.

8) What is the purpose of the FOOD DIRECT COLUMN on the Receiving Clerk's Daily Report?

9) Explain the difference between the Receiving Clerk's Daily Report and the Food Distribution Sheet.

10) Why should DIRECT PURCHASES be kept to a minimum?

LESSON 6

STORAGE AND ISSUE OF FOODS

LESSON 6 - PREVIEW

It is not the intent of this lesson to cover every single aspect of food storage. Many areas of the subject are learned easier and faster with, "on the job training". For example, there is no advantage in trying to teach the student all of the hundreds of storage times and temperatures for food items when he will be working with relatively few. The prime objective is to present pertinent facts and forms connected with the storage and issuing of food, in order to provide a foundation for the trainee.

Every establishment has its own particular forms for use in the storage and issuing of foods, and related items. The student should become thoroughly familiar with the forms presented in this lesson, such as, Inventory Sheets, Requisition, Stock Record Card, and Steward's Daily Report. Once the basic principles are understood, learning a modification of the form, in actual working conditions, will be simple.

FOOD STORAGE

The Four Principles of Food Storage. There are four primary rules connected with the storage of any type of food:

1. SAFETY. Large cases that do not fit on shelves, should be stored on the floor. Good quality aluminum step ladders should be provided for reaching high shelves. All walk-in refrigerators must have inside door releases.
2. SANITATION. All storage areas must be kept immaculate and free of insects and rodents. (Refer back to lesson 2 for information on insect and rodent control.)
3. SENSE. In this case, we mean sensible storage. Keep aisles free and clear of cases. Group like items together, such as canned fruits in one section, canned vegetables in another. Storeroom stock is usually placed in exactly the same order as the Inventory Sheet, starting at the door and going around the room. Keep stocks rotated by using the oldest stock first. Mark the cost price on everything to facilitate pricing inventories, requisitions, etc. Keep odor absorbing foods (e.g. eggs) away from strong odor foods (e.g. cheese).
4. SECURITY. Never leave the storeroom open while unattended. Key control is essential. There should be only one key in circulation, held by the man responsible for the inventory. A duplicate key is usually kept in the manager's safe, in a sealed envelope. The envelope must be dated and signed across the flap by both the man in charge of the storeroom and the manager. When a new man assumes responsibility of any security area, it is advisable to send him downtown to buy one good quality lock, with two keys, at company expense. This insures him no other keys are in existence.

Why Have A Storeroom? The storeroom exists for one purpose, the control of merchandise. If an operation does not know exactly how much stock is being received, stored, and issued, there can be no basis for cost control. Obviously, if there is no cost control, the amount of profit is doubtful. If the profit becomes nonexistent, there is no business.

Physical Set-up of Storerooms. Storerooms should be located between the receiving area and the preparation area. They must be well ventilated to retard spoilage. Good lighting is a must for easier reading of labels, record keeping, and proper sanitation. Racks should be used to keep merchandise off the floor, and make cleaning easier. Good quality adjustable metal shelving is advisable for the storage of broken case items.

Refrigerator Storage. Inspect all items frequently for spoilage, especially fresh fruits and vegetables. Maintain the proper temperature and humidity, as specified by the manufacturer. When moving merchandise in or out do so as rapidly as possible, to avoid coil icing, temperature drop, and overloading of compressors. The use of electric fans, or blowers, will insure proper air circulation and retard coil icing. Cases should be stored in such a manner to avoid contact with coils, fans, floors, or ceiling. Crates or cases with a bulge on top, such as melons must be stored on their side, to prevent crushing of products.

Storage Temperatures. Every establishment sets its own particular refrigerator storage temperatures. A general guide is presented on the following page.

Freezer: 0° F. or lower

Chill or Thaw Box: 40° F. to 45° F.

Fruit and Vegetable Box: 34° F. to 38° F.

Dairy Box: 32° F. to 34° F.

It is so important to maintain correct refrigerator temperatures many operations use a "Temperature Record Book", to make sure temperatures are checked and recorded at least twice daily. Any record book, about 5 x 8 inches can be used. Column headings and recordings should be in ink.

REFRIGERATOR TEMPERATURE RECORD BOOK

Date	5/9/66		5/10		5/11		5/12		5/13		5/14		5/15	
Time	8	4	8	4	8	4	8	4	8	4	8	4	8	4
Freezer	0	-1	0	+1	+1	+1	0	0	-1	-1	0	0	-1	0
Thaw	43	43	41	41	43	45	41	41	42	42	41	43	40	44
Fruit & Veg	36	36	36	36	42	42	36	36	36	37	36	38	36	38
Dairy	32	34	32	34	32	33	32	34	31	33	32	33	32	33

Management should make a determination as to how many degrees above and below desired temperatures is considered hazardous to food retention. Readings indicating those levels should be recorded in red ink, and the supervisor notified immediately.

Accuracy of recordings should be evaluated occasionally by checking the actual temperatures against those posted in the temperature record book. By reviewing the recordings daily, a supervisor can often detect erratic or malfunctioning compressors before food is damaged, or while only minor repairs are needed.

Inventories. There are many types of inventories and each one has its own place in operational improvement or cost control. Because inventory records are permanent records, frequently referred to, they must always be recorded in ink.

A SPOT-CHECK inventory is used to evaluate performance and efficiency of the Receiving Clerk, Storeroom Man, or other stores-handling personnel. Once or twice a week, two or three items are inventoried and compared with recorded entries.

Excessive food costs may indicate a need for a DAILY, WEEKLY or SEMI-MONTHLY inventory, to pinpoint the problem.

PERPETUAL inventories, when conscientiously recorded, show the exact balance on hand, of every item, at all times.

MONTH-END physical inventories are the foundation of food costing.

Month-End Inventory. A month-end inventory is the actual physical inventory, taken at the close of business, on the last day of every month. It is an exceptionally important inventory, for without an accurate count of each and every item, a true picture of food cost is impossible. Figure 6-A illustrates a typical inventory sheet.

INVENTORY

DATE TAKEN: 31 May 1966 PAGE 9

SHEET NO. 1 of 2 PRICED BY J. Amendola

CALLED BY John H. Bryetti Jr. DEPARTMENT STOREROOM EXTENDED BY J. Amendola

ENTERED BY J. P. Coffman LOCATION FREEZER EXAMINED BY L. Faber

ITEM NUMBER	QUANTITY	DESCRIPTION	√	PRICE	UNIT	EXTENSIONS	
	25	Baby Lima Beans	√	23	#	5 75	
	30	Cut Corn	√	23	#	6 90	
	37½	Cut Green Beans	√	25	#	9 38	
	24	Leaf Spinach	√	19	#	4 56	
	20	Brussel Sprouts	√	28	#	5 60	
	20	Broccoli Spears	√	28	#	5 60	
	17½	Asparagus Spears (medium)	√	60	#	10 50	
	44	Cauliflower	√	30	#	13 20	
	20	Orange Juice	√	85	qt.	17 —	
	37	Fruit Punch	√	85	qt.	31 45	
	41	Ground Beef	√	59	#	24 19	
	57	Lamb Chuck	√	44	#	25 08	
	8	Bologna (1)	√	47	#	3 76	
	8	Salami (1)	√	55	#	4 40	
	22½	Lobster Tails ½ 2½	√	1 50	#	~~23 75~~	33 75
	6	Dover Sole 1/18 oz	√	1 35	CN	8 10	
	10	Hamburger Buns	√	30	DZ	3 —	
	15	Lemon Juice 1/4 oz	√	28	CN	4 20	
	10	Unsliced Bread	√	30	LF	3 —	
	8	Lobster Meat 1/14 oz	√	3 —	CN	24 —	
	13	Frog Legs 4/1	√	1 75	#	22 75	
	12	Oysters	√	1 —	#	12 —	
	18	Swordfish	√	75	#	13 50	
	16	Halibut	√	60	#	9 60	
	68	Pot Roast	√	95	#	64 60	
	15	Ham Hocks	√	35	#	5 25	
	11	Pepperoni	√	79	#	8 69	
	32	Veal (Fore)	√	59	#	18 88	
		TOTAL THIS PAGE				~~388 69~~	398 69

Figure 6–A. Inventory Sheet.

Explanation of Columns. Most of the columns on the Inventory Sheet (Figure 6-A) are self explanatory. Those columns that may be confusing to the student are explained below.

Page. Refers to the page number in the Inventory Book.

Sheet No. The sheet number of the specific page of this inventory. Sheet numbers should always be written as a part of the group, such as 1 of 4, 2 of 4, 3 of 4, etc.

Called By. The name of the person doing the counting, and calling out the quantity, for the person entering the figures.

Item Number. Establishments often assign their own stock numbers to items to facilitate requisitioning, inventory, etc. This is particularly true of bottle goods.

✓. The check column is used by the examiner as he re-checks the figures.

Extension Columns. The student will note there are two extension columns. The original recordings are done in the left hand column. Any corrections are entered in the right hand column, as illustrated.

ISSUING OF FOOD

The primary objective of any issuing storeroom is to maintain daily control of merchandise used by the various departments. If an establishment knows exactly what is used each day, computing the daily food cost is easy. If the manager must "guesstimate" the cost of food used each day, by the time the month-end inventory is taken, and the actual cost calculated, the business could be bankrupt.

Some restaurants locate their Issue Room separately from the main Storeroom. Most units combines the two into one vecause it is more practical, saves time and labor, and is more efficient.

The man in charge of food issuing has a very important position. He must be honest, competent, and interested in his job. If he is not, he negates all the work and control of the Purchasing Agent and Receiving Clerk.

Issue Room Hours. Establishing specified hours for issuing merchandise to departments has many advantages. It allows time for re-stocking the shelves, record keeping, general cleaning, and any other work that may be required.

Date Stamps. All merchandise should have the "Date Received" stamped (or written) somewhere on the container. Date-stamping stock provides easier and simpler rotation. Items must be stored in such a manner as to permit easy reading of the label, and date received.

Pricing Merchandise. Pricing all items received prior to placing them on the shelf is extremely valuable. With the price on the item, accurate pricing of requisitions (when issuing) and inventories is relatively simple.

Requisitions. The most widely recognized method of controlling food issues is through the use of requisitions. A requisition, properly filled out, and signed by the head of the department, provides the authority for the release of merchandise from the storeroom. In addition, the requisition can be the basis of the daily food cost, because it shows the total money value of items used by a certain department, for a particular day. Figure 6-B illustrates a simplified requisition form used in many establishments.

REQUISITION ORDER

No. 101 Date 17 May 19 66

To Steward Angell Campus

Please deliver to PK-1

2	#10 Tomato Paste $1.13		2	26
2	#2½ Peaches (halves) .52		1	04
~~20~~ 15	# Potatoes .05			75
10	# Flour .08			80
			$4	85

Remarks

Alphonse S Marcello **Signature**

Printed in U.S.A.

Figure 6–B. Simplified Requisition.

A more sophisticated requisition is illustrated in Figure 6-C. Quite often the amount ordered, and the amount received, are not the same. This can be caused by erroneous ordering, unexpected stock demands, spoilage, etc. On the simplified requisition, when there is a difference between the amount ordered and the amount received, the figure must be scratched out and a new figure inserted. In addition, columns are not clearly defined. When using a simplified requisition, one department may use a particular section for an entry, such as the unit price, and a different department might use the same section for the container size. These problems are eliminated on the requisition shown in Figure 6-C.

CULINARY INSTITUTE OF AMERICA
Department Requisition

No. 101

To Steward *Angell* Campus

Date: *17 May* 19*66*

Deliver to: *PK-1*

Alphonse S. Marcello
Authorizing Signature

ITEM	UNIT OF ISSUE	AMOUNT ORDERED	AMOUNT RECEIVED	UNIT PRICE	EXTENSION
Tomato Paste	*#10 Can*	*2*	*2*	*$1.13*	*$2.26*
Peaches (Halves)	*#2½ Can*	*2*	*2*	*.52*	*1.04*
Potatoes	*lb.*	*20*	*15*	*.05*	*.75*
Flour	*lb.*	*10*	*10*	*.08*	*.80*

Issued by: *Fred A. Newhand S-8*
Storeroom Representative

Received by: *John Mislinski J-6*
Department Representative

Total: *$4.85*

Figure 6–C. Requisition.

Requisitions are usually made out with an original and one copy. Company policy may require additional copies. The original and duplicate are presented to the Storeroom Supervisor with only the "Item", "Unit of Issue", and "Amount Ordered" columns filled in. The Storeroom Representative, after issuing the merchandise, completes the remaining columns and retains the original copy for his file. The duplicate copy is returned to the originator, with the order.

Notice the spaces provided for signatures of the man actually issuing and the man actually receiving the merchandise. These signatures can provide valuable information when checking back through requisitions for shortages, errors, etc.

Stock Record Card. Stock Record Cards are also referred to as "Bin Cards", or "Perpetual Inventory Cards". They are a valuable tool of management because they show Receipts, Issues, and Balance on Hand, for each food item. Cards are printed on both the front and back. When a card is filled with entries a new card is started with, "BF" (Brought Forward), and the Balance on Hand figure, from the old card.

When there is more than one using department for an item, it is desirable to record the drawing department in the "Rec'd" column. This will provide fast reference should a question arise as to "how much" of a particular item is being used, by a specific department.

The "High Limit" is the maximum amount that should be in stock, at any one time. The "Low Limit" column serves as a "warning light" to order more stock. Both of these figures are established from usage date of past records and should be revised as necessary.

As explained in Lesson 5, some businesses use a number to identify certain items. If local stock numbers are being used, they would be recorded in the "Item Number" column, on the record card.

Because unit prices vary frequently, it is not practical to use the "Unit Price" column, unless the item was purchased in large quantity, or on term contract, where the price would remain stable, for long periods of time.

When properly posted, and kept up to date, the Stock Record Card becomes a "Perpetual Inventory Card". The recorded balance on hand should always equal the actual stock in the storeroom. To evaluate personnel efficiency, frequent spot-check inventories should be conducted to insure that actual stock on hand and the Balance figure on the card are in agreement. (See Figure 6-D.)

STOCK RECORD CARD

NAME OF ITEM: TOMATO PASTE		UNIT: #10 CAN
LOCATION: MAIN STOREROOM		UNIT PRICE
REMARKS: 1 co = 6/10 106 S. G.	ITEM NUMBER	HIGH LIMIT: 24
		LOW LIMIT: 6

DATE	REC'D	ISSUED	BALANCE	DATE	REC'D	ISSUED	BALANCE
4/28/66	BF		9				
4/29		2	7				
4/30	INV		7				
5/3		2	5				
5/5	18	1	22				
5/7		2	20				
5/9		1	19				
5/11		2	17				
5/13		2	15				
5/15		1	14				
5/17		2	12				

Figure 6–D. Stock Record Card.

Steward's Daily Report. The Steward's Daily Report is designed to provide management with a breakdown, by departments, of daily and to date food costs. At the end of each day, the total money value of all requisitions is posted in the "Today Column", alongside the department it is for. The "Today" cost figure is added to yesterday's "To Date" figure, to arrive at the new "To Date" total.

Whenever any form shows Today and To Date figures, the To Date Figure is always the most important, to the person doing the analysis. This is so because a legitimately high cost may be reflected in any department, for the day, without that department "operating in the red", in the To Date Column.

For example, let us assume faulty equipment has ruined a high-cost menu item, and it must be prepared again. The food cost for the department would be higher than normal that day. However, if the department has been exercising proper controls, their To Date cost would still be well within allowable limits.

With many forms, when an error occurs, it affects only one specific item, or one specific day. This is not true with the Steward's Daily Report. An undetected error, will be carried forward on all subsequent reports until the month-end inventory. For this reason, correct and accurate posting is essential. If the Receiving Clerk's Daily Report is wrong, if prices are incorrect, if issues are posted to the wrong department, if any mathematical errors occur, the Steward's Daily Report will be erroneous from that point on, and all the work involved is of no value.

Explanation of Columns in the Inventory Section:

Opening Inventory, Today. On the first day of each month, this figure would be the actual physical inventory amount, based on the month-end inventory taken at the close of business, the preceding day. On all other days, the Closing Inventory, Today, is brought forward from yesterday's Steward's Daily Report.

Purchases, Today. The total value of purchases, not including sundries, from the Receiving Clerk's Daily Report.

Total Available Stock, Today. Opening Inventory plus Purchases always equals Total Available Stock.

Issues, Today. The total money value of all issues, as determined from requisitions, or other sources.

Closing Inventory, Today. Total Available Stock minus Issues.

Opening Inventory, To Date. The money value of the actual physical inventory, taken at the close of business, on the last day of the month. This figure never changes. It remains the same on all Steward's Daily Reports throughout the month.

Purchases, To Date. The total of "Today's" Purchases added to Yesterday's "To Date" Purchases.

Total Available Stock, To Date. The cumulative total of Today's figure and yesterday's To-Date figure.

Issues, To Date. The total money value of Today's issues and yesterday's issues To Date.

Closing Inventory, To Date. The figure in this column must always be exactly the same as the Closing Inventory Today Figure.

Examine Figures 6-E and 6-F. Notice the Closing Inventory <u>Today</u> figure becomes the Opening Inventory Today Figure on the next report. As stated previously, this rule always applies, except on the first day of each month. The student must also remember that the Opening Inventory, To Date figure is always the same, during the entire month. It is the total money value of the actual physical inventory, taken at the close of business, on the last day of the month.

Depending on the rules of the establishment, the Steward's Daily Report may be required in the original only, or in the original with one or more copies in addition. Some operations require that information from the Steward's Daily Report be entered daily in a record book.

STEWARD'S DAILY REPORT — No. 11

ANGELL CAMPUS — Date. May 16, 1966

	TODAY	TO DATE
I. School Departments:		
PK: 1	22.75	523.57
PK: 2	29.56	471.68
PK: 3	16.51	472.34
PK: 4	18.34	448.43
PK: 5	31.99	543.14
PK: 6	30.39	550.63
DEMO: 1	33.74	299.64
BREAKFAST: 1	33.07	722.81
MEAT CUTTING:	—	—
TABLE SERVICE	28.07	364.30
BAKE SHOP	1.61	1027.12
AK: 4	98.82	819.72
AK: 5	36.42	1010.68
BREAKFAST: 2	21.67	395.74
VENDING:	—	114.86
TOTAL ISSUES:	402.94	7764.66
II. YALE AA	—	611.10
III. SPECIAL FUNCTIONS:		
HARTFORD SHOW 46.13		
HOLDEN PARTY 13.83		
	59.96	93.40
IV. MISCELLANEOUS:		
V. C.P.I.	10.24	184.07
VI. TRANSFERS:	35.02	351.15
TOTAL ISSUES:	508.16	9004.38
INVENTORY:		
Opening Inventory	3650.67	2749.14
Purchases	665.25	10 063.00
Total Available Stock	4315.92	12812.14
Issues	508.16	9004.38
Closing Inventory	3807.76	3807.76

Signature John H. Spatta Jr

Figure 6–E. Steward's Daily Report.

	STEWARD'S DAILY REPORT		No. *12*
	ANGELL CAMPUS		Date. *May 17, 1966*

1. School Departments:	TODAY	TO DATE
PK: 1		
PK: 2		
PK: 3	13.88	537.45
PK: 4	17.53	489.21
PK: 5	4.73	477.07
PK: 6	18.33	466.76
DEMO: 1	28.00	571.14
BREAKFAST: 1	59.15	609.78
MEAT CUTTING:	20.80	320.44
TABLE SERVICE	64.81	787.62
BAKE SHOP	—	—
AK: 4	13.00	377.30
AK: 5	3.43	1030.55
BREAKFAST: 2	57.84	877.56
VENDING:	40.35	1051.03
TOTAL ISSUES:	45.01	440.75
II. YALE AA	6.81	121.67
III. SPECIAL FUNCTIONS:	393.67	8158.33
EVENING SCHOOL		611.10
IV MISCELLANEOUS:	16.58	109.98
V. C.P.I.		
VI. TRANSFERS:	8.45	192.52
TOTAL ISSUES:	6.18	357.33
INVENTORY:	424.88	9429.26
Opening Inventory	3807.76	2749.14
Purchases	726.61	10789.61
Total Available Stock	4534.37	13538.75
Issues	424.88	9429.26
Closing Inventory	4109.49	4109.49

Signature *John H. Goguette Jr.*

Figure 6–F. Steward's Daily Report.

LESSON 6 - BRAINTEASER

When you are certain you understand the material in this lesson, answer the questions below. After you have completed the brainteaser, check your answers in the text. Use the following scale to evaluate your comprehension of this lesson:

10 Correct --- Outstanding
9 Correct --- Excellent
8 Correct --- Good
7 Correct --- Fair
6 Or Under
Correct --- Restudy the Lesson

1) Explain in detail the Four Principles of Food Storage.

2) What is the purpose of a "Refrigerator Temperature Record Book"?

3) List the recommended storage temperatures for each type of refrigerator.

Freezer:	______	to	______	degrees F.
Chill or Thaw:	______	to	______	degrees F.
Fruit and Vegetables:	______	to	______	degrees F.
Dairy Box:	______	to	______	degrees F.

4) Name the various types of inventories, and the purpose, or use, of each one.

5) Why are there two extension columns on an Inventory Sheet?

6) What are the advantages of having specified hours for issuing foods?

7) Name the two primary purposes for using requisitions.

8) Stock Record Cards are a valuable tool of management because they show

____________________, ____________________, ____________________, for each
(3 words)

food item.

9) What is the purpose of the Steward's Daily Report?

10) Why is accuracy especially important when computing the Steward's Daily Report?

What happens when an erroneous entry is made on a Steward's Daily Report?

LESSON 7

MENU PLANNING

LESSON 7 - PREVIEW

Preparing and serving food for the public is an art. A meal that is attractive, well balanced, palatable, and profitable does not just materialize out of thin air. It is developed from years of experience, hours of work, and a sincere interest in the company and the customer.

In this lesson the types of menus and the various rules of menu planning are explained. Acquiring a knowledge of these factors will aid the student in writing successful menus.

TYPES OF MENUS

Generally menus are divided into two main categories: the table d'hote and the a la carte.

The table d'hote offers the customer a complete meal and several courses at a fixed price. (See Figure 7-A.)

The "a la carte" menu lists each item with its own separate price. Because the entrees on the "a la carte" menu are less expensive, the customer often feels he will save money by using this menu. However, by the time the guest has ordered all the items he likes with his meal, he is often surprised at the size of the check. (See Figure 7-B.)

In addition to the previously mentioned menus, special menus are frequently used for breakfast, luncheon, dinner, banquets, holidays and specialty meals. (See Figures 7-C, 7-D, 7-E, 7-F, 7-G, 7-H.)

Famous Buttonwood Twin Dinners

CARVED AND FLAMED AT TABLE SIDE

CHATEAUBRIAND

— OR —

Prime DOUBLE SIRLOIN

GARNI

Asparagus, Broiled Tomato, Carrots, Duchess Potato, Mushroom Caps

Serves Two—
Seven dollars and fifty cents per person

CHAUVENET RED CAP SPARKLING BURGUNDY, BOTTLE 10.00, HALF 5.25 (11)

KOOPMAN CUT PRIME SIRLOIN STEAK: Specially aged Blue Ribbon Quality Steak, Broiled with the "Bone In" . . . The way Tom liked it . . . Mushroom Caps, Onion Rings . . . Five dollars and fifty cents.
B & G Chateauneuf Du Pape, Bottle 5.00, Half 2.75 (41)

FILET MIGNON, THE ROYALTY OF BEEFDOM: The most majestic and tender of all Steaks, Broiled . . . Topped with Mushroom Crowns and Onion Rings . . . Five dollars and fifty cents.
B & G Beaujolais Saint Louis, Bottle 5.00, Half 2.75 (47)

BUTTONWOOD'S SLICED BEEF TENDERLOIN: A popular feature of ours for years. Sliced Filet Mignon Sauted in Butter and Burgundy Wine. Served with our own Bordelaise Sauce . . . Four dollars and fifty cents.
B & G Pommard, Bottle 5.75, Half 3.00 (48)

FILET MIGNON EN BROCHETTE: Bite size chunks of the Queen of Steaks skewered with Tomatoes, Mushrooms, Peppers and Pearl Onions. Served flaming with Duchess Potato, Fresh Garden Peas and Wild Rice . . . Four dollars and fifty cents.
B & G Chateau-Pontet Canet, Bottle 5.75, Half 3.00 (43)

GREAT WESTERN, CHOPPED SIRLOIN: A generous serving of ground to order Steak, American Style with Mushroom Sauce and Onion Rings . . . Three dollars.
Almaden Grenache Rose, Bottle 3.25, Half 1.75 (81)

COUNTRY HAM STEAK, HAWAIIAN: Sugar cured ham from peanut-fed-pride-of-old-Virginia Porkers, flame broiled and linked to our 50th State by a broiled pineapple ring . . . Three dollars and fifty cents.
B & G Graves, Bottle 4.50, Half 2.50 (63)

Included with the Entrees . . . A Relish Dish, A selection of Baked Idaho or French Fried Potato, Tossed Garden Salad, Fresh Vegetable, Roll Basket, and Coffee

Figure 7–A. Table d'Hote Menu.
(Menu – Courtesy of Buttonwood Manor, Matawan, New Jersey.)
(Artwork and design – Courtesy of and Copyrighted by Yogg and Company, Newark, New Jersey.)

Roast Long Island BONED DUCKLING

Half a boned full breasted Long Island Duckling slowly roasted; basted with fruit juices and Burgundy Wine. Served with our own stuffing, Bing Cherries and sliced Orange Bigarade, in the manner that has become a Buttonwood tradition.

FOUR DOLLARS

CHATEAU ST. ROSELINE VIN ROSE, BOTTLE 4.50, HALF 2.75 (51)

SOUTH AFRICAN LOBSTER TAILS: Twin tails from Neptune's Locker along the South African Coast. Split and taken out of the shell, they are broiled with butter to a golden brown. Served with Drawn Butter . . . Four dollars and fifty cents.
Lancer's Crackling Rose, Bottle 6.50, Half 3.50 (3)

ALASKAN KING CRAB LEGS, BROILED AND SHELLED: The tenderest of meat from this denizen of the deep, broiled with White Wine and Butter . . . Four dollars and twenty-five cents.
Bernkastler Moselle, Bottle 4.50, Half 2.50 (66)

BAKED STUFFED WHITE PANAMIAN SHRIMP: Mammoth Butterfly Shrimp filled with our world famous Stuffing. Served on a bed of Lobster Sauce . . . Three dollars and fifty cents.
Liebfraumilch, Bottle 4.50, Half 2.50 (64)

STUFFED FILET OF JERSEY SOLE: America's foremost Sole, Broiled in Butter and White Wine and stuffed with Creamed Alaskan King Crabmeat . . . Three dollars.
B & G Sauterne, Bottle 4.75, Half 2.50 (65)

BUTTONWOOD SEAFOOD COMBINATION: A must for the craver of spectacular seafood sensations. A hot and cold combination with more than generous bounties of Alaskan King Crab Meat, Fresh Shrimp, Fried Scallops, Filet of Sole, Maryland Crabcake and Buttonwood's Deviled Clam . . . Three dollars.
B & G Chablis, Bottle 6.25, Half 3.50 (62)

WE WILL BE PLEASED TO SERVE ANY A LA CARTE ENTREE ON A COMPLETE DINNER FOR $1.00 ADDITIONAL. SELECT APPETIZER AND DESSERT FROM DINNER MENU.

Le repas sans vin est comme une jolie femme sans amour, ou comme un jour sans soleil—**Raymond**

SPORTS AFIELD CLUB

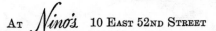

AT *Nino's* 10 EAST 52ND STREET :: NEW YORK CITY

HORS D'OEUVRES

Colossal Shrimps Grille, Raymond 2.35
Baked Oysters, Nino or Casino 2.00
Baked Clams, Nino 1.95 *Cherrystone Cocktail* 95
Nova Scotia Salmon 2.10
Melon with Prosciutto Ham 2.10
Imported Pate de Foie de Strasbourg 3.75
Coquille of Shrimps, Remick 2.00
Blue Point or Cape Cod Oysters 1.00
Crab Meat or Shrimp Cocktail 2.00
Hors d'Oeuvres, Parisienne 2.00
Delice Maison 2.00 *Beluga Caviar* 6.50
Celeris and Olives 95

SOUPS

Cream of Tomatoes 90
Cold Vichyssoise 90
Boula - Boula 1.00
St. German aux Croutons 85
Green Turtle 1.00
Consomme du Jour 70
Pauvre Homme (Poor Man's Soup) 1.00
Madrilene in Jelly 70

ENTREES

COLOSSAL SHRIMPS GRILLE, *Raymond, Wild Rice* 4.75
LOUISIANA FROG'S LEGS SAUTE, *Cote d'Azur* 4.50
MAINE LOBSTER GRILLE, *Maitre d'Hotel* 5.50
IMPORTED ENGLISH SOLE *aux Amandes* 4.50
SEA SCALLOPS AND LOBSTER, *Maison d'Or* 4.25
BROOK TROUT SAUTE, *aux Raisins, Champenoise* 3.95
FLORIDA POMPANO POCHE, *Marguery* 4.25
DOMESTIC VENISON SAUTE, *Grand Veneur* 5.75
ROAST PRIME RIBS OF BEEF AU JUS, *Moderne* 5.25
AFRICAN GUINEA HEN SAUTE, SMITHAINE, *Wild Rice* 5.50
BRIZOLA STEAK GRILLE *aux Echalottes* 6.25
LONG ISLAND DUCKLING, *Bigarade a l'Orange* 4.25
VEAL CUTLET SAUTE A LA FRANCAISE 4.25
NOISETTE OF LAMB GRILLE, *Princesse* 4.25
WESTERN PLAINS BUFFALO STEAK SAUTE, *Imperiale* 9.00
LLAMA STEAK OR CHOP GRILLE, *Sports Afield* 14.00

For Complete Enjoyment of These Superlative Culinary Achievements We Suggest "A WINE" of Your Choice

POTATOES

Lyonnaise 90
Jackson 1.00
Saute 85
Baked 90
French Fried 85
Souffles 1.00
Hashed Browned 85
Allumette 85

VEGETABLES

String Beans 90
Carrots 85
Zucchini Provencale 1.25
Broccoli Hollandaise or *Parmesan* 1.40
Peas 95
Cauliflower Polonaise 1.25
Spinach 95
Asparagus Hollandaise 1.50
Celeris Braised 1.25

SALADS

Shrimp Salad 3.75
Alma 1.25
Caesar Salad 2.75
Chicken Salad 3.75
Hearts of Palms 2.00
Mixed Green 1.00
Lobster Salad 4.00
Chiffonade 1.25
Kentucky Lettuce 1.50
Lettuce and Tomatoes 1.25

DESSERTS

Baked Alaska, Flambe au Brandy (for 2) 5.00
Coupe Diplomat 1.75
Strawberry Melba 1.50
Chocolate Mousse Maison 1.25
Parfait Maison 1.25
Macedoine de Fruit aux Liqueurs 1.75
French Pastry, Maison 1.00
Crepes Suzette, Rothschild 2.95

WE SUGGEST A RICH LUSCIOUS CHATEAU BOTTLING WHITE BORDEAUX WITH YOUR DESSERT

Cafe Diable or Royal 1.75
Coffee 60
Drambuie
Demi-Tasse des Princes 1.25
Espresso Cafe 70

CHOICEST SELECTION OF BRANDIES AND LIQUEURS

OPEN FOR LUNCHEON FROM 12:00 NOON — FOR RESERVATIONS CALL PLaza 3-6232—PLaza 3-9014

All prices are our OPS ceiling prices or lower. A list showing our ceiling price for each item is available for your inspection.

Figure 7–B. A la carte Menu.
(Courtesy Nino's Sports Afield Club, New York, N. Y.)

CATSKILL MOUNTAIN BLACK BEAR $8.50
Braised, Tavernier
(Sauce Poivrade, Imported French Mushrooms Bordelaise)
SPARKLING BURGUNDY, F. CHAUVENET

ROCKY MOUNTAIN ELK STEAK Grille $16.00 (for 2)
Garnitures des Chasseurs
CHATEAU AUSONE, (Saint Emilion), 1937

IMPORTED PTARMIGAN $12.00
Roasted sur Canape
(Au Fois Gras and Truffles, Celery Braise Flamande)
CHARLES HEIDSIECK CHAMPAGNE, 1943

IMPORTED BECASSINE Sur Crouton $9.00
Brillat-Savarin
(Buttered Toast, Orange, Essence of Truffles Sauce)
PERRIER JOUET, BRUT ENGLISH CUVEE, CHAMPAGNE, 1943

SCOTCH GROUSE $9.50
Roti a l'Anglaise, Riz Sauvage
MUMM'S CORDON ROUGE CHAMPAGNE, 1943

PRONG HORN MEXICAN ANTELOPE $14.00
Saute Mayaguez
MOET ET CHANDON, IMPERIAL, 1943

TROPICAL POSSUM (for 2 to 4) $55.00
au Vin Rouge, Chambertin
(Mushrooms and White Onions)
POMMERY-GRENO, CHAMPAGNE ROSE, 1943

AOUDAD STEAK OR CHOPS GRILLE $9.00
Imam Bayeldi
CHATEAU DE SELLE, VIN ROSE

We Are Frequently Able To Procure The Following Rare and Special Foods and Suggest That You Ask The Captain About Them

Mexican Armadillo (for 4) $150.00	Australian Kangaroo $95.00
Beaver & Beaver Tail $37.00	Moose $20.00
Big Horn $25.00	Muskrat $75.00
South American Boar $25.00	Woodchuck $25.00
Water Buffalo $18.00	Porcupine $75.00
Caribou $95.00	Ostrich Eggs (for 6) $125.00

VELTEVREDEN DUCKLING, FARCI $10.00
(for 2) *Western Style*
CHABLIS 1945

DOMESTIC VENISON STEAK GRILLE $8.50
Metternich, Puree de Marrons, Chatelaine
MUSIGNY BLANC, 1945

ENGLISH PARTRIDGE, ROTI $8.50
Sauce Champagne, Riz Sauvage
CHAMBERTIN, 1943

MAINE WILD MALLARD DUCK (for 2) $13.00
Rouennaise
LANSON, 1943

BOB WHITE QUAIL, SUR CANAPE $7.50
Veronique
(Seedless Grape)
CORTON CHARLEMAGNE, 1945

AFRICAN LANGUOUSTE TAILS GRILLE $5.00
Diavolo
ANJOU, COTEAUX DE SAUMUR, 1947

MOROCCO COAST BABY OCTOPUS $8.00
Saute Orientale
(White Tomatoes and Garlic Butter)
HERMITAGE BLANC, 1934

CARRIBEAN - WATERS BABY SHARK $17.00
Baked a l'Indienne
GRAVE LA TOUR BLANCHE, 1937

DIAMOND - BACK TERRAPIN, Baltimore $22.00
(for 2) *Amontillado*
BOLLINGER CHAMPAGNE 1943

NATIVE PHEASANT a l'Anglaise (for 2) $13.50
CHAMBOLLE MUSIGNY, 1934

ECUADOR SWORDFISH STEAK $6.50
Broiled
(South American Sauce)
MEURSAULT CHARMES, 1937

TURTLE EGGS $15.00
LES GRAND VINS D'ALSACE, TRAMINA, 1945

TIVOLI

CONTINENTAL

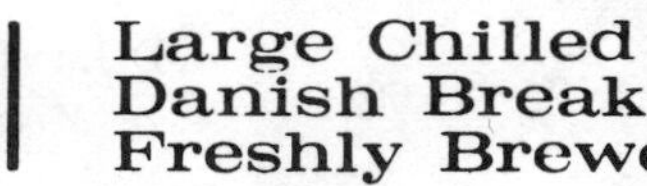

Large Chilled Orange Juice
Danish Breakfast Pastries
Freshly Brewed Coffee .95

TIVOLI CLUB BREAKFASTS

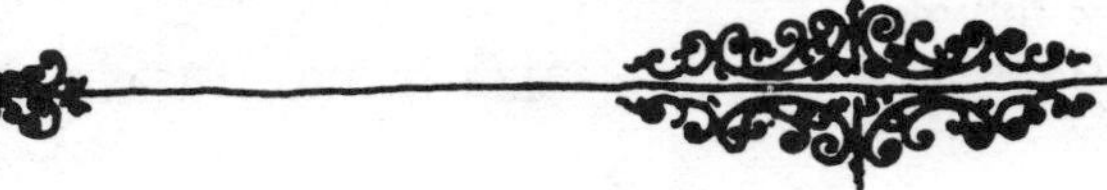

THE CAPITOL

Your favorite Cereal with Milk, Two Eggs any style, Buttered Toast and Tivoli Coffee 1.45

Price Includes Complete Breakfast

Choice of

Orange, Grapefruit, Tomato or Prune Juice
Sliced Bananas with Light Cream
Stewed Prunes Fresh Melon in season

No. 1 One Egg "As You Like It"	**1.15**
No. 2 One Egg with Bacon, Ham or Sausage	**1.55**
No. 3 Two Eggs, Any Style	**1.50**
No. 4 Two Eggs with Bacon, Ham or Sausage	**1.90**
No. 5. Griddle Cakes or Waffles	**1.50**
No. 6. French Toast	**1.50**

Choice of One

Danish Pastry Muffins
Buttered Toast

Coffee Tea Milk Sanka Chocolate

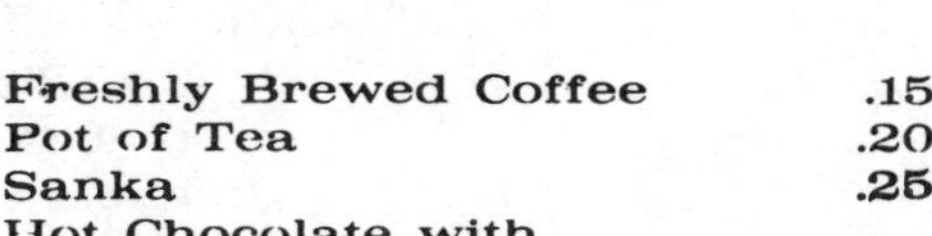

Freshly Brewed Coffee	.15
Pot of Tea	.20
Sanka	.25
Hot Chocolate with Whipped Cream	.30
Homogenized Milk	.20

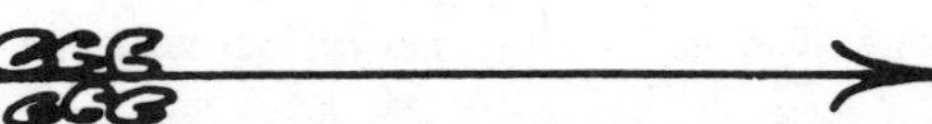

BEVERAGES

Figure 7–C. Breakfast Menu.
(Courtesy Hotel America, Hartford, Connecticut.)

FRUIT JUICES

Orange, Grapefruit, Tomato, Prune
Small Juice .30 Large Juice .45

FRUITS

Fresh Berries in Season - with Light Cream	.50
Fresh Sliced Bananas with Light Cream	.35
Chilled Melon in season	.50
Stewed Prunes	.40
Half Grapefruit	.45

CEREALS

Fresh, Crisp Cereals with milk -	.40
with Light Cream -	.55

Two Eggs with Buttered Toast	1.00
One Egg with Toast	.75
Rasher of Bacon (4 slices)	.70
Country Ham	.70
Sausages (3 links)	.65
Roast Beef Hash	.85
with poached egg	1.15
Plain Country Omelette with Buttered Toast	1.00
Cheese or Jelly Omelette with Buttered Toast	1.30
Western Omelette with Buttered Toast	1.35

WAFFLES served with

Syrup and Pure Creamery Butter	.95

PANCAKES

Golden Griddle Cakes with Butter and Maple Syrup	.95
Pancakes with Bacon or Sausage	1.40
French Apple or Strawberry Pancakes	1.15
Golden French Toast with Syrup and Butter	.95

TIVOLI PASTRIES

A selection of Fresh Danish Pastry	.30
Buttered Toast	.30
Oven Fresh Muffins	.30

Dinner at The Four Seasons

Cold Appetizers

ESCABACHE *of Cape Scallops* 1.85 *Small Clams with Green Onions and* TRUFFLE 1.65
Today's Melon .95 *Lobster Chunks on* SORREL 3.25 *Iced* BROCHETTE OF SHRIMP 2.25
SUMMER *Hors d'Oeuvres, A Sampling* 2.50 A TUREEN *of September Fruit* .95
Marinated Beef Salad 1.75 *Mousse of Chicken Livers* 2.25
BOUQUET OF CRUDITES, *Hot Anchovy Dressing* 1.75
STRASBOURG PATÉ *in Crock, Garnitures* 3.50

Mussels in a PINK *Sauce* 1.65 PERIWINKLES *Mignonette* 1.50 MINTED LOBSTER *Parfait* 2.
Cherrystone Clams 1.35 *Virginia* BLUE CRAB *Lump* 2.85 *Little Neck Clams* 1.35
Fresh AMSTERDAM *Herring, Pommes Vapeur* 2.25 *Avocado Shrimp* LOUIS 2.75
Sweet and Sour Pike in Tarragon Aspic 2.25 *Caviar, per serving* 7.50
A Service of SCOTCH SALMON OR SMOKED STURGEON 2.95
Prosciutto or Smithfield Ham and NEW FIGS 2.65

Hot Appetizers

Smoked Salmon Soufflé, ONION SAUCE 2.50 *Egg in* A ROBE 1.10 *Paupiette of Ham* 1.35
Chervil Stuffed MORELS 1.85 *Herb Dressed Mussels* 1.85
Riviera FEUILLETTE 1.85 SAGE SAUSAGE *in Puff Pastry* 1.85
BEEF MARROW *in Bouillon or Cream* 1.85 *Mussels Poulette* 2.25

THE FOUR SEASONS *Mousse of Trout* 2.50

Snails in POTS 2.25 SKEWERED SNAILS *with Garlic* 1.85 *Cocotte of Summer Game* 1.10
Our Coquille St. Jacques 2.25; *also with Snail Butter* *Crêpes with* FOIE GRAS 2.00
Crisped Shrimp Filled with Mustard Fruits 1.85 *Calamondin Crêpes with Ham Mousse* 1.
Snails in BRIOCHE 1.85 *Spiced Crabmeat Crêpes* 2.45

Tiny Trout à la POINT 2.65

Soups and Broths

Red Cherry Consommé, ALMOND PROFITEROLES 1.25
Bisque of Smelts 1.50 *A September Vegetable Potage* 1.10
COLD: ONION *Madrilène* .95 CARROT *Vichyssoise* 1.10 *Gazpacho* 1.25

Double Consommé with Sorrel 1.10
Tomato and Thyme Bisque 1.10 *Onion Soup with Cheese Gnocchi* 1.25
Watercress VICHYSSOISE 1.10 DANISH *Plum Soup* 1.25

Sea and Fresh Water Fish

Grilled SILVERSIDE SALMON, *Bordelaise* 4.65 *The Fillets of Sole* FOUR SEASONS 4.65
Frog's Legs in MOSELLE, *Garlic Cracklings; or prepared* EN CHEMISE, *Sauce Orly* 5.25
Crabmeat Casanova FLAMBÉ 5.65 *Barquette of Flounder with Glazed Fruits* 4.95

LIVE SEA BASS, *Broiled* 4.50 LIVE PERCH, *Pan Fried* 4.25 *Broiled* MAINE LOBSTER 6.50
The CLASSIC *Truite au Bleu* 5.25 POACHED LOBSTER *in Our Style* 6.75
Lobster Stuffed with MUSSELS 7.00 LOBSTER AROMATIC *Prepared Tableside* 6.50

A Variety of Seasonals

Baby Pheasant with GOLDEN SAUCE, *Nutted Wild Rice* 6.25 *Piccata of* PIGLET *in Pastry* 5.50
NEW DUCKLING *with Peaches, Sauce Cassis* 5.50 *Sautéed Calf's Liver with* AVOCADO 4.85
Rack of Lamb Persillé with ROBUST HERBS, *For Two* 14.00

Stuffed Breast of Chicken with TARRAGON, *Demi-Deuil* 4.95 *Rare* FILET STROGONOFF 6.50
A Cutlet of Meadow Veal with MORELS *in Light Cream* 4.85
THE QUEEN'S GROUSE, *Blackberries and Beignets* 8.50

THIS EVENINGS ENTREES * * * * * * * *

Grilled STRIPED BASS, *Mirabeau* 4.85 *Sautéed* VEAL STEAK, *Braised Romaine* 5.00
PARTRIDGE *with Summer Cabbage, Chartreuse* 6.75

ROAST SIRLOIN OF BEEF, *Cauliflower Gratiné* 6.50
Roast Carré of BABY LAMB, *Vevantine* 5.50

Steaks, Chops, and Birds

* * * * * * *
Two Triple Lamb Chops 5.75 *Jersey Poularde* 4.50
BEEFSTEAKS OF ALL KINDS *
SIRLOIN STEAK *or* FILET MIGNON *Served for One* 7.50; *for Two* 15.00
TWIN TOURNEDOS *with Woodland Mushrooms* 7.00
Filet of Beef POIVRE *Flambé* 8.00
* * * * * * *
The HEART *of the* PRIME RIB, *Sliced Thin* 5.50 *Poussin, Summer Savory* 5.00
SHASHLIK CAUCASSUS, *Wild Thyme* 4.75

* BROILED OVER CHARCOAL
Supreme of Baby Turkey 5.50 *Amish Ham Steak, Peach Knoedel* 4.65
* * * * * * *
Sirloin VINTNERS STYLE 7.75 SKILLET STEAK *with Smothered Onions* 7.50
Sirloin Steak Poivre EN PAPILLOTE 7.50
Beefsteak SCANDINAVIAN 7.25
* SPIT-ROASTED WITH HERBS
FARMHOUSE DUCKLING, *Fresh Sage, for Two* 12.00
Leg of Baby Lamb, LEAFY RUE, *for Two* 13.50

Some Summer Salads

AS A MAIN COURSE *
Buffet of Fruits 4.25 JULIENNE *of* PHEASANT *with Fruit Melangé* 5.25
Bouillabaisse Salad 4.75 *Beef in Burgundy Aspic* 4.75
* * * * * * *
MIDSUMMER *Greens* .95 *Onion and Ripe Olive* .85
Cooked Carrots, Fennel Dressing 1.25
OUR FIELD GREENS ARE PICKED EACH MORNING AND WILL VARY DAILY

* * * * * * *
Julep of Crabmeat in SWEET PEPPERONI 5.00 *Smoked Steak Slices and* RATATOUILLE 5.50
Avocado with Sliced WHITE RADISH 4.25 *Lobster and* WILD MUSHROOMS 5.50
* AS A DINNER ACCOMPANIMENT
Beefsteak Tomato, CARVED AT TABLE 1.25 NASTURTIUM *Leaves* 1.50
Raw Mushrooms, MALABAR *Dressing* 1.65
Salad Dressing with ROQUEFORT *or* FETA CHEESE .50 *additional*

Vegetables and Potatoes

TODAY'S GATHERINGS MAY BE SELECTED IN THEIR BASKETS *Beignets Varies* 1.25
Beets with SOUR CREAM 1.25 *Bouquet Platter, per Person* 1.50 *Petits Pois* MANGE TOUT 1.25
* * * *
POTATOES: *French Fried* .95 *Baked in Jacket* .95 *Vapeur* .95

Broccoli FLOWERS *Hollandaise* 1.95 *Soufflé of Spinach, for Two* 3.50 *Onions in Onions*
GREEN *Rice* .95 *Cracked Wheat, Forestière* .95 THE YOUNGEST *Carrots in Butter* 1.25
* * * *
Country Style .95 *Mashed in Cream* .95 NEW ONES *with Dill* .95

Figure 7–D. Dinner Menu.

(Courtesy The Four Seasons Restaurant, New York, N. Y.)

August Fruits and Cheese

Corbeille of Fruits, ON VIEW 1.00
Green Gage Plums IN ALMOND CREAM 1.25
Melon Melange AU PORTO 1.50 *Melons of the Day* .95
Peaches FLARED IN BOURBON 1.95
STUFFED GREEN ALMONDS *en Brochette* 1.85
Compote of Fresh Fruits, CART SERVICE 1.25
COEUR A LA CREME 1.35 *Vermont Store Cheese* .75
Bel Paese .90 *California Teleme* .85
A Tray of International Cheeses 1.90 *Gruyere* .90

Soufflés, Crêpes and Crèmes

SOUFFLES FOR TWO:
Minted Chocolate 4.00 *Semolina* 4.00
Berry Basket 4.25
SOUFFLES FOR ONE:
Cold Apricot Soufflé 1.85
Coffee Cup Soufflé 1.75 *Soufflé Praline Glacé* 1.65

Little Souffléed Crêpes 2.25 *Crêpes Suzette* 1.95
Crêpes Aurora 2.25 *Toasted Strawberry Crêpes* 1.95
PAIN PERDUE *Caprice* 2.25
Various Blossom Beignets 1.50
Savarin of Rice PRESERVED *Fruits* 1.50
Charlotte Royale 1.50 WINE SAPPHIRE 1.25
ROSE PETAL *Parfait* 1.25
SABAYON OF KIRSCH *Over Strawberries* 2.50

Frozen Desserts

Peach, Cantaloupe, Double Chocolate and
USUAL ICE CREAMS .95
Apricot Sherbet or Lemon Ice .95
FOUR SEASONS *Coupe Filigree* 1.65
Berry Glacier Flambé 2.50
Parfait Santos 1.25 *Café Granito* .95
Violets in Summer Snow 1.75
Frozen Mousse Cake 1.50

Pastries

Fruit Tarts 1.00 *Napoleon Nonpareil* 1.50
THE FOUR SEASONS *Fancycake* 1.35
Chocolate Velvet 1.50 *Petits Fours* 1.00
Rigi Kirsch Torte .95 *Hot Plum Tartlet* .95
Hazelnut Caramel Cake 1.10
Other Sweets from the Silver Wagon

Frosted Mocha 1.00 *Iced Tea, Spiced or Simple* .75
Iced Coffee, Whipped Cream .75; *with Rum* 1.50
Pot of English, Linden or Chinese Tea .50
Coffee Flamboyant 3.00; *Serves Two* *Pot of Coffee* .50
Espresso .75 *Irish Coffee* 1.50
Café Cognac Chantilly 1.70

Cover 1.00

Cafe Napoleon - Luncheon

Les Hors d'Oeuvres

Gulf Shrimp Cocktail	1.25	Pâte Maison	1.10
Choice of Juice	.40	Cherrystone Clams	1.40
Melon in Season	.60	Marinated Herring in Sour Cream	.80
Point Oyster	1.60		
Supreme of Fresh Fruits	.40		

Les Potages

Consommé Celestine	.50	Cream of Tomato	.50
French Onion Soup	.75	Chilled Vichyssoise	.60
New England Clam Chowder	.60		

Sandwiches Froids

Sliced Breast of Turkey	1.75
Smoked Beef Tongue	1.25
Premium Smoked Ham	1.35
Tuna Fish Salad	1.35
Swiss or American Cheese	.95

Sandwiches Chauds

Roast Prime Rib of Beef Sandwich with natural gravy and mashed potatoes	2.90
Hot Corned Beef or Pastrami on Rye with potato salad	1.90
Club Sandwich	1.85
Monte Carlo Sandwich — Smoked Sugar Cured Ham, Swiss Cheese, Sliced Chicken on White Bread — Dipped in batter and fried in butter	2.25

Les Salades

Chef's Salad Bowl — Mixed green salad, celery, radishes, julienne of chicken, tongue, ham, Swiss cheese, hard boiled egg, tomato	1.85
Selected Back Fin Crabmeat Salad — Garnished with asparagus tips, sliced tomato, hard boiled eggs	2.80
Florida Fruit Plate — Served with fruit jello — cottage cheese	1.60

Plats du Jour

Omelette "Park Plaza" with Chicken hash in cream and glazed	2.25
Sliced Breast of Turkey Argenteuil (Asparagus and Glazed)	2.50
Broiled Salisbury Chopped Steak with French Fried Onions	3.00
Fried Filet of Boston Sole with Tartare Sauce	2.25
Broiled Half Spring Chicken with Julienne Potatoes	2.25
Broiled Minute Steak Maitre d'Hotel (8)	4.00

Les Entremets

Fresh Fruit Pie	.50	Pie à la Mode	.75
French Pastries	.60	Ice Cream	.55
Sherbet	.55	Cake of the Day	.60
Caramel Custard	.75	Cheese Cake	.50
Rice Pudding	.75		

Coffee .20 Tea .20 Milk .30 Ice Tea .30 Sanka .20

Figure 7–E. Luncheon Menu.
(Courtesy Park Plaza Hotel, New Haven, Connecticut.)

MENU

Clear Green Turtle

Golden Cheese Straws

✓ ✓ ✓

Hearts of Celery **Ripe and Green Olives**

Salted Almonds and Nuts

✓ ✓ ✓

Great Lakes White Fish

Et Sa Garniture

✓ ✓ ✓

Filet Mignon Chasseur

Nest of Beignet Potatoes

New Stringbeans Saute

✓ ✓ ✓

Autumn Salad

✓ ✓ ✓

Bibescot Glace New Waldorf

Rhum Sabayon

Petits Fours

✓ ✓ ✓

Demi Tasse

✓ ✓ ✓

Château Rieussec 1940

Beaune Clos de l'Ecu 1943

Figure 7–F. Banquet menu used at a dinner given by the City of New York in honour of The President and Delegates to the General Assembly of the United Nations.
(Courtesy Waldorf Astoria Hotel, New York, N. Y.)

NOVEMBER 24, 1623, A. D.

To All Ye Pilgrims

Inasmuch as the great Father has given us this year an abundant harvest of Indian corn, wheat, beans, squashes, and garden vegetables, and has made the forests to abound with game and the sea with fish and clams, and inasmuch as He has protected us from the ravages of the savages, has spared us from pestilence and disease, has granted us freedom to worship God according to the dictates of our own conscience; now, I, your magistrate, do proclaim that all ye Pilgrims, with your wives and little ones, do gather at ye meeting house, on ye hill, between the hours of 9 and 12 in the day time, on Thursday, November ye 29th of the year of our Lord one thousand six hundred and twenty three, and the third year since ye Pilgrims landed on ye Pilgrim Roch, there to listen to ye pastor, and render thanksgiving to ye Almighty God for all His blessings.

WILLIAM BRADFORD
Ye Governor of Ye Colony

Ye Bill of Thanksgiving Fare

To Begin the Feaste

Harlow House Mulled Cider

and

An Appetite Whetter

Oysters on their half shell　The Clams with little necks　Plimoth Clam Pie
Fresh Fruits and Berries from the Harvest　Fall Melon from the Patch

And then a Soup

The Clam Chowder of New England　A Herb Soupe of Split Peas

Followed by The Main Course

Steak of Venison with a Jelly of Red Currants 6.75
Roasted Turkey with a Sauce of Cranberries and as ye may choose: a dressing of oysters or chestnuts 5.75
A Young Duck with a sauce of Spiced Apples 6.25
A Lobster fresh from the sea, Broiled and with Drawn Butter 7.75

And From the Community's Gardens

Smashed White Potatoes　Steamed Green Sprouts that have been buttered
Sweet Potatoes that are Candied　Butternut Squash from the Harvest
Small Onions in a Cream Sauce　Yellow Corn off the Hull

A Salad of Fresh Greens with Woodland Herbs

Accompaniments from the Baking Ovens

An abundance of Corn Breads, Rolls with Pecan meats and Hot Browned Popovers

To Compleat the Feaste

A Pie of Harvest Pumpkin　The Plum Pudding, Bradford style
A Pie of Apples and Mincemeat　Baked Pudding from the Indians

Coffee from the Indies　Tea from Auld England　Milk from the Colony's cows

Dinner for the Little Ones 3.25

The Rib Room in Ye Hotel America situated in Hartford in the Colonies

Figure 7–G. Thanksgiving Menu.
(Courtesy Hotel America, Hartford, Connecticut.)

BUFFALO STEAK
MENU

STEAK HOUSE
KNOTT'S BERRY FARM
BUENA PARK, CALIFORNIA

Figure 7–H: Specialty Menu.
(Courtesy Knotts Berry Farm, Buena Park, California.)*

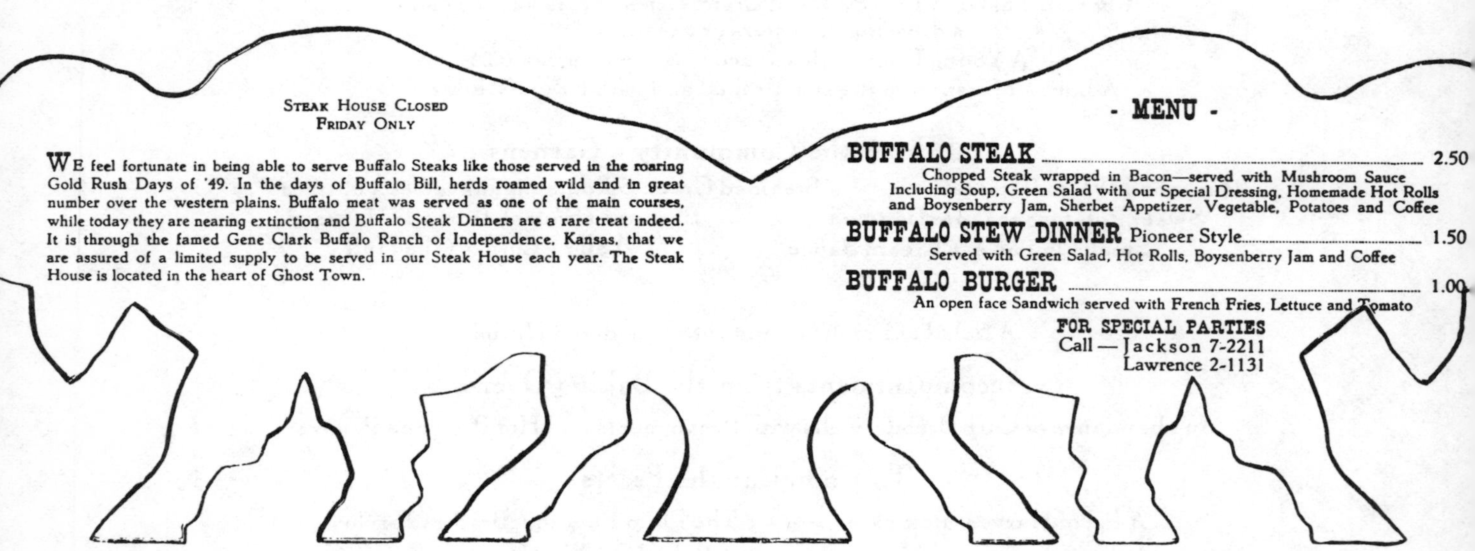

STEAK HOUSE CLOSED
FRIDAY ONLY
WE feel fortunate in being able to serve Buffalo Steaks like those served in the roaring Gold Rush Days of '49. In the days of Buffalo Bill, herds roamed wild and in great number over the western plains. Buffalo meat was served as one of the main courses, while today they are nearing extinction and Buffalo Steak Dinners are a rare treat indeed. It is through the famed Gene Clark Buffalo Ranch of Independence, Kansas, that we are assured of a limited supply to be served in our Steak House each year. The Steak House is located in the heart of Ghost Town.
- MENU -
BUFFALO STEAK 2.50
Chopped Steak wrapped in Bacon—served with Mushroom Sauce
Including Soup, Green Salad with our Special Dressing, Homemade Hot Rolls and Boysenberry Jam, Sherbet Appetizer, Vegetable, Potatoes and Coffee
BUFFALO STEW DINNER Pioneer Style........ 1.50
Served with Green Salad, Hot Rolls, Boysenberry Jam and Coffee
BUFFALO BURGER 1.00
An open face Sandwich served with French Fries, Lettuce and Tomato
FOR SPECIAL PARTIES
Call — Jackson 7-2211
Lawrence 2-1131

Figure 7–H. Specialty Menu (Inside View).
(Courtesy Knotts Berry Farm, Buena Park, California.)*

* Note: Buffalo steak is no longer served at Knotts Berry Farm due to difficulty in obtaining buffalo meat, and lack of customer acceptability. The menu is inserted merely for purposes of illustrating a way of advertising a specialty food.

MENU

WEEK OF: November 14—20, 1966

	MONDAY	TUESDAY	WEDNESDAY	THURSDAY	FRIDAY	SATURDAY	SUNDAY
BREAKFAST	Blended Juice French Toast w/ Hot Syrup Hot Cereal	Orange Juice Scrambled Eggs with Diced Ham	Pineapple Juice or Fresh Fruit Fried Eggs to Order	Orange Juice Hot Cakes with Hot Syrup Grilled Link Sausage	Grapefruit Juice Hard and Soft Boiled Eggs Hot Cereal	Apricot Nectar Ham Omelet Home Fried Potatoes	Orange Juice Fried Eggs to Order Grilled Bacon
	Note: Toast, Jam, Jelly, and Cold Cereal Served Every Breakfast						
LUNCH	Cream of Tomato Soup Stuffed Frankfurter Potato Sticks Cole Slaw Sheet Cake with Chocolate Icing	Vegetable Soup Canadian Bacon Creamed Potatoes Ambrosia Salad Bread Pudding with Lemon Sauce	Minestrone Soup Assorted Luncheon Sandwich Meats Maceroni Salad Pickles, Carrot Sticks Jello Cubes with Whipped Cream	Split Pea Soup Individual Pizza Pie French Fries Crisp Garden Salad Bowl Asst. Ice Creams	Vegetarian Vegetable Soup Baked Salmon Loaf with White Sauce Buttered Green Beans Citrus Salad Date Nut Squares	Cream of Mushroom Soup Fried Chicken Whole Kernal Corn Asst. Salads with Asst. Dressings Gingerbread with Vanilla Sauce	Tomato Juice Baked Ham with Raisin Sauce Marshmallow Candied Yams Buttered Peas Carrot-Pineapple Gelatin Peach Melba
DINNER	Veal Cutlets or Liver and Onions Mashed Potatoes Brown Gravy Buttered Sliced Carrots Lettuce Wedge w/ French Dressing Chilled Peach Half Dinner Rolls	Salisbury Steaks w/ Mushroom Sauce Rice Creole Broccoli Spears Combination Salad Asst. Ice Cream Hot Dinner Rolls	Leg of Lamb or Fresh Ham Boiled Potatoes w/ Country Gravy Stewed Tomatoes Blueberry Crisp Hot Dinner Rolls	Pre-Holiday Dinner Cranberry Cocktail Roast Tom Turkey Bread Dressing Whipped Potatoes w/ Giblet Gravy Peas w/Pearl Onions Buttered Squash Asst. Salads and Dressings Stuffed Celery - Olives - Pickles Dessert Buffet Nuts-Mints-Rolls	Grape Juice Swordfish Steak w/ Lemon Butter or Cube Steak w/ Onion Gravy Baked Potato w/ Sour Cream Cabbage, Carrot Slaw Strawberry Shortcake Dinner Rolls	Roast Beef on Kimmelwick Rolls Parslied Potatoes Julienne Beets Green Goddess Salad French Apple Pie Asst. Breads	

Figure 7–I. Typical College Menu.
(Courtesy Faculty Student Assoc., Food Service Department, State University College, Fredonia, New York.)

Different food operations require, and use, menus peculiar to their own particular needs. Many college menus list only the main items of the meal. Regular everyday accompanying items such as bread, butter, milk, coffee, tea, etc. are automatically added to the food lines, each meal. Colleges often do not serve a supper on Sunday. The normally lighter luncheon is increased on that day to a heavier full course meal. (See Figure 7-I.)

Hospital Menus are frequently written up in "cycles". A cycle usually consists of any odd number of menus, such as 3, 5, 7, etc. Sometimes cycle menus are written for an odd number of days, instead of weeks.

"In these menus (See Figures 7-J, 7-K, 7-L) all items are suitable for use in the full or normal diet. Those foods suitable for use in soft diets are marked by the letter (S). For patients on full or normal diets, a choice of entrees, vegetables, salads and desserts is given for noon and night meals, and a choice of fruit and cereal for breakfast.

Patients on soft diets are restricted to the items labeled (S). In some cases a choice of items is permitted, in others only one menu item is suitable for soft diets. The menus are planned so that one of the two items can also be used for other types of modified diets with adjustments in certain cases. For example, on diabetic diets, prescribed amounts of fresh fruits served without sugar or canned fruits sweetened by a noncaloric sweetener may be used. On sodium-restricted diets, foods may be prepared with little or no added salt, depending upon the degree of sodium restriction. In one case, ice cream and sliced oranges might be offered as dessert alternates for patients on full or normal diets. Ice cream would be permitted for patients on soft diets, and patients on certain other modified diets, such as diabetic and low-sodium, would receive oranges."*

*Courtesy HOSPITALS, Journal of the American Hospital Association. Issue of May 1, 1966.

SELECTIVE CYCLE MENUS

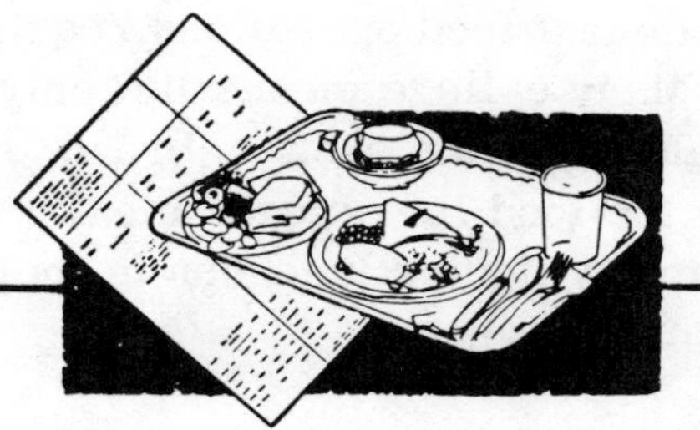

1st WEEK EAST SUMMER SELECTIVE CYCLE MENU — prepared by Mary C. Peck, assistant chief dietitian
(MENUS TO BE USED DURING JUNE, JULY, AND AUGUST) Yale-New Haven Hospital, New Haven, Conn.

	morning	noon	night
monday	Apricot Nectar (S) **or** Cantaloupe Oatmeal (S) **or** Puffed Wheat Cereal (S) Soft-Cooked Egg (S) Broiled Bacon (S)	Tomato Juice (S) Macaroni and Cheese en Casserole (S) **or** Hot Turkey Sandwich with Gravy (S) Brussels Sprouts **or** Mashed Butternut Squash (S) Tossed Salad with French Dressing **or** Pear and Cranberry Salad with Honey Cream Dressing (S) Strawberry Snow (S) **or** Watermelon	Cream of Celery Soup (Strained (S)) Roast Leg of Lamb with Mint Jelly (S) **or** Salisbury Steak with Gravy Whipped Potatoes (S) Whole Kernel Corn **or** Italian Green Beans (S) Black-Eyed Susan Salad with Mayonnaise (S) **or** Sliced Cucumber Salad with Piquante Dressing Caramel Custard (S) **or** Lemon Sponge Cake (S)
tuesday	Orange Juice (S) **or** Stewed Prunes Prepared Oat Cereal (S) **or** Cooked Enriched Wheat Cereal (S) Soft-Cooked Egg (S) Cinnamon Twist Cruller	Knickerbocker Soup Creamed Eggs on Toast Points (S) **or** Cold Sliced Beef, Potato Salad, Sliced Tomatoes Wax Beans (S) **or** Whole Baby Beets (S) Coleslaw **or** Carrot and Raisin Salad Fresh Bing Cherries **or** Lemon Ice (S)	Grape Juice (S) Porcupine Meatballs (S) **or** Broiled Chicken (S) Baked Idaho Potato (S) Fordhook Lima Beans **or** Chopped Spinach (S) French Salad Bowl with Oil and Vinegar Dressing **or** Perfection Salad with Mayonnaise Bread Pudding with Butterscotch Sauce (S) **or** Raspberry Gelatin
wednesday	Grapefruit Juice (S) **or** Banana (S) Cooked Malted Wheat Cereal **or** Prepared Rice Cereal (S) French Toast with Maple Syrup (S)	Pineapple Juice (S) Tuna Chop Suey on Chinese Noodles **or** Cottage Cheese Fruit Salad (S) French Sliced Green Beans (S) **or** Mixed Vegetables Vitamin Salad **or** Sunset Salad with Mayonnaise Danish Pudding with Whipped Cream (S) **or** Cantaloupe	Ruby Consomme (S) Roast Turkey (S) with Sausage Dressing, Giblet Gravy **or** Braised Liver (S) with Onions Paprika Potatoes (S) Peas (S) **or** Yellow Summer Squash (S) Chopped Romaine Lettuce with Blue Cheese Dressing **or** Cranberry Jewel Salad with Honey Cream Dressing Lime Sherbet (S) **or** Marble Cake (S)
thursday	Prune Juice (S) **or** Fresh Strawberries Cooked Whole Wheat Cereal **or** Corn Flakes (S) Scrambled Eggs (S) Sausage Links Hard Roll	Minestrone Soup Hamburger on Bun (S) with Catsup and Relish **or** Ham Salad, Pineapple Rings, Potato Sticks Corn on the Cob **or** Whole Leaf Spinach (S) Sliced Tomatoes **or** Laguna Slaw Bartlett Pear Halves (S) **or** Toffee Pudding (S)	Cream of Chicken Soup (S) Yankee Pot Roast with Brown Gravy (S) **or** Breaded Veal Cutlet (S) Au Gratin Potatoes (S) Wax Beans (S) **or** Parsley Cauliflower Lettuce Wedge with Russian Dressing **or** Pinwheel Salad with Chantilly Dressing Apple Pie **or** Mocha Ice Cream (S)
friday	Cantaloupe **or** Orange Juice (S) Cooked Enriched Wheat Cereal (S) **or** Puffed Wheat Cereal Soft-Cooked Eggs (S) Blueberry Muffin	New England Clam Chowder with Oyster Crackers Cheese Omelet (S) **or** Turkey Salad Sandwich with Potato Chips and Pickles Carrot Coins (S) **or** Stewed Tomatoes Marinated Cucumber Salad **or** Chef's Salad with Oil and Vinegar Dressing Peach-Plum Cobbler **or** Coffee Ice Cream (S)	Cream of Asparagus Soup (S) Broiled Swordfish with Lemon Wedge (S) **or** Beef Pot Pie with Biscuit Topping Oven-Browned Potatoes (S) Summer Squash (S) **or** Lima Beans Stuffed Celery **or** Garden Salad with Herb Dressing Boston Cream Pie (S) **or** Fresh Pineapple Chunks
saturday	Fresh Raspberries **or** Grape Juice (S) Oatmeal (S) **or** Prepared Whole Wheat Cereal Scrambled Eggs (S) Waffles and Honey (S)	Vegetable Soup with Crackers (S) Frankfurter and Baked Beans with Catsup **or** Italian Spaghetti with Plain Meat Sauce and Parmesan Cheese (S) Chopped Broccoli **or** Peas (S) Coleslaw **or** French Salad Bowl with Thousand Island Dressing Fruited Gelatin with Whipped Cream **or** Lemon Ice (S)	Scotch Broth Meat Loaf with Gravy (S) **or** Baked Pork Chop (S) Whipped Potatoes (S) Asparagus Spears (S) **or** Creamed Onions Pickled Beet Salad **or** Tomato Salad with French Dressing Nectarine **or** Banana Layer Cake (S)
sunday	Honeydew Melon **or** Blended Juice (S) Cooked Wheat-Oat Cereal **or** Prepared Rice Cereal (S) Scrambled Eggs (S) Broiled Sausage Butter Pecan Rolls	French Onion Soup with Croutons and Parmesan Cheese Roast Chicken with Cream Gravy (S) **or** Baked Ham with Orange Sauce Parsley Potatoes (S) Succotash **or** Chopped Spinach (S) Molded Lime-Apricot Salad (S) **or** Lettuce and Tomato Salad with Mayonnaise Angel Cake (S) **or** Chocolate Ice Cream (S)	Pineapple Juice (S) Hot Pastrami on Pumpernickel Bread **or** Creamed Tuna on Toast Points (S) Brussels Sprouts **or** Diced Carrots (S) Chef's Salad with French Dressing **or** Cucumbers with Sour Cream Dressing Vanilla Pudding with Grenadine Topping (S) **or** Watermelon

Any item on this menu is suitable for full or normal diets.
Items marked (S) are suitable for soft diets.

Bread, butter, and a choice of beverages are to be included with each meal.

Figure 7–J. Hospital Cycle Menu #1.
(Reprinted with permission from HOSPITALS, Journal of the American Hospital Association, May 1, 1966 Issue, Pages 132, 133, 134.)

2nd WEEK EAST SUMMER SELECTIVE CYCLE MENU — **prepared by Mary C. Peck, assistant chief dietitian**
(MENUS TO BE USED DURING JUNE, JULY, AND AUGUST) **Yale-New Haven Hospital, New Haven, Conn.**

	morning	noon	night
monday	Orange Juice (S) **or** Stewed Compote Cooked Enriched Wheat Cereal (S) **or** Prepared Oat Cereal (S) Poached Egg on Toast (S)	Fruit Punch (S) Stuffed Peppers with Mushroom Gravy **or** Sliced Cold Turkey with Molded Orange-Cranberry Salad (S) Corn Muffin Okra and Tomatoes **or** Whole Baby Beets (S) Vitamin Salad with French Dressing **or** Potato Salad Banana Cream Pie (S) **or** Fresh Plums	Ruby Consomme (S) Yankee Pot Roast (S) with Brown Gravy **or** Deep Sea Scallops and Tartar Sauce Franconia Potatoes (S) Wax Beans (S) **or** Peas (S) Golden Glow Salad with Honey Dressing **or** Shredded Romaine Lettuce with Blue Cheese Dressing Blueberry Cobbler **or** Mocha Ice Cream (S)
tuesday	Tomato Juice (S) **or** Kadota Figs Oatmeal (S) **or** Prepared Corn-Soy Cereal Soft-Cooked Egg (S) Cinnamon Coffee Cake	Corn Chowder Hamburger on Bun (S) with Catsup, Relish **or** Cheese Fondue (S) with Cream Sauce Italian Green Beans (S) **or** Mixed Vegetables Sliced Tomatoes **or** Golden Glow Salad Rice Pudding (S) **or** Seedless Grapes	Apple Juice (S) Roast Loin of Pork (S) with Sweet-Sour Sauce **or** Beef Pot Pie Lyonnaise Potatoes Broccoli Spears **or** Mashed Butternut Squash (S) Red and White Slaw **or** Stuffed Prune Salad with Mayonnaise Peach Pie **or** Vanilla Ice Cream (S)
wednesday	Cantaloupe **or** Grapefruit Juice (S) Cornmeal (S) **or** Prepared Whole Wheat Cereal Scrambled Eggs (S) Bacon (S) Blueberry Muffin	Potage Printaniere (S) Hot Open-Faced Beef Sandwich (S) with Gravy **or** Shrimp Salad Plate with Ripe Olives, Perfection Salad, Whole Wheat Wafers Yellow Summer Squash (S) **or** Baby Lima Beans Garden Salad with French Dressing **or** Banana-Nut Salad with Cream Dressing Lemon Pudding with Fudge Sauce (S) **or** Fruit Cocktail	Cranberry Juice (S) Broiled Chicken (S) **or** Savory Meat Loaf with Gravy Whipped Potatoes (S) Creamed Carrots (S) **or** Paprika Cauliflower Green Island Salad (S) with Mayonnaise **or** Lettuce Wedge with Russian Dressing Jelly Roll (S) **or** Orange Ice (S)
thursday	Blended Juice (S) **or** Chilled Apple-sauce (S) Cooked Malted Wheat Cereal **or** Puffed Rice Cereal (S) Soft-Cooked Egg (S) Toasted English Muffin	Apricot Juice (S) Cold Plate: Sliced Ham, Potato Salad, Dill Pickle, Poppy Seed Roll **or** Eggs a la Goldenrod on Toast (S) Peas (S) **or** Stewed Tomatoes Blushing Pear Salad with Mayonnaise (S) **or** Mixed Greens Salad with Oil and Vinegar Dressing Bing Cherries **or** Vanilla Ice Cream (S)	Grape Juice (S) Veal Parmigiano (S) **or** Roast Turkey with Corn Bread Dressing (S) Creamed Potatoes (S) Green Summer Squash (S) **or** Corn on the Cob Peach-Cranberry Jelly Salad with Mayonnaise (S) **or** Chef's Salad with Blue Cheese Dressing Gingerbread with Whipped Cream (S) **or** Danish Pudding (S)
friday	Orange Juice (S) **or** Banana (S) Cooked Whole Wheat Cereal **or** Corn Flakes (S) Scrambled Eggs (S) Broiled Bacon (S)	Tomato Bisque (S) Tuna Salad Plate with Radish Rose, Cucumber Fingers, and Potato Chips **or** Baked Macaroni and Cheese (S) Whole Leaf Spinach (S) **or** Succotash Celery Seed Coleslaw **or** Pinwheel Salad with Mayonnaise Watermelon **or** Lime Snow (S)	New England Clam Chowder Seafood Creole **or** Rib Eye Steak with Gravy (S) Steamed Rice (S) Asparagus Tips (S) **or** Sliced Buttered Beets (S) Ginger Ale Salad with Honey Cream Dressing **or** Vitamin Salad with French Dressing Frosted Brownie **or** Lemon Sherbet (S)
saturday	Cantaloupe **or** Prune Juice (S) Cooked Enriched Wheat Cereal (S) **or** Shredded Wheat Cereal Soft-Cooked Egg (S) Cinnamon Cruller	Vegetable Soup with Crackers (S) Hot Corned Beef Sandwich on Pumpernickel **or** Veal Patty (S) with Currant Jelly Brussels Sprouts **or** Mashed Butternut Squash (S) Waldorf Salad **or** Perfection Salad Nectarine **or** Orange Custard (S)	Tomato Juice Cocktail (S) Steak Sukiyaki **or** Roast Leg of Lamb with Gravy (S) Buttered Noodles (S) Wax Beans (S) **or** Mixed Vegetables Minted Pear Salad (S) with Mayonnaise **or** Lettuce Wedge with Russian Dressing Fruit Turnover **or** Coffee Fluff (S)
sunday	Blended Juice (S) **or** Honeydew Melon Cooked Whole Wheat Cereal **or** Prepared Oat Cereal (S) Scrambled Eggs (S) Sausage	Scotch Broth Rib Roast of Beef au Jus (S) **or** Roast Duck with Orange Glaze (S) Baked Idaho Potato (S) Cauliflower au Gratin **or** Buttered Peas (S) Molded Vegetable Salad **or** Stuffed Prune Salad with Mayonnaise Lemon Meringue Pie **or** Whole Peeled Apricots (S)	Cream of Chicken Soup (S) Bacon, Lettuce, and Tomato Sandwich with Dill Pickle, Potato Sticks **or** Manicotti with Tomato Sauce (S) Asparagus Spears (S) **or** Mexican Corn Orange-Coconut Salad with Chantilly Dressing **or** Garden Salad with Piquante Dressing Caramel Custard (S) **or** Peach Betty (S)

Any item on this menu is suitable for full or normal diets.
Items marked (S) are suitable for soft diets.

Bread, butter, and a choice of beverages are to be included with each meal.

Figure 7–K. Hospital Cycle Menu #2.
(Reprinted with permission from HOSPITALS, Journal of the American Hospital Association, May 1, 1966 Issue, Pages 132, 133, 134.)

3rd WEEK EAST SUMMER SELECTIVE CYCLE MENU — **prepared by Mary C. Peck, assistant chief dietitian**

(MENUS TO BE USED DURING JUNE, JULY, AND AUGUST) **Yale-New Haven Hospital, New Haven, Conn.**

	morning	noon	night
monday	Cantaloupe **or** Prune Juice (S) Oatmeal (S) **or** Bran Flakes Soft-Cooked Egg (S) Danish Pastry	Mongol Soup Chicken and Rice Casserole (S) **or** Meat Biscuit Roll with Cream Gravy Whole Baby Beets in Orange Sauce (S) **or** Cut Green Beans (S) Assorted Relishes **or** Blushing Pear Salad with Salad Dressing (S) Peanut Butter Pudding (S) **or** Fresh Strawberries	Chilled Apple Juice (S) Fresh Roast Ham (S) with Raisin Dressing and Gravy **or** Old-Fashioned Meat Loaf (No Onions (S)) with Gravy Scalloped Potatoes (S) Chopped Spinach (S) **or** Creamed Onions Carolina Slaw **or** Tomato Aspic Salad with Mayonnaise (S) Blueberry Cobbler **or** Chocolate Mousse (S)
tuesday	Orange Juice (S) **or** Pineapple Tidbits Cooked Whole Wheat Cereal **or** Prepared Rice Cereal (S) Scrambled Eggs (S) Broiled Bacon (S)	Grape Juice (S) Ravioli (S) with Parmesan Cheese **or** Open-Faced Hot Sliced Turkey Sandwich (S) with Giblet Gravy Zucchini Squash (S) **or** Baby Lima Beans Stuffed Peach Salad (S) with Chantilly Dressing **or** Marinated Cucumber Slices Fresh Plums **or** Lime Snow (S)	Consomme Royale (S) Sauerbraten **or** Chicken Paprika (Plain Baked Chicken (S) Whipped Potatoes (S) Peas (S) **or** Okra and Tomatoes Banana-Nut Salad with Honey Dressing **or** French Salad Bowl with Blue Cheese Dressing Rum Sponge Cake (S) **or** Raspberry Sherbet (S)
wednesday	Tomato Juice (S) **or** Blueberries Cooked Enriched Wheat Cereal (S) **or** Prepared Corn-Soy Cereal Poached Egg (S) Whole Wheat Muffin	Potage Printaniere (S) Knackwurst **or** Minute Steak with Mushroom Gravy (S) Sauerkraut **or** Buttered Asparagus Tips (S) German Potato Salad **or** Garden Salad with Thousand Island Dressing Apple Taffy Pudding (S) **or** Watermelon	Alphabet Soup (S) Veal Scallopini **or** Swedish Meatballs (S) Lyonnaise Potatoes **or** Whipped Potatoes (S) Stewed Celery **or** Mashed Squash (S) Antipasto Salad **or** Black-Eyed Susan Salad with Mayonnaise (S) Cherry Whip (S) **or** Bread Pudding with Butterscotch Sauce (S)
thursday	Cantaloupe **or** Apricot Juice (S) Cooked Whole Wheat Cereal **or** Corn Flakes (S) Soft-Cooked Egg (S) French Toast with Maple Syrup (S)	Cream of Mushroom Soup (S) Sea Squab (S) with Lemon Butter **or** Corned Beef Hash with Catsup Mixed Vegetables **or** Wax Beans (S) Under-the-Sea Salad with Mayonnaise **or** Chef's Salad with Oil and Vinegar Dressing Rice Pudding with Whipped Cream (S) **or** Fresh Peach	French Onion Soup with Croutons Beef Stroganoff (S) **or** Braised Liver with Bacon (S) Buttered Noodles (S) Shoestring Carrots (S) **or** Chopped Broccoli Pickled Beet Salad **or** Lettuce Wedge with Russian Dressing Strawberry Pie **or** Mocha Ice Cream (S)
friday	Sliced Peaches (S) **or** Grapefruit Juice (S) Cooked Whole Wheat Cereal **or** Puffed Rice (S) Scrambled Eggs (S) Sausage German Coffee Cake	Mixed Fruit Punch (S) Welsh Rabbit on Toast (S) **or** Open-Faced Meatball Sandwich with Tomato Sauce (S) Fried Eggplant **or** Peas (S) Caesar Salad **or** Molded Lime-Apricot Salad with Mayonnaise (S) Honeydew Melon **or** Peppermint Ice Cream (S)	Manhattan Clam Chowder Deep Sea Scallops with Lemon Wedge **or** Turkey Pot Pie (Hot Sliced Turkey Sandwich and Gravy (S)) Parsley Potatoes (S) Yellow Summer Squash (S) **or** Fordhook Lima Beans Tomato Salad with Mayonnaise **or** Pear-Cranberry Jelly Salad with French Dressing (S) Lemon Chiffon Pudding (S) **or** Frosted Brownies
saturday	Banana (S) **or** Blended Juice (S) Oatmeal (S) **or** Prepared Rice Cereal (S) Soft-Cooked Egg (S) Corn Muffin (S)	Cranberry Juice (S) Date-Nut Cream Cheese Sandwich and Fruited Gelatin **or** Creamed Chicken on Toast (S) French Green Beans (S) **or** Diced Rutabaga with Chopped Parsley Garnish Pinwheel Salad (S) with Mayonnaise **or** Vitamin Salad with French Dressing Cherry Pie **or** Orange Sherbet (S)	Philadelphia Pepper Pot Barbecued Spareribs **or** Pot Roast of Beef (S) with Onion Gravy Whipped Potatoes (S) Brussels Sprouts **or** Sliced Carrots (S) Assorted Relishes **or** Garden Salad with Blue Cheese Dressing Banana Layer Cake (S) **or** Chocolate Pudding (S)
sunday	Pineapple Juice (S) **or** Cantaloupe Cooked Enriched Wheat Cereal (S) **or** Bran Flakes Scrambled Eggs (S) Waffles with Honey (S)	Fresh Fruit Cup Roast Turkey (S) with Herb Dressing and Gravy **or** Swiss Steak (S) Franconia Potatoes (S) Succotash **or** Asparagus Spears (S) Golden Glow Salad with Mayonnaise **or** French Salad Bowl with Zero Dressing Vanilla Pudding (S) with Creme de Menthe Sauce **or** Old-Fashioned Strawberry Shortcake with Whipped Cream	Vegetable Soup Lasagna (S) **or** Hot Open-Faced Roast Pork Sandwich (S) with Gravy Broccoli Spears **or** Sliced Beets (S) Stuffed Apricot Salad with Mayonnaise **or** Tossed Green Salad with Piquante Dressing Elberta Peach with Melba Sauce (S) **or** Coconut Custard

Any item on this menu is suitable for full or normal diets.
Items marked (S) are suitable for soft diets.

Bread, butter, and a choice of beverages are to be included with each meal.

Figure 7–L. Hospital Cycle Menu #3.
(Reprinted with permission from HOSPITALS, Journal of the American Hospital Association, May 1, 1966 Issue, Pages 132, 133, 134.)

Children's Menus for little customers can mean big money. Restaurants catering to the whole family are very popular, particularly in suburban areas. Specially designed children's menus not only encourage family trade, they frequently provide something for the child to do while waiting for food to be served. Although not apparent in the illustrations, children's menus are usually printed in bright colors. (See Figures 7-M, (1), (2), (3), and 7-N, (1), (2).)

Figure 7–M. Children's Menu (1) Front Page.
(Courtesy of, and Copyrighted by Yogg and Company, Newark, New Jersey.)

YOUNG MEMBERS' MENU

Your Choice 99c

TINY TIM likes
Cup of Soup or Juice
Mashed Potato and Vegetable
with Gravy
Rolls and Butter
Chocolate Ice Cream Sundae
Milk or Hot Chocolate

MARY HAD A LITTLE
Cup of Soup or Juice
with Little Lamb Chop
Mashed Potato and Vegetable
Rolls and Butter
Ice Cream Cake Roll
Milk or Hot Chocolate

DICK TRACY likes
Cup of Soup or Juice
Ham Steak
Whipped Potatoes and Vegetable
Rolls and Butter
Chocolate Ice Cream Sundae
Milk or Hot Chocolate

DENNIS THE MENACE likes
Cup of Soup or Juice
Sliced Turkey with Gravy
Mashed Potato and Vegetable
Rolls and Butter
Butterscotch Sundae
Milk or Hot Chocolate

SUPERMAN likes
Cup of Soup or Juice
Grilled Hamburg Pattie
Mashed Potato and Vegetable
Rolls and Butter
Butterscotch Ice Cream Sundae
Milk or Hot Chocolate

Figure 7–M. Children's Menu (2) Inside Page.
(Courtesy of, and Copyrighted by Yogg and Company, Newark, New Jersey.)

FOLLOW THE DOTS AND COLOR WITH CRAYON

Figure 7–M. Children's Menu (3) Back Page.
(Courtesy of, and Copyrighted by Yogg and Company, Newark, New Jersey.)

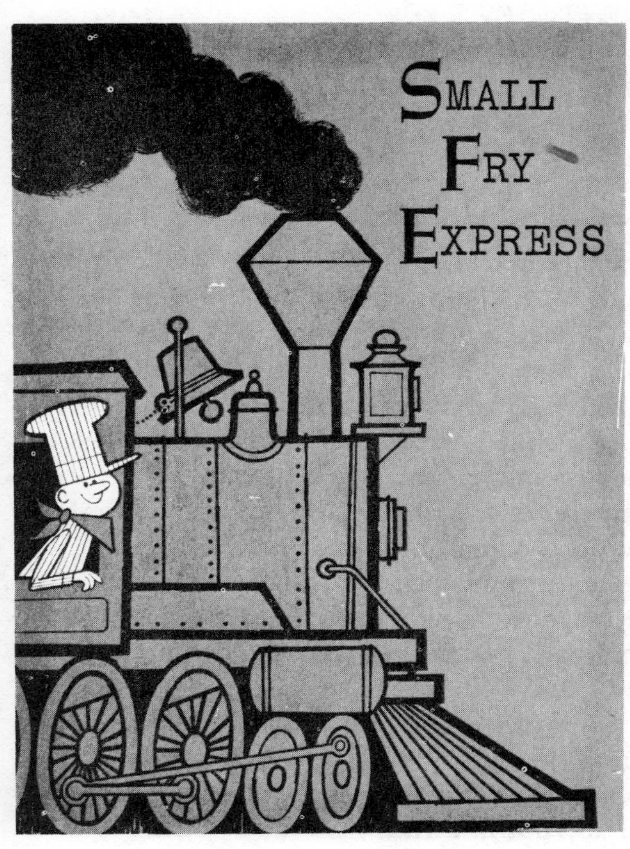

Figure 7–N. Children's Menu (1) Front Page.
(Courtesy of, and Copyrighted by Yogg and Company, Newark, New Jersey.)

CHILDREN'S MENU

FOR CHILDREN UNDER TWELVE

PLEASE ORDER BY NAME PLEASE ORDER BY NAME

Casey Jones

Soup or Juice
Roast Young Turkey
Potato Vegetable
Rolls and Butter
Ice Cream or Cake
Milk Coca-Cola
1.25

Whistle Stop

Soup or Juice
Hamburger Patty
Potato Vegetable
Rolls and Butter
Ice Cream or Cake
Milk Coca-Cola
.90

Caboose

Soup or Juice
Roast Beef au Jus
Potato Vegetable
Rolls and Butter
Ice Cream or Cake
Milk Coca-Cola
1.50

Round House

Soup or Juice
Broiled Red Snapper
Potato Vegetable
Rolls and Butter
Ice Cream or Cake
Milk Coca-Cola
1.35

Locomotive

Soup or Juice
Peanut Butter and Jelly Sandwich
Ice Cream or Cake
Milk Coca-Cola
.75

Engineer

Soup or Juice
Ice Cream or Cake
Milk Coca-Cola
.60

Figure 7–N. Children's Menu (2) Inside Pages.
(Courtesy of, and Copyrighted by Yogg and Company, Newark, New Jersey.)

THE MENU FROM DIFFERENT VIEWS

From The Customer's Viewpoint. The menu is often the first thing a customer REALLY sees after entering a restaurant. This is especially true when he comes in with friends. Usually there is extensive conversation going on, and it continues until guests are seated, and menus are passed out. Once the customer picks up, and begins to study, the menu, he becomes acutely conscious of the establishment.

A menu must always be spotlessly clean. Smudge marks, bits of food or other dirt on a menu make the customer strongly suspicious about the sanitation of the kitchen, and the rest of the establishment. Waiters and waitresses must be trained to check menus for cleanliness BEFORE giving them to customers. Menus should be ordered from the printer in sufficient quantity to allow immediate discarding of any that become soiled. Some operations use a plastic coated paper that can be easily wiped off. In other establishments, a transparent menu cover is used to keep menus clean.

In addition to being clean, a menu must be attractive. With the possible exception of certain specialty restaurants, "loud" or bright colors should be avoided. Pastels or soft colors are more conducive to good atmosphere and, consequently, good dining.

It is important for a menu to state in a clear manner the merchandise for sale. Prices must be clearly indicated so as to prevent misunderstandings with the customers. Dishes should be named in such a way as to be easily understood. If a foreign language is used, an explanation should follow underneath. Some restaurants use menus written in two languages. One page is devoted to listings in French, and the opposite page has the same menu written in English. While a few customers may consider a menu written entirely in French to be fashionable, the average man, not familiar with the French language, would much prefer to know exactly what he is ordering.

If the decor and atmosphere calls for a menu written in French, or some other foreign language, waiters and waitresses should know the ingredients of each dish, exactly how it is prepared, and the correct wine to be served with it. If a waiter must relay a question concerning a menu item to the headwaiter, captain, or chef, guests are kept waiting unnecessarily.

From The Manager's Viewpoint. To a food manager, the menu represents hard work. Writing a menu entails much more than merely listing food items in a certain order. Listed below are additional points that must be taken into consideration:

a. Color: Foods should always be of contrasting colors. A menu offering creamed chicken, boiled rice, cauliflower, and cottage cheese, may provide many of the required nutrients in the diet, but it will hardly smash any sales records. Many times meals are sold, or not sold, by one customer observing another customer's order.

b. Variety: The word "variety" has two different uses in connection with menu construction. First of all, it means a variety of foods for your customers to choose from. This is not to imply a menu should have an excessive number of entrees, but rather a good selection. For example, one selection of beef, pork, lamb, fish or seafood, poultry, veal, and a casserole dish should provide something for everyone, without "cluttering up" the menu. A second meaning of "variety", in relation to menu planning, is variety of preparation methods. The same foods can be made quite different by using various gravies and sauces, or varying the preparation method. It is important for the menu planner to consider the production capabilities of the kitchen employees and food preparation equipment, when working variety into a menu. Production of foods must be spread over the ENTIRE kitchen, utilizing as many machines and as much of the personnel as possible.

c. Quality: For a restaurant to maintain and expand the repeat business so necessary to its survival, a high standard of quality must be maintained. Only the very best foods, consistent with the end product being developed and the menu price, should be used. As stated in Lesson 5, no dish can be acceptable if the original product is of poor quality.

   The menu planner must always be honest and give his customers exactly what he has promised them. NEVER underestimate the intelligence of your customers. If the menu states, "U.S.D.A. Prime Sirloin Steaks", the guest has every right to expect that particular grade, and nothing else. Taste and yield tests should be made continually to insure that quality is constant.

d. Appearance: The often repeated phrase, "We eat with our eyes" is true. If food looks good, the customer will try it. If it tastes good, the customer will eat it. Plates must be large enough to prevent crowding of foods. In addition to the color mentioned earlier, foods should have different textures and shapes. A plate made up of all soft foods may be "just what the doctor ordered" for a hospital patient, but it is hardly suitable for a healthy restaurant customer.

e. Taste: Even the newest culinary student realizes food must taste good, but there are other factors equally important pertaining to taste. Flavor contrasts must be incorporated into each meal. When selecting foods for the menu, use combinations that provide changes in flavor, such as sweet, tart, bland, strong, mild, etc.

f. Acceptability: The high priority of customer acceptability is obvious. If guests are not pleased, they do not return. Menus must be designed to give the customer precisely what he will buy, and equally important, at a price he can afford to pay.

ANALYZING MENU SALES

Many years ago the trend in menu writing was to offer as many entrees as could be crowded on the menu, in an effort to please every single customer that entered the establishment. Today, modern menu planners limit menus from seven to ten entrees. Not only does this keep the inventory down by requiring less stock on hand, it also increases seat turnover, because customers do not have to spend as much time reading and reaching a decision on what to order. In addition, payroll costs are reduced due to less preparation, and profit is increased because there is less waste.

In order to use a limited menu, it is important to know which items sell and which items do not sell. With this information available, slow moving items can be omitted, and replaced by foods the customer will buy. To determine which foods customers prefer, it is necessary to analyze sales carefully.

An accurate count of sales, by individual items, is recorded on a copy of the menu, by the cashier or checker. The TOTAL number of each item sold is transferred to an Item Sales History Form. Columns and entries on the Item Sales History Form are explained on following page. (See Figure 7-O.)

Brought Forward (Sales to Date, % to Date): Figures entered in these columns are carried forward from the last entries in the preceding form.

Item: The specific item on the menu, classified by appetizers, soups, entrees, potato, vegetable, salad, dessert.

Number Sold Today: The exact number of each item sold, as recorded on the menu by the cashier or checker.

Percentage of Sales Today: The number of each item sold divided by the total number of customers for the day.

Number Sold To Date: The number of each item sold today added to yesterday's Sales to Date figure.

Percentage of Sales To Date: The number of each item sold to date divided by the Total Customers To Date.

Total Customers Today: Determine the total number of customers from guest checks, cover count, or other means, and enter figure. Total customers ALWAYS equal 100%.

Total Customers To Date: Today's customer count added to yesterday's TO DATE customer count.

Weather Conditions: Weather conditions are important to sales analysis and should be recorded in this section.

Special Events: Record any special event having an effect on sales. This would include sporting events, holidays, conventions, etc. If there are no known special events, write "none" in the space provided.

Remarks: This section can be used to record any information considered pertinent to sales analysis. For example, if a cycle menu was being used, the number of the menu could be recorded.

ITEM SALES HISTORY FORM

	Brought Forward			Date: January 10, 1967 Day: Tuesday									
	Sales To Date	% To Date	Specific Menu Item	# Sold Today	% Sales Today	# Sold To Date	% Sales To Date	# Sold Today	% Sales Today	# Sold To Date	% Sales To Date	# Sold Today	% Sales
APPET	892	32	Shrimp Cocktail	93	30	985	32						
APPET	163	6	Choice of Juices-	22	7	185	6						
APPET	443	16	Melon w/ Proscuitto	50	16	493	16						
APPET	394	14	Escargots	37	12	431	14						
APPET	1892	68	Totals	202	65	2094	68						
SOUP	392	14	Chilled Vichyssoise	40	13	432	14						
SOUP	334	12	Turtle Soup	34	11	368	12						
SOUP	219	8	Potage Paysanne	28	9	247	8						
SOUP	945	34	Totals	102	33	1047	34						
ENTREES	327	12	Broiled Lobster	43	14	370	12						
ENTREES	252	9	Cornish Hen	25	8	277	9						
ENTREES	772	28	Prime Ribs	90	29	862	28						
ENTREES	249	9	Roast Duckling	28	9	277	9						
ENTREES	308	11	Tournedos	31	10	339	11						
ENTREES	582	21	Sirloin Steak	65	21	647	21						
ENTREES	280	10	Frogs Legs	28	9	308	10						
ENTREES	2770	100	Totals	310	100	3080	100						
POTATO	834	30	Duchess	90	29	924	30						
POTATO	194	7	Au Gratin	22	7	216	7						
POTATO	1167	42	Baked w/ Sour Cream	127	41	1294	42						
POTATO	462	17	Parslied	62	20	524	17						
POTATO	2657	96	Totals	301	97	2958	96						
VEG	579	21	Green Beans	68	22	647	21						
VEG	699	25	Peas	71	23	770	25						
VEG	803	29	Corn, W.K.	90	29	893	29						
VEG	548	20	Asparagus	68	22	616	20						
VEG	2629	95	Totals	297	96	2926	95						
SALAD	499	18	Stuffed Tomato	55	18	554	18						
SALAD	319	12	Lettuce Heart	51	16	370	12						
SALAD	865	31	Chef's	90	29	955	31						
SALAD	547	20	Mixed Vegetable	69	22	616	20						
SALAD	2230	81	Totals	265	85	2495	81						
DESSERTS	243	9	French Pastry	34	11	277	9						
DESSERTS	218	8	Cherries Jubilee	28	9	246	8						
DESSERTS	330	12	Crepes Suzette	40	13	370	12						
DESSERTS	160	6	Rum Pie	25	8	185	6						
DESSERTS	477	17	Ice Cream	47	15	524	17						
DESSERTS	1428	52	Totals	174	56	1602	52						
	2770		Total Customers:	Today: 310		To Date: 3080		Today:		To Date:			
			Weather Conditions:	Snow Flurries									
			Special Events:	None									
			Remarks:										

Figure 7–O. Item Sales History Form.

(On this form the sales and percentage figures have been rounded off to the nearest whole number. Some establishments prefer to list figures carried out one place past the decimal point.)

ADDITIONAL PERTINENT POINTS

Menu Layout. Regardless of the type of menu, items should be listed in order of service. The following examples illustrate correct listing procedures:

Breakfast	Luncheon and Dinner
Fruits and Juices	Appetizers
Cereals	Soups
Eggs, Meats	Entrees
Additional Items (Griddle	Vegetables
Cakes, Waffles, etc.)	Salads
Hot Breads	Breads
Toast	Desserts
Beverages	Beverages

Hot and cold sandwiches are usually listed separately. One method is to print the hot sandwiches down one side of the menu and cold sandwiches down the other side of the menu.

The daily (or chef's) special is normally listed first. In order to merchandise a daily special, bold (heavy) type is sometimes used. A "clip-on" may be used to call attention to the specials and suggestions, provided it is properly handled so as not to obliterate part of the remaining menu from the customer's view. Some menus are designed with a blank space to allow room for clip-ons. (See Figure 7-P.)

With the exception of the daily special, it is not good business to list low priced items first on the menu. If the restaurant specializes in a particular item, it should be placed in such a manner that it will catch the customer's eye. This can be accomplished by the use of different colors, borders, bold type, and/or proper location.

Beverage Suggestions

MANHATTAN .85 **WHISKEY SOUR .85** **BLOODY MARY .85** **VODKA MARTINI .85**

Appetizers

A Cocktail of Fresh Florida Shrimps 1.15 (75c additional on Complete Dinner)

Fresh Fruit Cocktail	.35	Chilled Tomato Juice	.30
Chopped Chicken Livers	.45	Chilled Melon in season	.50

Cherrystone Clams on the half shell (6) .85 (50c extra on Complete Dinner)

SOUPS Chef's Soup du jour .30 Jellied Madrilene .35 Chilled Cream Vichyssoise .35

Fish and Sea Food

SERVED WITH CHOICE OF POTATO AND VEGETABLE, CHOICE OF SALAD, ASSORTED HOT BREADS AND RELISH TRAY

	DINNER	A LA CARTE
Broiled Block Island Swordfish WITH ANCHOVY BUTTER	3.30	2.45
Golden Brown Fried Filet of Boston Sole CRISP ON THE OUTSIDE; FLAKEY AND JUICY INSIDE	3.10	2.25
Mariner's Choice Seafood Platter FILET OF BOSTON SOLE, SHRIMPS, SCALLOPS, CRAB CAKE, SERVED WITH TANGY TARTAR SAUCE	3.60	2.75
Fried Florida Shrimps and Scallops GOLDEN BROWN — SERVED WITH TANGY TARTAR SAUCE	3.50	2.65
Broiled Whole Brook Trout Amandine WITH ALMONDS TOASTED IN BUTTER AND SEASONED WITH LEMON JUICE	3.35	2.50
Curried Shrimps with Chutney FROM A WORLD FAMOUS RECIPE	3.35	2.50
Alaska King Crab Cakes WITH TANGY TARTAR SAUCE	3.30	2.45

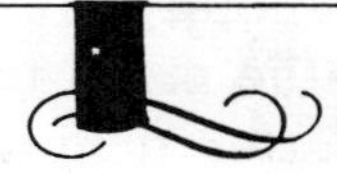

OUR SUGGESTIONS FOR TODAY

For the Salad Mood

CHEF'S SALAD BOWL 2.35
Julienne White Meat Turkey, Ham, Swiss and American Cheese, Crisp Tossed Greens, Tomato and Egg Garni. Choice of Dressing

ASSORTED COLD CUTS 2.65
with Potato Salad Garni. Served with chilled Tomato Slices

FRESH FRUIT BOUQUET 2.25
Chilled Fresh Fruit and Creamy Cottage Cheese on crisp Lettuce Leaves with Schrafft's Fresh Fruit Sherbet

CHILLED WHOLE TOMATO FILLED WITH SHRIMP SALAD 2.85
with Cucumber Slices and crisp Potato Chips

Figure 7–P. Menu Illustrating a Specially Designed Clip-on Holder. (Courtesy of, and Copyrighted by Yogg and Company, Newark, New Jersey.)

The wording of a menu requires a great deal of thought. Carefully chosen words that are tempting, descriptive, and true, will bring higher checks, happier guests, and more profit. Avoid the use of worn-out words and old cliches. Try to find synonyms, or new words, for delicious, luscious, tender morsels, etc.

Menu Advertising: In a food establishment everyone must read the menu before they can order food. Because of this fact, the menu affords an excellent advertising media. The name, address, city, state, and telephone number of the restaurant should always be printed on the menu in a conspicuous place. If the restaurant specializes in any particular functions, such as banquets, wedding receptions, parties, etc., this too should be properly noted on the menu.

Customers should be encouraged to take menus home with them. If the printing cost puts a strain on the budget, miniature menus can be printed at a much lower price.

Menu Substitution: Menus should be planned to allow for sensible substitution. Sensible substitution is defined as substitution between items of approximately the same wholesale cost. Not every customer prefers brussel sprouts with his dinner. When preparing the menu, allow for customer preference by offering two or three potatoes and vegetables. Let the customer decide which one he prefers. Some managers feel this system creates excessive waste, but if vegetables are prepared in small quantities, just before serving, this need not be so.

Plan In Advance: Menus should always be written well in advance of production. A minimum of 7 to 10 days is standard, but some operations prepare menus much further ahead. Advance planning allows time for purchasing and delivery, as well as providing early notice for production personnel. It is also good practice to go over menus with production personnel as early as possible to obviate any problems.

Expect The Unexpected: Always be ready for those last minute changes brought about by equipment failure, non-delivery of items, and other emergencies. If Maine lobsters do not arrive when needed, it may be necessary to change the menu to lobster tails. This may not satisfy the true lobster connoisseur, but it is better than no lobster at all.

Experiment and Change: Everyone becomes bored with the same foods, no matter how well they are prepared. Do not be afraid to experiment with new recipes and ideas. Obviously the menu planner should not remove good selling dishes from the menu just to try out new items. However, slow moving items can and should be deleted from the menu, and replaced with something new and exciting. Needless to say, a new recipe should be thoroughly tested before it becomes a part of the menu. Always get several opinions on a new dish. Do not be prejudiced by your own likes and dislikes.

Try to do something special for holiday meals. If possible, bring out special holiday menus, decorate the dining room in accordance with the holiday, and provide the best, most unusual meal you can afford.

Just as people become bored with eating the same foods, they also get tired of seeing the same old menu. Change the cover, style, color, design, and interior of the menu every few months to break the monotony.

Special Diet Customers: Guests with special diet problem are often reluctant to eat out because they feel a restaurant cannot provide the foods they must have. No one expects a restaurant to use a hospital menu, but being able to serve your guests a few basic diet foods often wins friends and repeat business. For example, keeping a few cans of salt-free foods, low calorie foods, and sugar-free foods in stock will be most appreciated by patrons with heart trouble, weight problems, or diabetes.

Basic Four Food Groups: Foods are divided into four groups based on the nutrients they provide in the human diet. The menu planner must be fully aware of these groups and be sure to incorporate them into the menu. This is particularly true in institutional feeding operations because the customer frequently cannot afford, or is unable, to go elsewhere for his food.

Group I - Milk. In addition to milk, Group I includes cheese and ice cream. The function of this group is to supply calcium, protein, and riboflavin in the diet. Group I also supplies other vitamins and minerals, but in smaller amounts. Foods in Group I should be served 2 or more times a day.

Group II - Meat. Includes all meats, fowl, fish and eggs. Group II foods should be served 2 or more times per day. These foods are important sources of protein, iron, thiamine, riboflavin, niacin, and fat. They also provide smaller quantities of other vitamins and minerals.

Group III - Vegetables and Fruits. Group III foods furnish vitamin "C" and carotene, which the body converts to vitamin "A". Four or more servings of this group should be incorporated into the diet daily. One of the four servings should include a good source of vitamin "C", and one serving, at least every other day, should include a good source of vitamin "A". (Refer back to Lesson 4 to refresh your memory as to which fruits and vegetables supply these vitamins.)

Group IV - Bread and Cereals. This particular group includes all bread and cereals, either whole grain, enriched, or restored. Group IV foods provide iron, thiamine, riboflavin, and niacin, in the diet. Foods in Group IV should be served 4 or more times a day.

Other Foods. Any food not listed in the basic four is classified as "Other Foods". These are the extra items that go along with the meal, such as sugar, butter, oils, etc. Their major contribution to the diet is providing calories.

LESSON 7 - BRAINTEASER

After you are certain you understand the material in this lesson, answer the questions below. When you have completed the brainteaser, check your answers in the text. Use the following scale to evaluate your comprehension of this lesson:

10 Correct --- Outstanding
9 Correct --- Excellent
8 Correct --- Good
7 Correct --- Fair
6 or Under
Correct --- Restudy the Lesson

1) Name the two main types of menus and explain how they differ from each other.

2) If a foreign language is used in a menu the best practice is to:______________________ ______________________. What additional knowledge should waiters have for a menu written ENTIRELY in a foreign language?

3) Explain the two uses of the word, "variety" in connection with menu planning.

4) Define "flavor contrasts", as used in menu planning.

5) What is meant by the term "menu analysis"? How is this accomplished? What is the name of the form used?

6) In the space provided below list the correct menu layout for breakfast and dinner.

BREAKFAST | DINNER

7) In menu planning, the term "sensible substitution" means?

8) Smart restaurant managers plan for customers on special diets. Name the three more common diets that customers would likely request.

9) Why is it most important for a college food manager to know, understand, and use, the Basic Four Food Groups in menu planning?

10) List the MAIN FOODS that make up the Basic Four Food Groups.

GROUP I:

GROUP II:

GROUP III:

GROUP IV:

LESSON 8

FOOD PROCESSING

LESSON 8 - PREVIEW

In Lesson 8, four aspects of food processing - canning, freeze-drying, liquid nitrogen freezing and future food processing are discussed. In the study of food preparation, a culinary student should acquire a knowledge of how a given food was processed before it is delivered to the establishment. For example, in studying the various steps involved in the commercial canning of food, you will learn why foods are "vacuum packed" and what this does to the container and for the product.

In the section on freeze-dried foods, you will find out exactly what freeze-drying is, what the foods look like, and how they are dried. The complete process of freeze-drying is explained from beginning to end, including the advantages and disadvantages of this processing method.

Liquid nitrogen freezing is relatively new in the industry: A special piece of equipment capable of dropping temperatures to a minus 320° F. freezes an amazing amount of food, extremely fast.

Future food processing explains new methods of preserving foods for later use. Some of the methods are still in the laboratory stage while others are already in commercial or military use.

COMMERCIAL CANNING

Commercial canning has been traced back to the early 1800's when a Frenchman, Nicolas Francois Appert, preserved a few foods in glass bottles. From this modest beginning, the canning industry has grown to such magnitude that in the 1960's the United States had an annual output of approximately 17,000,000,000 cans of almost every conceivable type of meat, fish, fruit, vegetable and miscellaneous product.

Specific Steps in Commercial Canning. Although the sequence of steps will vary with the particular product being processed (canned), there are certain basic steps applicable to all canning operations. Regardless of the method utilized, the basic principle remains the same, i.e.: To develop temporary or permanent conditions that prevent the growth of harmful bacteria.

Product Cleaning is usually done by special washing machines. The raw food may be cleaned by the use of high pressure sprays or streams of water while moving along on a belt or tumbling on a revolving screen. Prior to washing, certain products may receive dry cleaning from air blasting or agitation screens.

Pre-preparation of products for canning is identical in purpose to the pre-preparation of foods for production. The objective is to remove any part or parts of the item deemed undesirable or not edible. This is accomplished by trimming, slicing, peeling, coring, cutting, pitting, etc. as necessary, depending on the particular product being processed. Most of these operations are performed by special types of machinery, although some foods still require hand work.

Grading and sorting by size and quality is necessary for many canned products. In sizing, an item may be dropped through screens with different mesh sizes, or the food may be passed over differently spaced rollers.

Blanching is done by submerging certain raw foods in warm or hot water, or occasionally by exposing foods to live steam. Blanching is done primarily to improve color and flavor. It also provides another cleaning for the product.

Filling is done by machine whenever possible. Some products, particularly those canned in large pieces, such as peaches, require hand fillings of containers. (See Figure 8-A.)

Certain types of mechanical filling can be accomplished at the rate of 1200 or more containers a minute.

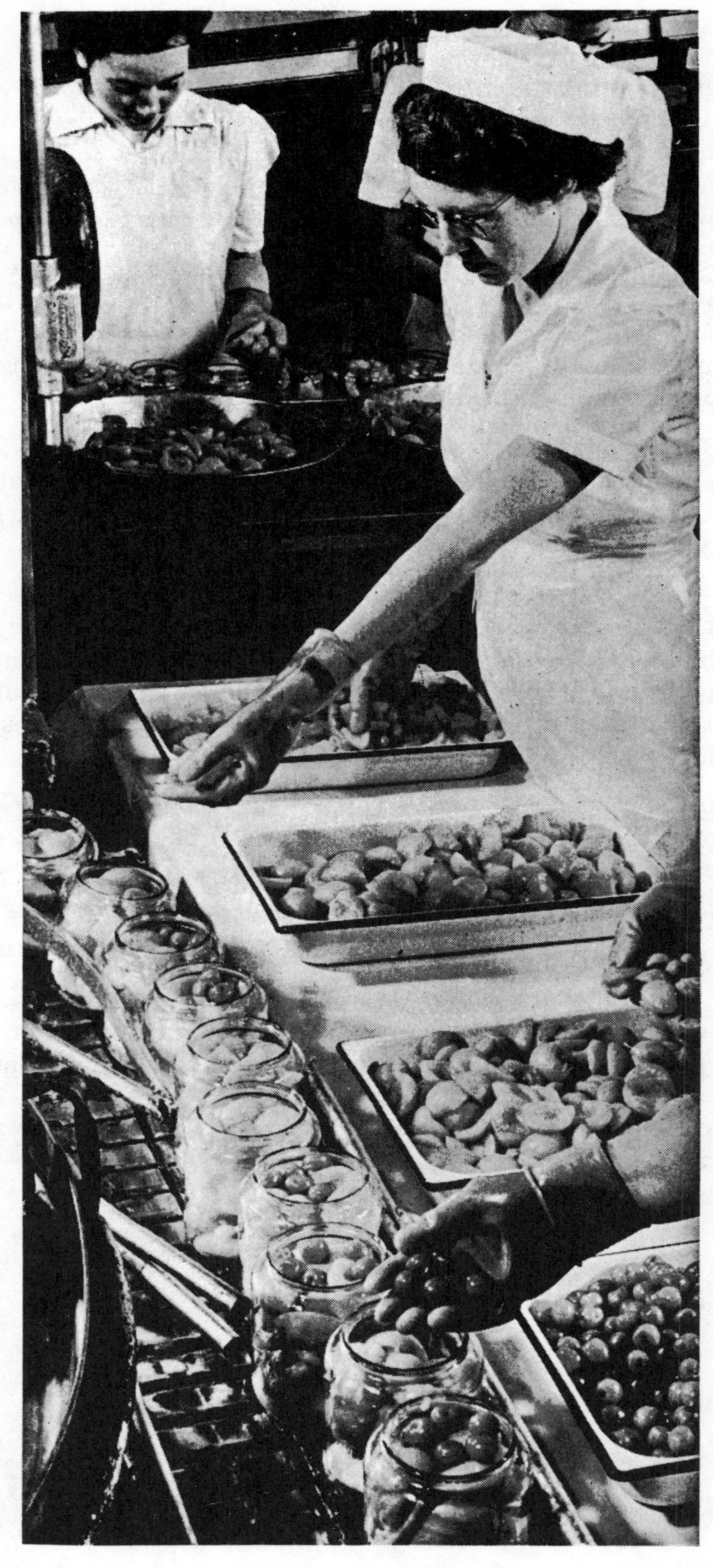

Figure 8–A. Fruit Cocktail is created as glass containers move along automatic runway.
(Courtesy National Canners Association, Washington, D. C.)

Vacuum in containers must be attained in order to remove air and gas. This is necessary to insure that interior can pressure is less than atmospheric pressure. A low interior pressure (vacuum) accomplishes the following:

1) Helps keep can ends drawn in, an indication of a safe product.
2) Reduces strain on containers during processing.
3) Minimizes discoloration or flavor effects of oxygen remaining in headspace.
4) Prolongs shelf live of some products.
5) Prevents bulging at high altitudes or in high temperatures.
6) Is necessary to keep some styles of lids on glass containers.

Sealing the container is done by a closing machine. In sealing lids on metal cans, a double seam is created by interlocking the curl of the lid and flange of the can. (See Figure 8-B.)

Figure 8–B. Sealing Machine. This machine is capable of placing and sealing 1200 lids per minute on cans. (Courtesy National Canners Association, Washington, D.C.)

Heat processing is a treatment to which foods are subjected after hermetic sealing in containers. In the industry, this heat treatment is referred to as the "process". During this process micro-organisms which would cause spoilage are destroyed by heat. The amount and length of heat varies with the product being processed and the size of the container. (See Figure 8-C.)

Figure 8–C. Continuous Cooker for Heat Processing of Foods After Canning.
(Courtesy National Canners Association, Washington, D.C.)

Cooling containers must be done quickly to prevent overcooking. It can be accomplished by cold water tank, cold water spray or a combination of cold water and air cooling.

Labeling is done by high speed machines which apply glue and labels in one operation.

Casing involves moving the cans (usually along conveyor belts) to devices which pack them into shipping cartons.

Canned Food and Nutrition. Nutritional knowledge of canned foods, based on years of research, has developed the following significant facts.

1. Foods high in proteins, carbohydrates and fats in the raw state retain these nutritive factors completely when canned. These nutrients are not adversely affected by canning. On the contrary, the cooking process makes certain plant or animal tissues easier to digest. In some cases, the canned food is higher than the fresh in caloric values due to such additions as sugar syrup to fruits and to some vegetables.

2. Vitamin C is well retained in canned foods because of the nature of the canning procedure, wherein as much air as possible is expelled from the products and the cans are sealed prior to sterilization. Vitamins A and D are little affected by cooking. Vitamin A is retained substantially in the solid portions of vegetables and fruits canned in a liquid medium. Both Vitamins A and D are retained in the solid portions of fish canned in a liquid medium. (See pp. 274 to 276.)

Flash Canning of Foods. One of the newest and most revolutionary canning procedures to be developed is "flash" canning of foods. "In the session on Trends in Food Processing, Warren Schack (Swift & Co.) outlined the theories involved in 'flash' canning of foods. He described the operation of a plant designed, in sequence, to heat food rapidly by steam injection, to cool it slightly, to fill it into cans, and to complete the sterilization upon closing. These last steps necessitate use of a pressurized room which workmen enter and leave through locks. The process minimizes heating and permits production of heat-sensitive foods with a minimum of deterioration. Several foods produced by the "Flash-18" process were shown to have better retention of heat labile vitamins than similar products canned by conventional means."*

Common Container Sizes. The container sizes illustrated in the following chart provide valuable information on the number, size, approximate weight and products of various containers. For the approximate servings per can or jar see pp. 277 to 279.

*Courtesy Food Technology Magazine, Page 25, Vol. 21, 831, June 1967 Issue.

• *COMMON CONTAINER SIZES*

The labels of cans or jars of identical size may show a net weight for one product that differs slightly **from the net weight on the label of another** product, **due to the difference in the density of the food. An example would be pork** and **beans (1 lb.), blueberries (14 oz.), in the same size** can.

Container			Products
Industry Term	Consumer Description		
	Approximate Net Weight (check label)	Approximate Cups	
8 ounce	8 oz.	1	Fruits, vegetables, *specialties. 2 servings.
Picnic	10½ to 12 oz.	1¼	Condensed soups, small quantities of fruits, vegetables, meat and fish products, *specialties. 2 to 3 servings.
12 oz. (vacuum)	12 oz.	1½	Used largely for vacuum packed corn. 3 to 4 servings.
No. 300	14 to 16 oz.	1¾	Pork and beans, baked beans, meat products, cranberry sauce, blueberries, *specialties. 3 to 4 servings.
No. 303	16 to 17 oz.	2	Fruits, vegetables, meat products, ready-to-serve soups, *specialties. 4 servings.
No. 2	1 lb. 4 oz. or 1 pt. 2 fl. oz.	2½	**Juices, ready-to-serve soups, *specialties, and a few fruits and vegetables. No longer in popular use for most fruits and vegetables. 5 servings.
No. 2½	1 lb. 13 oz.	3½	Fruits, some vegetables (pumpkin, sauerkraut, spinach and other greens, tomatoes). 5 to 7 servings.
No. 3 Cyl.	3 lb. 3 oz. or 1 qt. 14 fl. oz.	5¾	Fruit and vegetable juices, pork and beans, condensed soup and some vegetables for institutional use. 10 to 12 servings.
No. 10	6½ lb. to 7 lb. 5 oz.	12–13	Fruits, vegetables and some other foods for restaurant and institutional use. 25 servings.

Strained and homogenized foods for infants, and chopped Junior foods, come in small jars and cans suitable for the smaller servings used. The weight is given on the label.

Meats, Poultry, Fish and Seafood are almost entirely advertised and sold under weight terminology.

*SPECIALTIES: Usually a food combination such as macaroni, spaghetti, Spanish style rice, Mexican type foods, Chinese foods, tomato aspic, etc.

**Juices are now being packed in a number of can sizes.

Substitution of various can sizes may be accomplished in the following way:

• *SUBSTITUTING ONE CAN FOR ANOTHER SIZE—for institutional use*

		Approx.	
1 No. 10 can equals	7 No. 303	(1 lb.)	cans
1 No. 10 can equals	5 No. 2	(1 lb. 4 oz.)	cans
1 No. 10 can equals	4 No. 2½	(1 lb. 13 oz.)	cans
1 No. 10 can equals	2 No. 3 Cyl.	(46 to 50 oz.)	cans

(Courtesy National Canners Association, 1133 20th St., N.W., Washington, D.C. 20036)

FREEZE-DRIED FOODS

Dehydrating foods has long been an established means of preserving them. This was always done through evaporation of liquid by the application of heat. Although this method of processing improved the keeping quality and lowered the weight and volume to reduce shipping charges, it almost invariably meant an irreplaceable loss of quality.

Freezing food is not a new process. "In 1842 a patent was granted H. Benjamin in England for freezing foods by immersion in an ice and salt brine." In the early days primitive freezing of baked goods was accomplished by placing trays in a freezer. Not only did this require many hours, in addition the outside of the product was stale by the time the center was frozen. New blast freezing tunnels, with forced cold air, reduced freezing time from many hours to about 1/2 hour. This of course depended on the particular type and cut of food to be frozen, its temperature at the time it was placed in the freezer, etc.

What is freeze-drying? Freeze-drying is a technique which involves freezing incidentally, but the primary object of which is the drying. The end product is dry, not frozen. The name comes from the fact that the material to be dried is also frozen and remains frozen during the whole drying period. The drying process is called sublimation and sometimes occurs naturally. (A snow bank that disappears without melting into run-off water has sublimated.)

After it is dry, the food may be stored at room temperature for two years or more, so long as it is packaged to protect it from oxygen, light, and moisture. After water is added back to the dried food, it is treated as a thawed frozen food. When compared with other dried foods, quality is high.

What do the foods look like? Freeze-dried foods may be recognized by their appearance. They look somewhat like the initial frozen product in so far as shape and size are concerned. But, they are much lighter in weight and have a spongy texture. Generally, their color lightens, but returns to normal when we add back water during rehydration. They are so dry as to be brittle. Some freeze-dried foods are so friable that they may be completely pulverized between two fingers.

The product shrinks little during the drying process so it has almost the same volume as when it was frozen. Theoretically, there should be no shrinkage of the food, but in actual practice some shrinkage -- perhaps as much as five percent -- does occur.

A few flavors and nutrients are lost during freeze-drying, but these losses are negligible when compared with losses occurring with most other freezing or drying methods. However, if drying and packaging are done correctly, the process allows a food to maintain more original product characteristics than any other drying method.

The drying process. The freeze-drying process is unique in that ice in the frozen product goes directly from the solid state to the gaseous form. This type of drying allows little flavor and nutrient loss to take place because only distilled water moves out of the food. Solids that had been dissolved in the water of the original food were frozen out as the water solidified during the freezing. During drying, these important solids and oils are left in the food where they were frozen out of the water.

The most important difference between freeze-drying and evaporative drying methods is that, although both are water removal methods, freeze-drying dries from the solid ice where the others dry from liquid. This is the secret of the high quality foods produced by freeze-drying. Heat is applied to the food at a low pressure causing the ice in the food to change to water vapor. The ice in the food does not melt. Sublimation occurs under low pressure at a lower temperature, thereby protecting flavor.

The complete process. Briefly, the steps involved in freeze-drying are as follows:

1) Preparing the food in the form that is wanted after it is dried. This may include trimming, peeling, sizing, grading, and portion-control. Also, it may include blanching or cooking. Or, it may mean dicing, slicing, pulverizing, or otherwise changing particle size.

2) Freezing the food. The temperature and method of freezing is important as it changes the ice crystal size. The food must be kept frozen until the drying cycle is completed.

3) Drying the food. Steps include placing frozen food on trays, putting trays on the heating shelves, and closing the cabinet door. Meanwhile, the condenser plates are chilled to about -40° F. When the moisture on the equipment surfaces in the cabinet is removed, the vacuum pump is turned on. Pressure is then lowered to evacuate air from the cabinet. We then add heat to the heating plates.

In this low pressure situation, water vapor from the ice in the food now flows to the colder condenser plates. These plates attract, collect and freeze the vapor. It is held in a frozen state until the plates are defrosted.

When all the ice has been sublimated from the food, we stop the process. We then break the vacuum (increase the pressure) with nitrogen gas. This is done so that oxygen and moisture do not re-enter the cabinet and get back in the food. Finally, the food is removed from the cabinet. (See Figure 8-D, 8-E.)

Figure 8–D. System Used for Freeze-Drying Coffee.
(Compliments of Frick Company, Waynesboro, Pennsylvania)

Figure 8–E. System Used for Freeze-Drying Coffee.
(Compliments of Frick Company, Waynesboro, Pennsylvania)

4) Package the food in air-tight, water-proof containers. This is done in a moisture-free room. We nitrogen-gas or vacuum-pack the food package to eliminate oxygen and moisture.

5) Rehydrate by placing the food in water or some other liquid. Use as you would use a thawed frozen food.

Principal Advantages. Low temperatures and sublimation avoid chemical and flavor losses. Physical changes are minimized. Nutrients remain dispersed in their original position within the food with little loss. Case-hardening does not take place. Bacteria, molds, and yeasts have little chance to multiply. Food items have a long shelf-line. They rehydrate quickly, permitting simplified food preparation. Refrigeration is not required, as in the case of frozen or fresh products. Meat items are all meat, with no fat or bone.

Principal Disadvantages. Costs of processing are high. The foods require a tight package that is expensive. The foods are easily damaged and processors must package and handle them carefully. Quality of the dried foods, although good when compared with other dried foods, is usually not as good as frozen or canned food. These foods are not beauty contest winners, although some, like strawberries, look appetizing even when dry. Their market is limited.

LIQUID NITROGEN FREEZING

One of the newest innovations in the freezing of food products is the use of liquid nitrogen as the freezing agent. One such system is marketed under the trade name of "Cryotransfer". (See Figure 8-F.)

Figure 8–F. Cryotransfer Liquid Nitrogen Flash Freezer.
(Courtesy General Dynamics, Liquid Carbonic Division, Chicago, Illinois)

Because of its ability to freeze products very rapidly, liquid nitrogen is ideally suited to I.Q.F. (individually quick frozen) work. One company reports it is able to freeze 1500 pounds of individual fish fillets or portions per hour, with excellent quality.

The rapid freezing action of liquid nitrogen demands a few minor changes over older freezing methods. For example, products requiring breading must be breaded PRIOR to freezing to make the breading hold better. A pre-cooling operation has been found necessary, in most cases, to prevent splitting of the product under the action of the intense cold, flash freezing being done at a temperature of approximately -320°F.

Freezing by liquid nitrogen is not as complicated as one might suppose. A conveyor belt carries the product through the whole machine.

The products to be frozen are met by a gaseous nitrogen curtain wall just as they enter the machine. This nitrogen curtain seals the interior of the machine from infiltration of outside air and moisture. In addition, the gaseous nitrogen subjects the product to a -50° F. This provides an immediate crust freeze, locking in flavor and quality.

After passing the gaseous nitrogen, products move through a "liquid nitrogen mist" chamber where low pressure spray nozzles shoot a heavy spray which surrounds them. The temperature in this area reaches -320°F.

A major advantage of the Cryotransfer machine is liquid nitrogen recirculation. Excess liquid nitrogen is re-collected in the collector pan, and flows back out to the external reservoir for recirculation. (See Figure 8-G next page.)

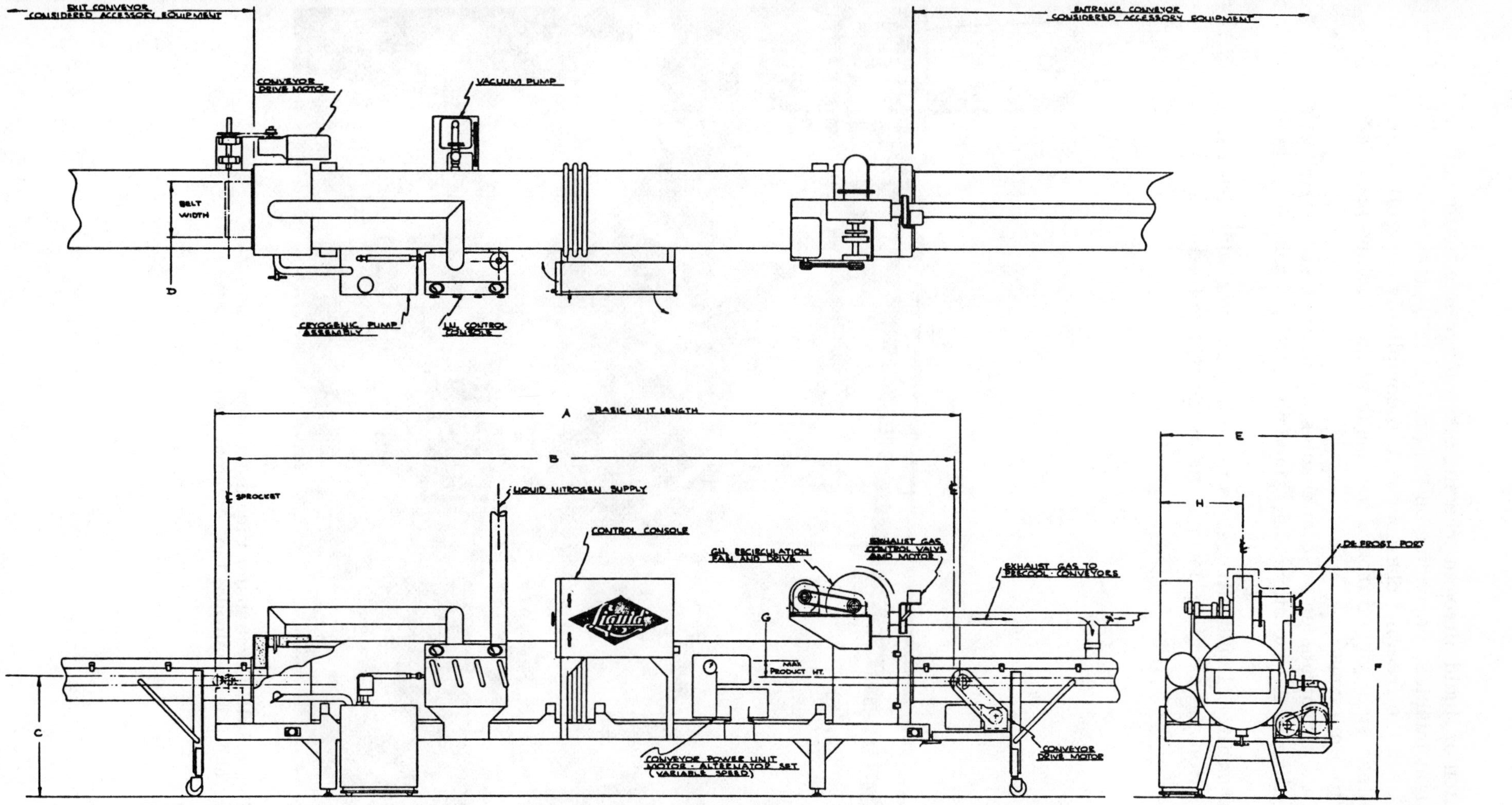

BELT CONVEYOR CONSIDERED ACCESSORY EQUIPMENT
ENTRANCE CONVEYOR CONSIDERED ACCESSORY EQUIPMENT
CONVEYOR DRIVE MOTOR
VACUUM PUMP
BELT WIDTH
D
CRYOGENIC PUMP ASSEMBLY
LN. CONTROL CONSOLE
A BASIC UNIT LENGTH
B
℄ SPROCKET
LIQUID NITROGEN SUPPLY
CONTROL CONSOLE
GAS RECIRCULATION FAN AND DRIVE
EXHAUST GAS CONTROL VALVE AND MOTOR
EXHAUST GAS TO PRECOOL CONVEYORS
G
MAX. PRODUCT HT.
C
CONVEYOR POWER UNIT MOTOR · ALTERNATOR SET (VARIABLE SPEED)
CONVEYOR DRIVE MOTOR
E
H
DE-FROST PORT
F

Figure 8–G. Schematic Drawing of Cryotransfer Machine.
(Courtesy General Dynamics, Liquid Carbonic Division, Chicago, Illinois)

STANDARD CONVEYOR BELT WILL BE STAINLESS STEEL POSITIVE DRIVE WITH THE FOLLOWING SPECIFICATIONS

CHAINS: (ON EACH SIDE OF BELT) RC 40

RODS: .156 D. SPACED ON 2" CENTERS AND DRILLED FOR COTTER KEYS

MESH: SPECIFICATION 72-24-16

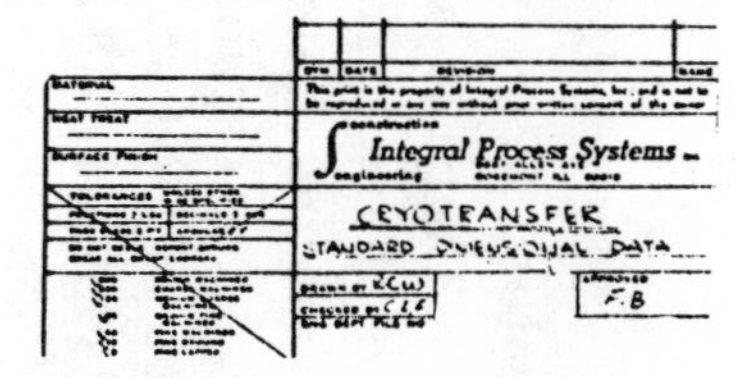

The whole operation of liquid nitrogen freezing takes place in a matter of minutes, at the most eight minutes, depending on the product to be treated.

There is no oxygen in the freezing chamber. It is completely controlled nitrogen atmosphere. The stainless steel jacket around the length of the machine provides a vacuum insulation of 1 to 5 microns.

The capability of the Cryotransfer system enables the ultra-fast freezing of all types of food stuffs, sealing in the moisture and, since no air is present, eliminating any risk of oxidation.

Because of its versatility, liquid nitrogen is providing an ever widening range of products for consumption and creating new phases of the frozen food industry. (See Figure 8-H.)

Figure 8–H. Cryotransfer Liquid Nitrogen Freezer
in use at Viking Seafoods, Inc., Boston, Massachusetts.

FOOD PROCESSING IN THE FUTURE

In the past few years a processing revolution has taken place within the food industry. New and startling concepts are being developed to change a fresh perishable product into one that is storable, edible, and, hopefully, palatable. Many of these ideas, such as freeze-drying and cryogenics, have already been tested and are now in limited use. Other concepts are still in the laboratory stage and may, or may not, turn out to be practical.

To be successful, a new food processing method should accomplish at least one or more of the five requirements listed below:

1) Perform an old job at a lower cost
2) Produce a better quality
3) Produce a new product
4) Yield a food with special application
5) Use some new product as raw material

Osmotic Dehydration. Developed by the U.S. Department of Agriculture, this new method of dehydration appears practical for various foods, including those fruits high in sugar content.

By using the osmosis* principle certain foods have been reduced to "50 percent of their original weight in 24 hours at 70°F., or 3 hours at 120°F." Obviously each food has its own drying requirements. The weight reduction causes little damage to flavor or color. (Some loss of color, flavor and nutrients is always inherent in any dehydration procedure.)

One product produced by osmotic dehydration that may be useful is maple syrup. Seventy-five percent of the sap's moisture has been successfully removed.

Cost studies show considerably lower figures than amounts expended for regular evaporation methods.

Dehydrofreezing and Dehydrocanning. In this processing method about half the moisture is first removed, and the products then are either frozen or canned. There is little difference in nutrition, flavor, or appearance of these foods compared with similar frozen or canned products. Dehydrofrozen peas, apple sauce, apple pieces, and slices are now in use by the U.S. Navy and other large outlets.

Explosive Puff-drying. A new combination drying method. Convection hot air driers partially dry the item. An explosion gun causes the product to expand by changing from high to low pressure. Foods finish drying in bins. Carrots, beets, blueberries, and apple pieces have been dried by this method but so far sales have been poor.

Freeze-Concentration. Foods processed by this method must be in liquid form. The processor first freezes the liquid to be concentrated into a slurry. While the ice crystals are held below freezing, but above their lowest melting point, a machine centrifuges the ice crystals to separate them from the liquid concentrate.

*Osmosis is the selective passage of fluids through semipermeable substance or membrane. The absorption of water by plant roots is an example of osmosis in its simplest form. Osmotic pressure develops as a result of differences in concentrations of substance on opposite sides of a membrane. It increases with heat.

Freeze-concentration is currently in use for removing water from vinegar. Several soluble (instant) coffee companies use this system to remove water from their coffee extract. French wine processors use this system to increase the alcohol content of their wines. It is also being considered as a method of beer concentration.

Compaction. Food cost is based in part on transportation costs. Since transportation rates are based on both weight and bulk, compaction may prove to have commercial value.

Dried foods are being compressed at 1000 to 3000 pounds per square inch. A new compression technique is to roll the dried food in thin sheets. Sheets of catsup, barbecue sauce, gravy, syrup and pickle relish are possible. The sheets are easy to chew and easily rehydrated in the mouth with saliva. Some of the freeze-dehydrated foods being compacted in the laboratory are chicken, cooked beef, raw beef, stew, shrimp, chili con carne, scrambled eggs, onions, rice, spinach, and peaches. One compacted food, with rapid rehydration ability, is a disc 1 1/2 inches in diameter and 1/2 inch thick.

Irradiation. In this method of food processing, ionizing radiation preserves food through sterilization. The most widely used source of energy to date is Cobalt 60, although X-rays, electron guns, and Cesium 37 may be used.

Radiation dosages range from 1 million to 5.6 million rads of energy. Meat, poultry, marine products, and wheat flour are the only products currently undergoing sterilization evaluation. High dosages have created a problem because to attain a radiation level sufficient to destroy bacteria may also damage structure and texture molecules.

Pasteurization of foods and dairy products including milk, cheese, sour cream, and milk powders can be accomplished with smaller dosages (about 1/4 to 1 million rads) of irradiation energy. Poultry products may be treated for Salmonellae, and the trichinoe worm in pork can be killed with low dosage levels of irradiation energy.

To pasteurize fresh foods, dosages of about 200,000 to 500,000 rads are used. Under refrigeration, these foods maintain their freshness longer than usual. Examples are strawberries, cherries, peaches, coleslaw, cabbage, and tomatoes. Meats include prepared items such as sausage, bologna, and weiners. Oysters and shrimp have their refrigerated shelf-lives doubled.

Pasteurization extends the shelf-life of non-refrigerated products such as asparagus, brussel sprouts, green beans, ham, and other cured meat products. Frozen foods, too, extend their shelf-life through use of irradiation. Dried foods have their keeping qualities improved and improvements in their physical structure improve rehydration. Costs of irradiation pasteurization are said to be about 1/2 to 1 1/2 cents per pound, but since commercial foods are not yet produced, little is known about actual processing costs.

Dosages of 50,000 to 100,000 rads are useful for killing insects in food. Research on tropical fruits such as mangos and papayas, and on wheat shows disinfestation to be possible and economically feasible. Wheat flour has been difficult to disinfect with chemicals - particularly so when packaged. (See Tables 1 and 2 on following pages.)

Table 1. Items from the food irradiation program approved by the Food and Drug Administration (FDA) as of June 1966

Product and purpose of irradiation	Radiation Source	Dose range (Megarad)
Bacon:		
Purpose, sterilization	Cobalt 60	4.5 to 5.6
	Electron Beam (5 & 10 Mev)	4.5 to 5.6
	Cesium 137	4.5 to 5.6
	X-ray from electron beam (5 Mev)	4.5 to 5.6
Wheat and wheat flour:		
Purpose, insect disinfestation ..	Cobalt 60	0.02 to 0.05
	Cesium 137	0.02 to 0.05
	Electron beam (5 Mev)	0.02 to 0.05
White potatoes:		
Purpose, sprout inhibition	Cobalt 60	0.005 to 0.015
	Cesium 137	0.005 to 0.015
Packaging materials:		
Purpose, food contactants for use in radiation preservation of prepackaged foods	Cobalt 60	1.0 maximum
	Cesium 137	
Vegetable parchment paper:		
Purpose, food contactants for use in radiation preservation of prepackaged foods	Cobalt 60	6.0 maximum
	Cesium137	6.0 maximum
	X-rays from electron beam (5 Mev)	6.0 maximum

Source: United States Congressional Record 1965.

Table 2. Items from the food irradiation program pending before the Food and Drug Administration (FDA) as of July 1966

Product and purpose of irradiation	Radiation Source	Dose range (Megarad)
Oranges:		
Purposes, inhibition of surface and subsurface microorganisms	Cobalt 60	0.075 to 0.20
	Cesium 137	0.075 to 0.20
Strawberries:		
Purpose, shelf-life	Cobalt 60	0.10 to 0.25
	Cesium 137	0.10 to 0.25
Dehydrated Vegetables:		
Purpose, shelf-life and to speed up rehydration	Gamma or Electron Omitters	0.3 to 4.0
Ham:		
Purpose, sterilization	Cobalt 60	3.5 to 5.6
	Cesium 137	3.5 to 5.6
Fish:		
Purpose, pasteurization	Cobalt 60	0.10 to 0.20
Includes: Haddock, Codfish,	Cesium 137	0.10 to 0.20
Sole, Flounder, Pollock and	Electrons (10 Mev)	0.10 to 0.20
Ocean Perch.	X-rays from electron beam (5 Mev)	0.10 to 0.20
Packaging materials:		
Purpose, food contactants for use in radiation preservation of prepackage foods	Cobalt 60	1.0 to 6.0 maximum
	Cesium 137	1.0 to 6.0 maximum

Source: United States Congressional Record 1965.

Protein Foods From Plants. Synthetic meats now manufactured use plants as the source of their protein. Researchers are able to spin the resulting protein fibers into threads using a technique similar to that used in the production of rayon. These threads, when woven, provide the fiber structure of synthetic meats. An advantage is that the protein content of the "meat" may be adjusted and controlled.

Synthetic meats come close to duplicating real meats (chicken, beef, ham, and bacon) in flavor, texture, and nutritional value. Some of the new foods produced are fibrous. Others are powders and extruded grits. They may be used as meat loaf, hamburger patty, and other meat substitutes. Artificially flavored and colored, they resemble real meats.

Simulated chicken, ham, beef, bacon, or sea foods are now available on the market, but prices are high since volumes are low. Main purchasers to date are vegetarians, certain religious groups, and persons on special diets.

Synthetic Foods. In the years ahead, we may be eating more foods derived from sources not usually thought of as food today. One of the more promising raw materials sources is petroleum. Processes now being developed use petroleum as a cheap and abundant source of energy for the growth of microorganisms such as yeasts, bacteria, and molds. These minute plants are efficient and work with great speed. An often quoted example is as follows:

"In a 24 hour day, a 1,000 pound steer produces 0.9 pounds of protein (roughly four pounds of meat). One thousand pounds of soybeans, planted and cultivated under optimum conditions, produces on the average 82 pounds of protein every 24 hours. But, 1,000 pounds of yeast, given sufficient raw material, can produce 100,000 pounds of protein in 24 hours."

The principal prospect of large-scale production is using the Champagnat's process. Microorganisms consume unwanted waxy components of petroleum and so refine the oil as they produce food. A semi-commercial plant, treating 500 tons of gas oil per day, may produce 450 tons of refined oil and 50 tons of dried yeast containing 40-50 percent protein.

Bibliography:

Commercial Canning. Courtesy National Canners Association, Washington, D.C.

Freeze-Dried Foods. Courtesy Kermit Bird, United States Department of Agriculture.

Liquid Nitrogen Freezing. Courtesy Emery Newton Jr., General Dynamics, (Liquid Carbonic Division) Chicago, Illinois, and Quick Frozen Food Magazine, November 1965.

Food Processing in the Future. Courtesy Kermit Bird, United States Department of Agriculture.

LESSON 8 - BRAINTEASER

When you are certain you understand the material in this lesson, answer the questions below. After you have completed the brainteaser, check your answers in the text. Use the following scale to evaluate your comprehension of this lesson:

10 Correct --- Outstanding
9 Correct --- Excellent
8 Correct --- Good
7 Correct --- Fair
6 Or Under
Correct --- Restudy the Lesson

1) Explain "how" and "why" Blanching is done in commercial canning.

2) In commercial canning certain types of mechanical filling can be accomplished at the rate of:

a. 1200 or more containers per minute
b. 1000 " " " " "
c. 1400 " " " " "
d. 800 " " " " "
e. 1600 " " " " "

3) There are six basic reasons for maintaining a low interior pressure (vacuum) when canning foods. The first one is named for you. Name three of the remaining five below.

a. Helps keep can ends drawn in, an indication of a safe product.

b.

c.

d.

4) A snow bank that disappears without melting is said to have ____________________.

5) In packaging FREEZE-DRIED foods why is it necessary to use "nitrogen gas" or to "vacuum-pack" the food package?

6) Name three DISADVANTAGES of freeze-dried processing of foods.

a.

b.

c.

7) Why is it necessary for most products to be pre-cooled prior to being frozen by liquid nitrogen?

8) Flash freezing is being done at a temperature of approximately:

a. Minus 340°F.
b. " 300°F.
c. " 360°F.
d. " 320°F.
e. " 280°F.

9) When using compaction processing, dried foods are compressed at ________________ to________________pounds per square inch.

10) State the basic principle of Irradiation food processing.

LESSON 9

GENERAL PRINCIPLES OF FOOD PRODUCTION

LESSON 9 - PREVIEW

With some basic knowledge, and relatively little training, it is possible to follow a recipe. However, there is much more to the food industry than merely reading a recipe, and combining the ingredients. This does not mean recipes are unimportant. On the contrary, they are extremely necessary to the successful business and a considerable amount of time and space in this lesson, is devoted to the necessity of standard recipes, and recipe conversion. Never-the-less, there are other factors that must be taken into consideration. Understanding and applying the general principles outlined and explained in this lesson, together with an appreciation of the importance and use of standard recipes, will materially aid the student in becoming more proficient in his chosen field.

GENERAL PRINCIPLES OF FOOD PRODUCTION

In the preparation of food, from appetizers to desserts, there are certain fundamental rules that apply. Such things as quality ingredients, correct cooking methods, the time lapse between preparation and service, gearing production to demand, and the prevention of waste, loss and theft, must all be under constant evaluation if food is to be appetizing in appearance, palatable in taste, nutritious in content, and profitable to the business.

Ingredients. The rule for ingredients is simply to use the best quality possible, consistent with what the customer is willing to pay, and in line with producing the desired item. For example, it may be more sensible to use a smaller size peach for a peach and cottage cheese salad, and use a larger size peach for a peach and whipped cream dessert. Grilled or charcoal broiled steaks should be obtained from high grade beef while an excellent swiss steak, or roulade, can be cut from a lower grade beef.

Cooking Methods. The cooking method is normally determined by the cut of meat being used (and other factors discussed in Lesson 10), the specific dish to be prepared, or occasionally for the effect desired.

Less tender cuts of meat are cooked by moist heat. More tender cuts are prepared by dry heat. Specific dishes may call for poaching, steaming, blanching, etc.* Obviously, it is important to follow the cooking method stated in the recipe, if best results are to be obtained.

Specialty dishes are often prepared to create an effect and impress the customer. A good example of this is found in flambe dishes prepared at the customer's table. In most all instances, the item could be done just as well in the kitchen, but the effect would be lost.

Time Between Preparation And Service. With very few exceptions, the time between preparation and service should be held to an absolute minimum. When possible, foods should be cooked to order. For dishes that must be prepared ahead, the rule is to prepare small quantities, at frequent intervals. Naturally this rule does not apply to soups, most sauces, and gravies, which are often better tasting when prepared in advance.

Overproduction. There are many causes of waste in the food business. Certainly overproduction ranks high on the list. Sometimes overproduction cannot be avoided, or is the result of unexpected events such as cancelled banquets, snowstorms, etc. Unfortunately, overproduction occurs too frequently without a legitimate reason.

One way of keeping overproduction to a minimum is by using the Item Sales History Form explained in Lesson 7, (Figure 7-O). In the restaurant business, as in any business, future predictions are based on past performance. To use the Item Sales History Form for anticipated sales, simply multiply the last recorded Percentage of Sales Today, for a particular item, times the number of expected customers, as shown in the following sample.

* See Glossary for definition of cooking terms, pp. 261 to 266.

ITEM	% SALES TODAY	No. Customers Expected	No. Portions Needed
Broiled Lobster	14	325	46
Cornish Hen	8	325	26
Prime Ribs	29	325	94
Roast Duckling	9	325	29
Tournedos	10	325	33
Sirloin Steak	21	325	68
Frog Legs	9	325	29

Use and Storage of Leftovers. In the food industry the difference between the expected profit, and little or no profit, may be the leftovers. Needless to say, the ideal situation would be to buy exactly what we can sell and never have leftover food. Unfortunately, ideal situations seldom exist so the utilization of leftovers is mandatory. Leftovers can be used in a variety of ways such as casserole dishes, ground meat dishes, hors d'oeuvres, canapes, soups, sauces, gravies, etc. When storing leftovers, place them in shallow pans, not over 4 inches deep to permit thorough chilling, cover, (cool slightly if hot) and refrigerate immediately. Management and chefs must be continually alert to find new and interesting ways to change leftover foods into dishes with customer appeal.

Waste, Loss and Theft. One area that should, and probably will, occupy a good deal of management's time is trying to prevent waste, loss, and theft. There is no allowance in the budget for these things, nor can there be one. Any merchandise that "disappears", regardless of the reason, ends up being charged to food cost. Since there is obviously no monetary return on waste, loss or theft, the food cost becomes higher than it should be and the margin of profit drops.

Besides overproduction, other causes of waste or loss may be:

a. Oversize portions. It is of small importance how many portions a given recipe will produce unless employees are very conscientious about following portion sizes. In other words, all portions must be carefully weighed or measured if any degree of control over cost is to be maintained.

Portion size lists should be typed and posted in each department for every employee to read and adhere to. Where applicable the size should be given by scoop number, or ladle, rather than ounces.

In the case of pre-portioned meats, specifications should be stringent enough to allow for only a minimum variation of weight. For example, specifications for steaks should state, "---no more than 1/2 ounce over or under the specified weight." Besides the fact that many customers get irritated if the person next to them receives a larger portion, some steaks can cost as much as $.25 per ounce. In a year, just one extra ounce over the portion size could cost the restaurant several hundred dollars.

It is the responsibility of management to insure that portion sizes are followed. Oversize portions cause waste and undersized portions cause loss of customers. To carry out this responsibility requires constant spot-checking and evaluation. If employees realize the supervisor is concerned, they will be concerned. If employees believe the manager does not care, they will not care.

b. Poor purchasing procedures. There are many ways in which waste and loss are associated with poor purchasing procedures such as not obtaining competitive quotations when buying, buying poor quality merchandise, over purchasing a perishable item, accepting bribes, etc. Any of these can result in higher food cost and profit loss.

c. Improper receiving, storing and issuing of merchandise. The importance of good receiving, storing, and issuing procedures, in relation to waste, loss and theft should be obvious. Review Lessons 5 and 6 to refresh your memory on correct methods of performing these tasks.

d. Not using standardized recipes. Failure to use standard recipes will result in needless loss and waste. The three main reasons for using standard recipes are covered later in the lesson.

e. Employees giving away food. As in other forms of waste and loss, food given away is subtracted from profit. Unfortunately there is no magic formula to prevent this from happening. One method employed to keep this problem to a minimum is the use of "checkers", to check trays and plates as they leave the kitchen.

Among other things, checkers insure portion sizes are correct, everything on the tray is recorded on the guest check, and the guest check is accurately priced, extended and totaled. In some operations the checker actually prices, extends and totals the guest check.

Another method in common use is duplicate checks. One check is turned in with the order and the other is retained by the waiter or waitress, and turned in at the end of the shift, at which time the two are compared.

Sometimes both methods are combined into one. In this case the "duplicate" procedure is followed exactly as stated above but, as the food leaves the kitchen, the checker runs a tray check and rings up the actual guest check in accordance with the items on the tray. This combination method provides a three-way test and evaluation between the two duplicates and the guest check. Naturally, food should never leave the kitchen under any circumstances, without something in writing to substantiate the order.

f. Theft. Theives fall into two distinct categories. One type will steal anything not bolted down, from money to merchandise. The other type has a peculiar sense of value and while he or she would never consider taking actual cash, feels that anything else belonging to the company also belongs to him.

In the food industry the greatest problem develops from the latter type of thief. This is probably because in most all instances proper security is given to cash in the form of locked registers, good safes, regular bank deposits, etc.

Strangely enough the same manager, so careful of the company's cash, frequently appears to have little or no interest in equally pilferable merchandise. Storerooms are often left unlocked all day; requisition systems are non-existent; and employees are allowed to wander in and out with bags and parcels.

In the past few years many excellent control systems have been developed to point out problem areas where theft might exist. These systems will provide a warning that something is wrong and can be of great value as an aid to management. However, in the final analysis, it is the observant manager and department heads using good common sense, together with proper supervision, that keep theft at its lowest attainable level.

Importance of Using Standard Recipes. For many years food recipes were filed in the chef's head. They were jealously guarded and never given to anyone. Today, owners and managers have come to realize the necessity of maintaining a standard recipe file, with ALL recipes printed on cards, (usually 5 x 8 inches), showing each ingredient to be used, the amount of each ingredient needed, and the order in which they should be mixed or blended. (See Figure 9-A below and Figures 9-B and 9-C on the following page.)

Fruit Stuffed
LEG OF LAMB

Lamb

In every season . . . in every locality, Roast Leg of Lamb is a favorite among diners who know and select the finest in foods. Here is a taste-tempting, mouth-watering roast that will add to your reputation for delicious and unusual gourmet dinners.

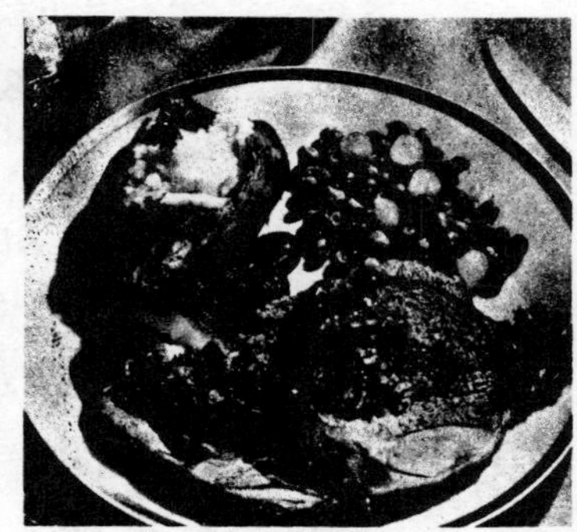

INGREDIENTS	AMOUNTS 25 SERVINGS	50 SERVINGS	100 SERVINGS	CHEF'S VARIATIONS	METHOD
Chopped pitted dried prunes	1 C.	2 C.	1 qt.		1. Combine prunes, dates, figs, pine nuts, onion, bulgar, parsley, *3 cups stock or bouillon, salt, coriander and pepper.
Chopped pitted dates	1 C.	2 C.	1 qt.		
Chopped figs	1 C.	2 C.	1 qt.		2. Mix well, fill lamb with mixture and secure with skewers.
Pine nuts	¼ C.	½ C.	1 C.		
Chopped onions	¾ C.	1 ½ C.	3 C.		3. Place on rack in shallow roasting pan and bake in slow oven 325° F. 2½ to 3 hours or until meat thermometer registers 175-180°, depending upon desired degree of doneness.
Bulgar (cracked wheat)	2 C.	1 qt.	2 qts.		
Chopped parsley	¼ C.	½ C.	1 C.		
Stock or bouillon	1 qt.	2 qts.	1 gal.		
Salt	1 Tbsp.	2 Tbsp.	¼ C.		4. Baste lamb occasionally with remaining cups of stock or bouillon during cooking period.
Coriander	½ tsp.	1 tsp.	2 tsp.		
Pepper	½ tsp.	1 tsp.	2 tsp.		*For 50 servings, combine 6 cups stock or bouillon with fruit mixture; for 100 servings, combine 12 cups.
Lamb legs — 5 lbs. after boning	3	6	12		

Figure 9-A. Standard Recipe.
(Courtesy American Lamb Council, Denver, Colorado.)

WHITE BREAD

YIELD: 30 Loaves (47½ Pounds of Bread) (20 Slices Per Loaf)				DAILY RATION: 6 Slices
INGREDIENTS	**WEIGHTS**	**MEASURES**	**% ON FLOUR BASIS**	**METHOD**
Yeast, active, dry Water, warm (110° F) Sugar	5 oz . 2 oz	15 tbsp 1½ pt 4½ tbsp	1.11	1. Sprinkle yeast on top of water. Let stand 5 minutes, then stir. Add sugar and stir until dissolved. Let stand 10 minutes longer, then stir again.
Water (68° F) variable Salt Sugar Milk, nonfat, dry	 11 oz 1 lb 13 oz 1¾ lb	2⅛ gal (variable) 1 cup 4¼ cups 5¾ cups	65.49 (Total) 2.43 6.86 (Total) 6.19	2. Place water in mixer bowl. Add salt, sugar, and milk and mix on low speed to break up any lumps.
Flour, hard wheat, sifted Shortening, soft	28¼ lb 1 lb 6 oz	28¼ qt 3¼ cups	100.00 4.87	3. Add flour, yeast suspension, and shortening and mix until dough is smooth and elastic, (approximately 15 minutes, on medium speed). 4. FERMENTATION: Set in warm place (78° to 80° F), free from drafts, until double in bulk, (approximately 2 hours). 5. PUNCH: Let stand 30 to 45 minutes. 6. MAKE UP: Scale loaves at 28 ounces, round up and let rest 10 minutes. Mould and place one loaf into each bread pan (11 by 5¼ inch). 7. PROOF: Place in a warm place until double in bulk, approximately 1¼ hours. 8. Bake at 425° F approximately 35 to 40 minutes.

NOTE: 1. 10 oz of compressed yeast may be substituted for active dry yeast.
2. Temper water to yield a dough temperature of 80° F.
3. A ½ inch bread slicer will yield 20 slices (plus 2 end slices); a 7/16 inch slicer will yield 23 slices (plus 2 end slices).

Figure 9-B. Standard Recipe.
(Courtesy United States Navy, Bureau of Supplies and Accounts)

STUFFED LOBSTER PESARO (10 PORTIONS)

INGREDIENTS	AMOUNT	METHOD
Lobsters, Live	10 (1¼ – 1½ pounds each)	1. Split lobsters down middle from head to tail but do not cut through shell. 2. Remove and discard intestinal track and stomach just in back of head. 3. Remove tomalley (liver) and save for stuffing. 4. Wash lobsters in clear water, turn right side up and allow to drain.
Bread Crumbs, coarse Salt Pepper, Black Salad or Olive Oil* Tomalley (from lobster)	5 cups 2½ teasp. ¾ teasp. 1¼ cups	5. Mix bread crumbs, salt, pepper, oil and tomalley until crumbs are uniformly moistened.
Lemon Juice, fresh Water	2½ tbsp. 7½ tbsp.	6. Mix lemon juice and water and stir into bread crumb mixture.
Garlic, fresh Parsley, fresh, heavy stems removed.	2½ small cloves 12 sprigs	7. Crush garlic in garlic press. Discard pulp. Dice parsley fine. Add garlic and parsley to bread crumb mixture and stir.
Shrimp, raw	1¼ pounds	8. Shell and devein shrimp. Dice fine and stir into bread crumb mixture.
Butter*	As required	9. Divide stuffing into ten portions and fill lobsters.
* Note: If pure olive oil is used, omit butter, and sprinkle extra teaspoon of olive oil over stuffing prior to placing lobster in oven.		10. Lay thin strips of butter* over stuffing. 11. Bake in 325 degree oven. Allow 50 minutes for a 1¼ pound lobster and 10 additional minutes for each extra ¼ pound.

Figure 9-C. Standard Recipe.
(Courtesy Gene Travaglini, New Haven, Connecticut.)

Perhaps the most important reason for using a standard recipe is quality control. If ingredients are properly weighed, blended together, and cooked at the specified heat in accordance with the recipe, the finished dish should taste the same each and every time it is produced. This can be extremely important for retaining critical repeat business.

It is certainly logical to expect a customer to return because he enjoyed a specific meal or dish, prepared in a certain manner. In restaurants where only the chef has the recipes, a serious profit loss could occur if that chef were suddenly hospitalized or disabled, or if he quit his job.

Another paramount reason for using standard recipes is cost control. If ingredients are thrown into a dish in a sloppy haphazard manner, accurate costing is virtually impossible to attain. Accurate weighing of ingredients is essential to calculating recipe cost and, subsequently, portion cost. If the exact portion cost is not determined, the menu price may be under or over what it should be.

A third reason for using standard recipes is portion control. When the CORRECT AMOUNT of ingredients are blended into a recipe, the chef or manager knows it will yield* a certain volume or weight, thereby producing a certain number of portions. The yield can easily be converted into number of portions by dividing it by the portion size. For example, if a finished recipe yields 6 pounds 12 ounces, the number of 6 ounce portions would be determined as follows:

6 pounds 12 ounces times 16 = 108 ounces.
108 ounces divided by 6 ounces = 18 portions.

Table of Weights And Measures. The following Table of Weights and Measures is only a partial listing. A complete Table is included at the end of the textbook. (See pages 267 and 268.)

1 Gallon:	4	quarts	1 Quart:	2	pints
	8	pints		4	1/2 pints
	16	1/2 pints		4	8 oz. cups
	16	8 oz. cups		2	pounds (water)
	8	pounds (water)		32	ounces (water)
	128	ounces (water)			
1 Pint:	2	1/2 pints	1 Cup:	16	level Tablespoons
	2	8 oz. cups		48	level teaspoons
	1	pound (water)		8	ounces (water)
	16	ounces (water)			

1 Tablespoon: 3 level teaspoons.

Generally accepted abbreviations are as follows:

Gallon - gal.	Cup - c.
Quart - qt.	Tablespoon - T., or Tbsp.
Pint - pt.	Teaspoon - t., or tsp.
Pound - lb., or #.	Ounce - oz.

Reducing And Increasing Units of Measure. The following rules apply to REDUCING measures:

Gallons to Quarts:	Multiply by 4
Quarts to Pints:	Multiply by 2

*Yield is the amount left after all losses (boning, cooking, carving, etc.) have been subtracted.

Pints to Cups:	Multiply by 2
Cups to Tablespoons:	Multiply by 16
Tablespoons to Teaspoons:	Multiply by 3
Pounds to Ounces:	Multiply by 16

To INCREASE measures to larger units, simply divide by the number of small units in the larger measure. For example: 1 cup equals 16 Tablespoons. To change 48 T. into cups the formula is: 48 ÷ 16 = 3 c.

Converting Recipes. Recipes are made up in various quantities, or sizes, yielding 2, 5, 10, 25, 50, and 100 portions. Most quantity cooking recipes yield 25 or 50 portions. It is common for recipes to state the yield, portion size, and number of portions to be expected. As stated previously, to obtain the number of portions stated on the recipe it is necessary to follow directions exactly and serve the portion size called for. Increasing or decreasing the portion size will require a new calculation.

Unless the recipe is for an extremely large number of servings, it is easier and better to convert all pounds to ounces, prior to the calculation. The formula to provide different numbers of servings is:

a. Number of Required Portions DIVIDED BY Number of Portions Per Recipe
b. The Resulting Answer Times Each Ingredient.

For example, suppose we wanted to reduce the following recipe to provide 32 pie crust tops for Individual Chicken Pies:

Pie Crust (50 Tops)

Flour, Sifted	3 lbs. 12 oz.
Shortening	2 lbs. 4 oz.
Salt	2 oz.
Water, Cold (Approx.)	3/4 Qt.

First convert everything possible to ounces:

Flour	3 lbs. 12 oz.	times 16 equals	60 oz.
Shortening	2 lbs. 4 oz.	times 16 equals	36 oz.
Salt	2 oz.	- - - - - - - - - -	2 oz.
Water	3/4 Qt.	equals	24 oz.

Divide Required Portions by Number of Portions Per Recipe:

32 ÷ 50 = .64

Multiply the answer (.64) times each ingredient:

Flour	60 x .64 = 38.4 oz.	or 38 1/2 oz.	or 2 lbs. 6 1/2 oz.
Shortening	36 x .64 = 23.04 oz.	or 23 oz.	or 1 lb. 7 oz.
Salt	2 x .64 = 1.28 oz.		or 1 1/4 oz.
Water	24 x .64 = 17.9 oz.	or 18 oz.	or 1 lb. 2 oz.

Increasing a recipe is accomplished the same way, using the same formula. If we wanted to increase the pie crust recipe to 129 portions:

129 ÷ 50 = 2.58
2.58 x each ingredient

Recipes in Decimals. Some quantity feeding operations make up recipes with the amount specified in decimals. The main advantage in using decimals is the ability to compute high speed quantity changes by running these figures through a calculator. Figure 9-D illustrates a recipe using the decimal system. Many of the columns are self-explanatory. Columns that may be confusing to the student are explained below.

Total Yield: The total weight of the original recipe or formula. This figure is obtained by adding the pounds and ounces on the left hand side of the sheet. (These figures, and the ingredients, are usually put on the paper permanently by means of mimeograph or printing.)

Times Factor and Equals: The amount of times the original recipe is to be increased or decreased, and the new expected yield.

✓ Column: For checking off each item as it is scaled (weighed) to prevent accidentally omitting an ingredient from the formula.

Cost-Unit and Amount: The cost per unit of each ingredient and the extension. For example, the first ingredient is 6x Sugar, with a unit of pounds. If the price were $.16 per pound, the $.16 would be entered in the Unit Column and multiplied by total weight of 10 lbs. 5 oz. giving an amount of $1.65. The $1.65 would be entered in the Amount Column. (See Figure 9-D.)

CULINARY INSTITUTE OF AMERICA

Formula Number: 807

ITEM: CHOCOLATE ICING (NON-STICKING) | Production Date: 12/23/66

Total Yield: 10 lbs.			Times Factor: 3 Equals: 30#				Cost	
Preparation Method	lbs.	oz.	Ingredients	lbs.	oz.	✓	Unit	Amount
Mix	3.4375		6X Sugar	10	5			
	1.625		Fudge Base	4	14			
Add:	1.5		Boiling Water	4	8			
Add:	3.375		6X Sugar	10	2			
		1.5	Shortening		4½			
Additional Instructions:								
1. Be sure water is boiling.								
2. Icing must be applied at 85° - 90°.								
3. After icing product let stand 45 minutes or longer before wrapping.								

Perfect Yield:	Raw Ingredient Weight:	Formula No. 807
Actual Yield:	Cooked & Cooled Weight:	Item: Choc. Icing Non-Sticking
Difference:	Difference:	Date First Used: 12/20/66
Total Cost: $	Cost Per Pound: $	Approved By: [signature]

Figure 9-D. Recipe Using Decimal Equivalents of Fractions.

Decimal Equivalent Charts. Small pocket size charts showing the decimal equivalents of fractions can be obtained free from machinery and drill manufacturers, toolmakers, etc. Frequently, wall size charts are obtained and hung up in the formula room.

When working with decimal equivalent charts certain basic rules must be kept in mind.

1. Always remember when you are working in pounds or ounces. For example, notice the formula in Figure 9-D calls for 1.5 (1 1/2) POUNDS of Boiling Water and 1.5 (1 1/2) OUNCES of Shortening. In other words, when working with decimal equivalents it is very possible to have identical figures, (for different ingredients) in both the pound and ounce columns.

2. Any figure to the left of the point is always a whole unit. Whether it is a whole unit of pounds or ounces depends on the column it is in.

3. When working in POUNDS the following chart applies:

Fraction	Decimal	Equivalency
1/16	.0625	1 oz.
1/8	.125	2 oz.
3/16	.1875	3 oz.
1/4	.25	4 oz.
5/16	.3125	5 oz.
3/8	.375	6 oz.
7/16	.4375	7 oz.
1/2	.5	8 oz.
9/16	.5625	9 oz.
5/8	.625	10 oz.
11/16	.6875	11 oz.
3/4	.75	12 oz.
13/16	.8125	13 oz.
7/8	.875	14 oz.
15/16	.9375	15 oz.

4. When working in POUNDS all decimal equivalents of sixty-fourths and thirty-seconds would be quarters, halves, or three-quarters of an ounce, OF THE OUNCE THAT IMMEDIATELY PRECEDES IT! For example, the decimal equivalent of 29/32 is .90625. If after multiplication the answer derived was 3.90625, it would be written on the right-hand side of the formula as:

lbs.	oz.
3	14 1/2

5. When working in OUNCES, Rule #2 is still applicable. Figures to the right of the point are fractions of an ounce. On most scales the smallest measurement is 1/4 of an ounce. If ounce decimals work out in between quarters there are two possible solutions to the problem. A special scale giving measurements smaller than a quarter of an ounce may be purchased, or, round the figure up or down to the nearest quarter. (See Figure 9-E on the following page.)

DECIMAL EQUIVALENTS OF FRACTIONS

1/64 — .015625	17/64 — .265625	33/64 — .515625	49/64 — .765625
1/32 — .03125	9/32 — .28125	17/32 — .53125	25/32 — .78125
3/64 — .046875	19/64 — 2.96875	35/64 — .546875	51/64 — .796875
1/16 — .0625	5/16 — .3125	9/16 — .5625	13/16 — .8125
5/64 — .078125	21/64 — .328125	37/64 — .578125	53/64 — .828125
3/32 — .09375	11/32 — .34375	19/32 — .59375	27/32 — .84375
7/64 — .109375	23/64 — .359375	39/64 — .609375	55/64 — .859375
1/8 — .125	3/8 — .375	5/8 — .625	7/8 — .875
9/64 — .140625	25/64 — .390625	41/64 — .640625	67/64 — .890625
5/32 — .15625	13/32 — .40625	21/32 — .65625	29/32 — .90625
11/64 — 171875	27/64 — .421875	43/64 — .671875	59/64 — .921875
-3/16 — .1875	7/16 — .4375	11/16 — .6875	15/16 — .9375
13/64 — .203125	29/64 — .453125	45/64 — .703125	61/64 — .953125
7/32 — .21875	15/32 — .46875	23/32 — .71875	31/32 — .96875
15/64 — .234375	31/64 — .484375	47/64 — .734.375	63/64 — .984375
1/4 — .25	1/2 — .5	3/4 — .75	1 — 1.

Figure 9-E. Decimal Equivalents of Fractions.

SOURCES OF RECIPES

Quality tested recipes may be obtained from various sources. Trade magazines, cookbooks, and even newspapers publish many fine recipes. Food processing companies often publish recipes on standard 5 x 8 cards, frequently with the number of portions, and the portion cost included. For quantity feeding operations, a set of over 700 U.S. Navy Recipes, all pre-tested and designed to yield 100 portions each, is available at nominal cost (currently about $8.25 per set) from the United States Government Printing Office, Washington, D.C.

While recipes from any of the above sources may not provide exactly what a food service operation is looking for, they can be an excellent foundation to build on. Management should constantly review and evaluate recipes with a view towards improving the menu and increasing customer satisfaction.

Regardless of the source, any recipe should be tested prior to use. Even recipes that claim to be pre-tested, should be re-tested, because of the possibility of typographical or printing errors.

LESSON 9 - BRAINTEASER

When you are certain you understand the material in this lesson, answer the questions below. After you have completed the brainteaser check your answers in the text. Use the following scale to evaluate your comprehension of this lesson:

10 Correct --- Outstanding
9 Correct --- Excellent
8 Correct --- Good
7 Correct --- Fair
6 Or Under Correct --- Restudy the Lesson.

1) Define the rule for "quality ingredients".

2) Basically the cooking method is determined by:

a.

b.

c.

3) From the standpoint of palatability, the time between preparation and service of most foods should be:

a. Two to four hours
b. As little as possible
c. One to two hours
d. As long as possible
e. One-half to three hours

4) To use the Item Sales History Form for anticipated sales, simply multiply

_______________ times _______________.

5) Any merchandise that "disappears" is charged to _______________.
(2 words)

Because there is no monetary return on this merchandise, the result is

_______________.
(2 words)

6) Name three things that can be done to prevent oversize portions:

7) Explain the combination "Checker and duplicate check" procedure.

8) Convert the following recipe to 22 portions.

FRENCH ONION SOUP

Ingredient	50 Portions	22 Portions
Onions, Peeled, sliced fine	8 lb.	
Butter or margarine	8 oz.	
Beef Stock, warm	1 1/2 gal.	
Chicken Stock, warm	1 1/2 gal.	
Dry Sherry (optional)	6 oz.	

9) Convert the following recipe to 163 portions.

BASIC WHITE STOCK

Ingredient	50 Portions	163 Portions
Beef Bones	25 lb.	
Water, to cover	6 gal. (approx.)	
Mirepoix:		
Onions	2 lb.	
Celery	1 lb.	
Carrots	1 lb.	
Bay Leaves	3	
Thyme	1 t.	
Peppercorns, crushed	1 t.	
Cloves, whole	1 t.	
Parsley Stems	-------	

10) On a separate piece of paper, convert the recipe for Chocolate Icing. (Figure 9-D) from a ten pound yield to a 65 pound yield.

LESSON 10

SPECIFIC PRINCIPLES OF FOOD PRODUCTION

LESSON 10 - PREVIEW

This lesson covers important principles of food production concerning appetizers, stocks and soups, meat cookery, microwave oven cooking, vegetable preparation, salads, and coffee brewing.

Due to the high wholesale cost of meats and their importance on the menu, the major portion of the lesson deals with meat cookery. It is extremely important that all food preparation personnel understand the various ways meat can be cooked.

APPETIZERS, STOCKS AND SOUPS

Appetizers. The word, "appetizer" is defined as, "....... a small portion of food or drink, normally highly seasoned and designed to stimulate the appetite. They are usually served before a meal, or as snacks at parties."

Almost any type of food or drink can be made into an appetizer. Because of the importance of "eye appeal", in relation to appetite, appetizers should be especially colorful and attractively arranged. Since appetizers are designed to stimulate the appetite, as opposed to filling the stomach, they should be small and easy to eat, with multiple varieties offered.

In the United States appetizers are classified as COCKTAILS (seafoods, fruits, vegetables, juices), APPETIZER SALADS, HORS D'OEUVRES, CANAPES (tiny open faced sandwiches), and RELISHES. Cocktails and appetizer salads are usually served at the guest's table. The remaining appetizers are most often served from a buffet table.

Stocks and Soups. The definition for "stock" is, "The liquid derived from cooking water, meat and/or bones, vegetables, and seasoning". The foundation of nearly every soup, and an important ingredient of sauces and gravies, is one of the four basic stocks: a) brown; b) white; c) chicken; d) fish.

Normal cooking time for stocks is about 5 to 6 hours. The recommended method is to bring the stock to a boil, reduce the heat and barely simmer for the remaining time. Because of liquid reduction during cooking, salt is usually omitted. In order to extract the most flavor, bones should be cut with a saw prior to use.

After cooking, stocks should be cooled as rapidly as possible, and refrigerated. Rapid cooling is accomplished by placing the stock pot on bricks or blocks in a sink and allowing cold water to circulate around the outside of the stock pot. As stock cools, a layer of fat rises to the top and hardens. This fat should not be removed until just before the stock is to be used.

Basically there are two types of soups: a) clear; b) thick. Clear soups include broths, bouillons and consommes. Thick soups include cream soups, purees, chowders, and bisques. A clear or thin soup is normally served with a heavy entree and a thick soup is usually served with a light entree. Other factors influencing the type of soup to be served would include weather conditions, customer preference, locale of the restaurant, etc.

MEAT COOKERY

Meat is cooked for various reasons such as attractiveness, tenderizing, improving flavor, aroma, and destroying bacteria and parasites. The particular type of cooking method chosen depends on the cut, kind, quality, and grade of meat being used. The amount of time required to cook meat depends on such factors as cooking temperature, raw meat temperature, weight of the cut, shape of the cut, amount of meat being cooked at one time, desired degree of doneness, and the amount of fat on the meat.

Whether a given piece of meat will be tender or tough depends on how much, and what type of connective tissue it contains. Lower grades of meat, and meat from older animals contain a larger percentage of connective tissue than high grade meats, and meat from younger animals. Elastin, one type of connective tissue, is not affected to any degree by cooking. Tougher pieces of meat, with high elastin content, must be chopped, ground, aged, or otherwise tenderized prior to cooking, if they are to be suitable for the American public.

When meat is cooked many things take place. Cell and tissue pigments break down, causing color to change. As proteins in the muscle fibers become thickened, the meat gradually becomes more firm. Collagen, a chief unit of another type of connective tissue, changes to gelatin, causing tenderization.

METHODS OF MEAT COOKERY

In recent years a controversy has developed over the names applied to the various methods of cooking meat and, in addition, to the number of ways meat can be cooked. Many authorities contend the two basic methods are MOIST HEAT and DRY HEAT. Technically of course, it is not the heat which is wet or dry, it is the liquid in which the food is cooked, or the air surrounding it, which is wet or dry.

Dry heat includes roasting, broiling, sauteing, deep fat frying, and other methods where no liquid (other than grease or oil) is used. Moist heat includes braising, simmering, boiling, steaming, and other forms of cooking where a liquid is used.

Other experts believe there are three separate categories of meat cookery, i.e.: MOIST HEAT, DRY HEAT, and any type of FRYING. A third group of professionals lists six basic ways of cooking meat - ROASTING, BROILING, PANBROILING, (or griddle-broiling), FRYING, BRAISING, and COOKING IN LIQUID.

It is not the intent of this textbook to debate the pros and cons of different ways of categorizing methods of cooking meat. The student is at liberty to accept the theory set forth by any authority he prefers. In the final analysis, it will be the student's ability to prepare different cuts of meat, using the correct cooking method needed for the cut, that will determine his value to the establishment. (See Figures 10-A, B, C, D.)

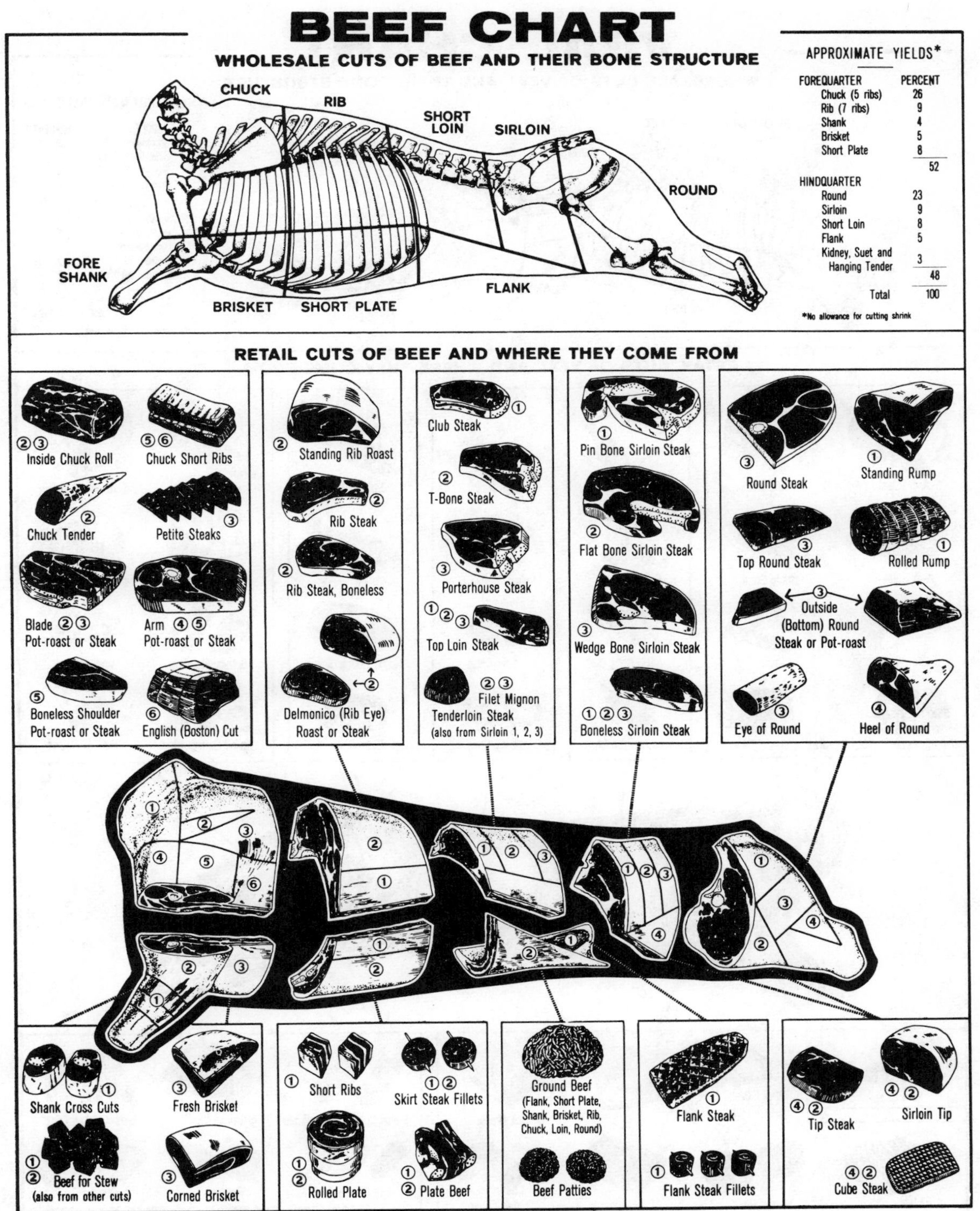

BEEF CHART
WHOLESALE CUTS OF BEEF AND THEIR BONE STRUCTURE
CHUCK
RIB
SHORT LOIN
SIRLOIN
ROUND
FORE SHANK
BRISKET
SHORT PLATE
FLANK
APPROXIMATE YIELDS*
FOREQUARTER PERCENT
Chuck (5 ribs) 26
Rib (7 ribs) 9
Shank 4
Brisket 5
Short Plate 8
52
HINDQUARTER
Round 23
Sirloin 9
Short Loin 8
Flank 5
Kidney, Suet and Hanging Tender 3
48
Total 100
*No allowance for cutting shrink
RETAIL CUTS OF BEEF AND WHERE THEY COME FROM
②③ Inside Chuck Roll
⑤⑥ Chuck Short Ribs
② Chuck Tender
③ Petite Steaks
Blade ②③ Pot-roast or Steak
Arm ④⑤ Pot-roast or Steak
⑤ Boneless Shoulder Pot-roast or Steak
⑥ English (Boston) Cut
② Standing Rib Roast
② Rib Steak
② Rib Steak, Boneless
② Delmonico (Rib Eye) Roast or Steak
① Club Steak
② T-Bone Steak
③ Porterhouse Steak
①②③ Top Loin Steak
②③ Filet Mignon
Tenderloin Steak
(also from Sirloin 1, 2, 3)
① Pin Bone Sirloin Steak
② Flat Bone Sirloin Steak
③ Wedge Bone Sirloin Steak
①②③ Boneless Sirloin Steak
③ Round Steak
① Standing Rump
③ Top Round Steak
① Rolled Rump
③ Outside (Bottom) Round Steak or Pot-roast
③ Eye of Round
④ Heel of Round
① Shank Cross Cuts
③ Fresh Brisket
①② Beef for Stew (also from other cuts)
③ Corned Brisket
① Short Ribs
①② Skirt Steak Fillets
①② Rolled Plate
①② Plate Beef
Ground Beef
(Flank, Short Plate, Shank, Brisket, Rib, Chuck, Loin, Round)
Beef Patties
① Flank Steak
① Flank Steak Fillets
④② Tip Steak
④② Sirloin Tip
④② Cube Steak
NATIONAL LIVE STOCK AND MEAT BOARD

Figure 10-A. Beef Chart.
(Courtesy National Live Stock and Meat Board, Chicago, Illinois.)

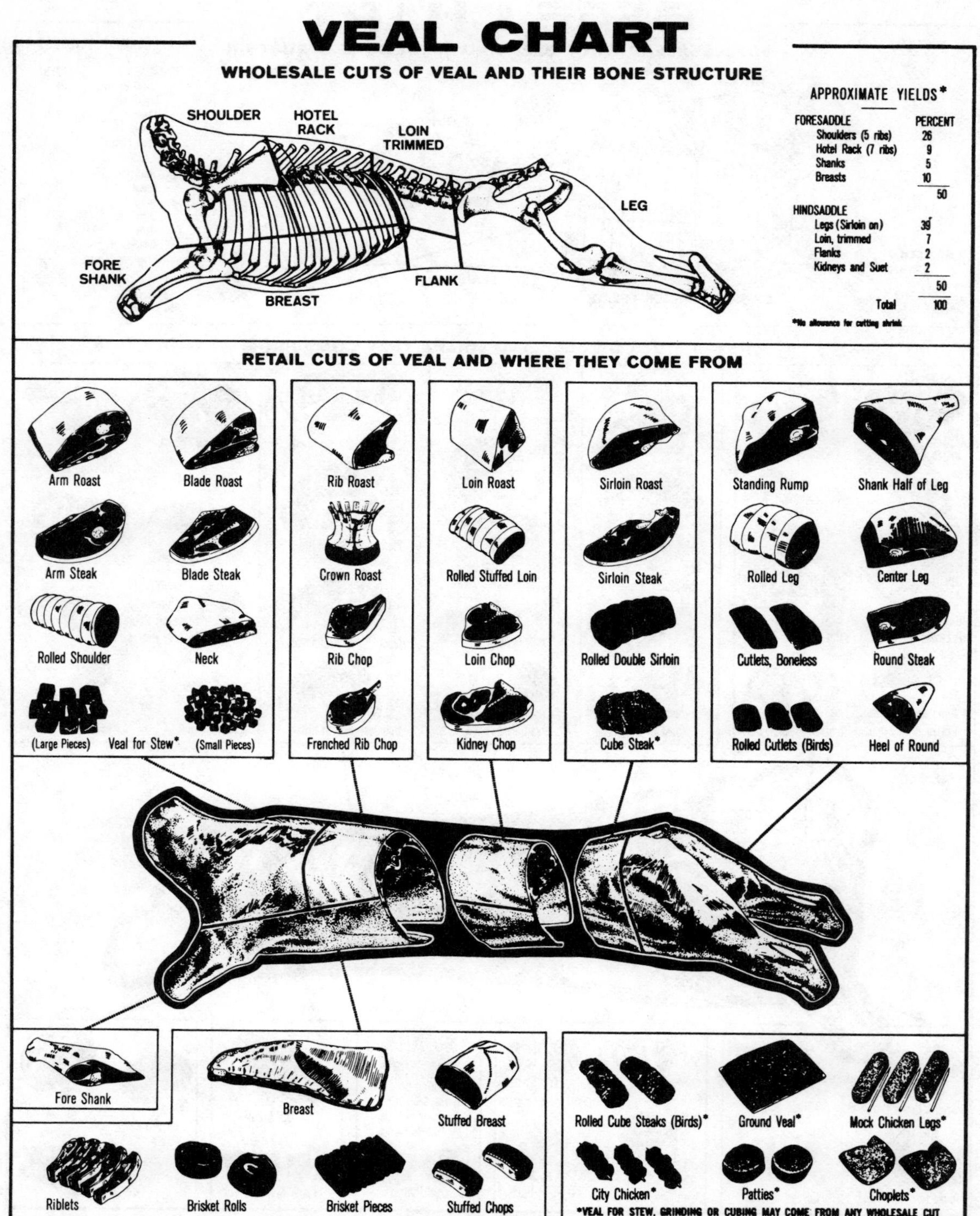

Figure 10-B. Veal Chart.
(Courtesy National Live Stock and Meat Board, Chicago, Illinois.)

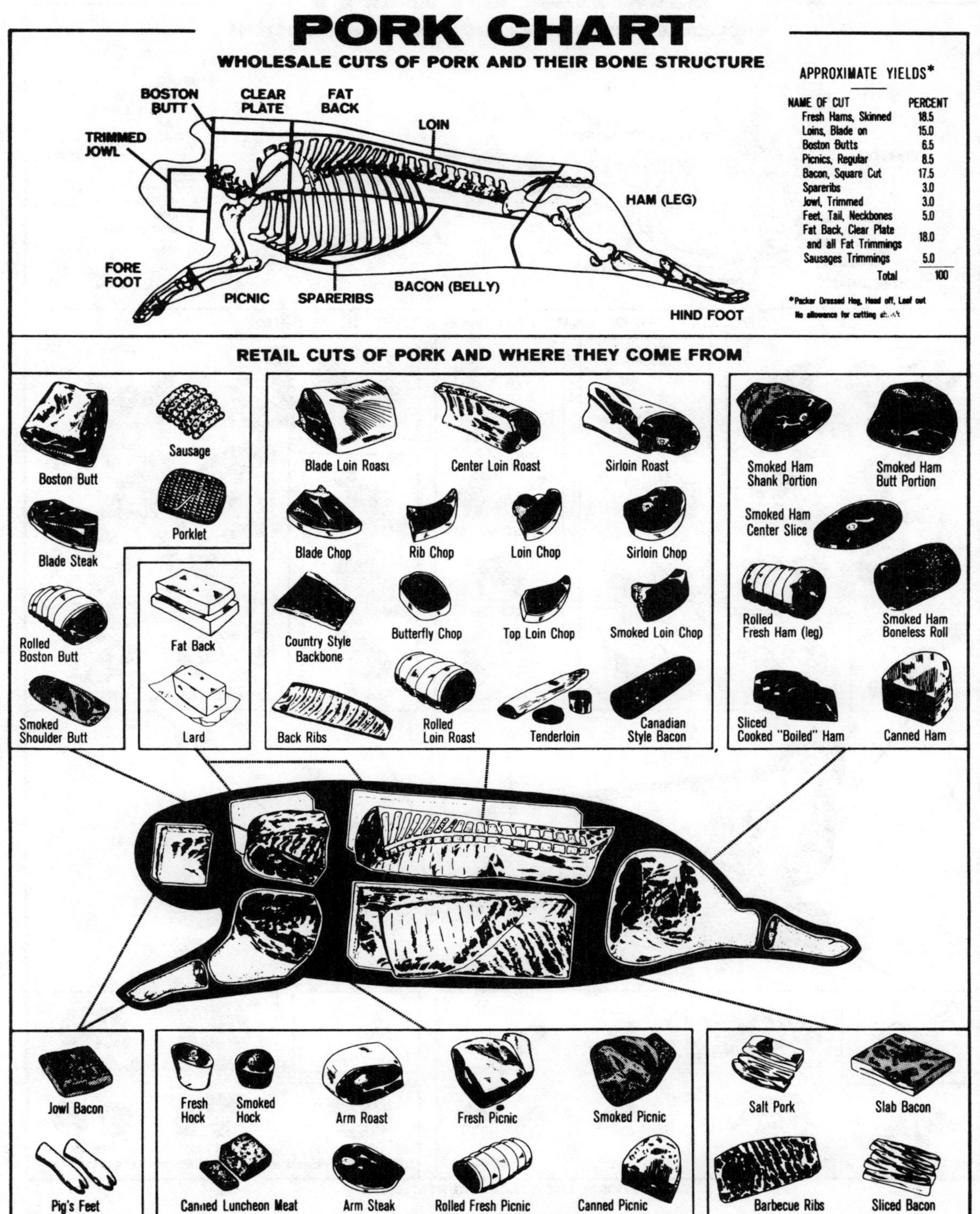

Figure 10-C. Pork Chart.
(Courtesy National Live Stock and Meat Board, Chicago, Illinois.)

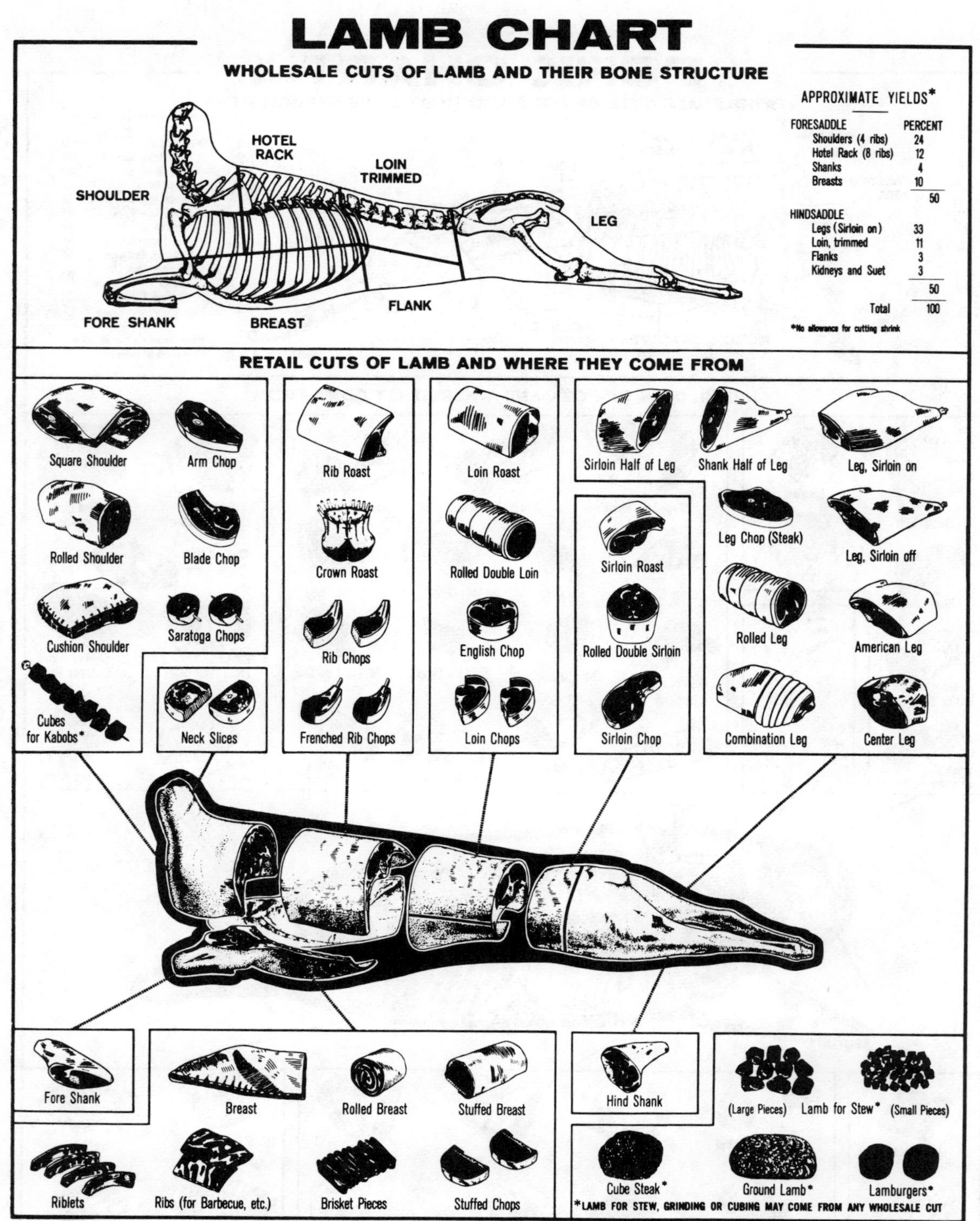

Figure 10-D. Lamb Chart.
(Courtesy National Live Stock and Meat Board, Chicago, Illinois.)

Roasting. For roasting, place the meat with the fat side up on a rack, in an open pan. By placing the fat side up, the meat will baste itself while cooking.

Meat may be seasoned with salt and pepper before, during or after cooking. The old theory that meats must be rubbed with salt and pepper prior to roasting is no longer followed.

Roasting temperatures will vary in accordance with the different factors discussed earlier in the lesson. In general, meat should be roasted in a slow oven - 300 to 325 degrees F. A meat thermometer inserted into the largest muscle, without touching bone or resting in fat, is the most accurate means of determining doneness. (See Figure 10-E.)

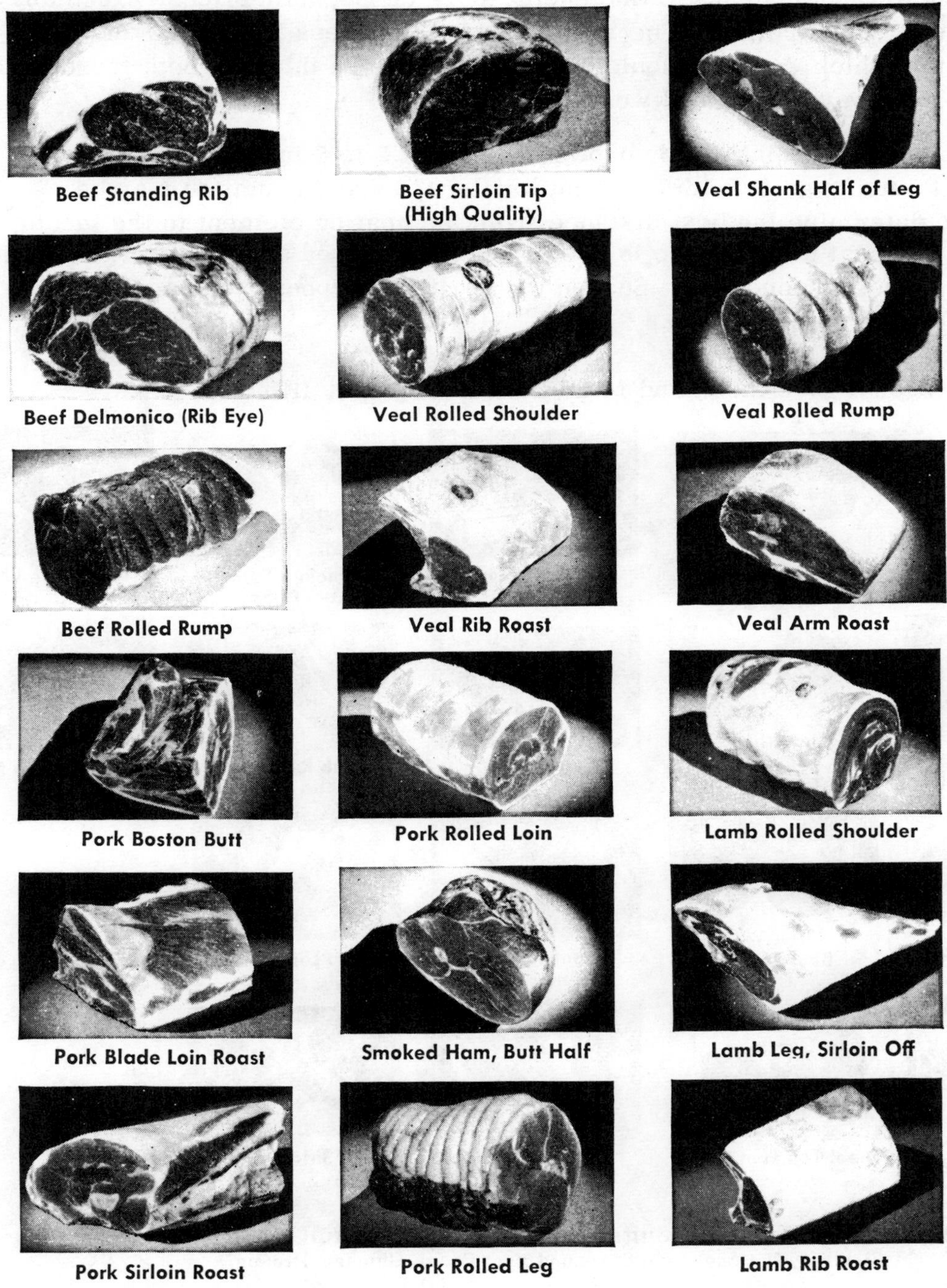

Figure 10-E. Some Meat Cuts Suitable for Roasting.
(Courtesy National Live Stock and Meat Board, Chicago, Illinois.)

Searing Meat Prior to Roasting. Years ago all meat was seared before placing it in the oven. "The practice of searing roasts was based on the theory that the coagulation of the protein on the surface in browning formed a coating which prevented the escape of the meat juices and thus decreased cooking losses. This has proved to be a fallacy because meat which is seared, whether at the beginning or the end of the roasting period, loses more than meat which has not been seared. This loss is due to fat loss rather than to the loss of juices. The old idea of 'searing to keep in juices' has been discarded. Searing develops aroma and flavor in outside slices and produces drippings of a richer brown color".*

Broiling. Tender steaks, lamb chops, pork chops, ham slices, bacon and ground meats may be broiled. The recommended thickness for steaks and chops is at least 3/4 inch thick.* Ham should be at least 1/2 inch thick.* Both fresh pork and veal should always be cooked well done.

Place the meat on a rack or broiler pan about 2 to 5 inches from the heat. Because heat output varies with different broilers, experimentation may be necessary to determine the best distance from the heating element to the meat.

Broil the meat until the top is brown and it is cooked about halfway through to the desired degree of doneness. Season with salt and pepper, turn and broil the other side. (See Figure 10-F.)

*Courtesy National Live Stock and Meat Board, Chicago, Illinois.

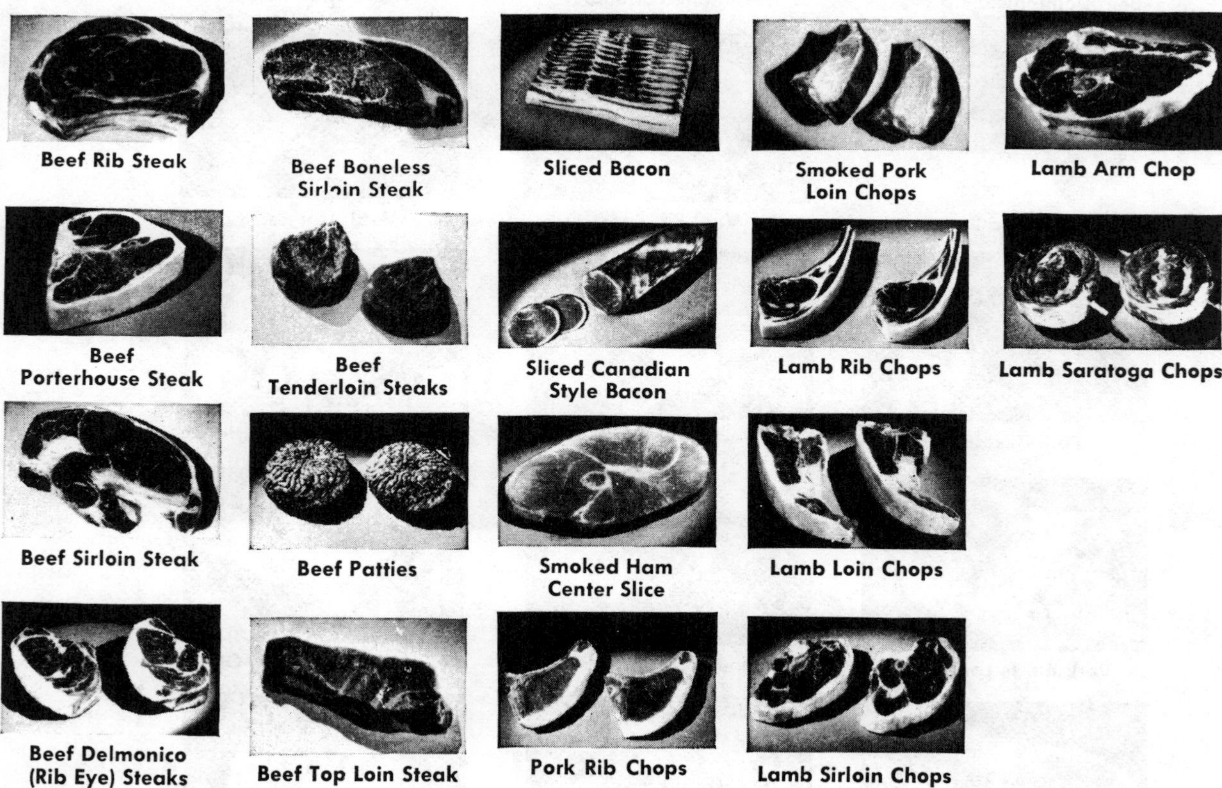

Figure 10-F. Some Meat Cuts Suitable for Broiling, Panbroiling and Panfrying.
(Courtesy National Live Stock and Meat Board, Chicago, Illinois.)

Panfrying (Sauteing). Cooking in a small quantity of fat is called panfrying or sauteing. Comparatively thin pieces of tender meat, those made tender by pounding, scoring, cubing or grinding, or leftover meat, may be prepared in this manner. (See Figure 10-G.)

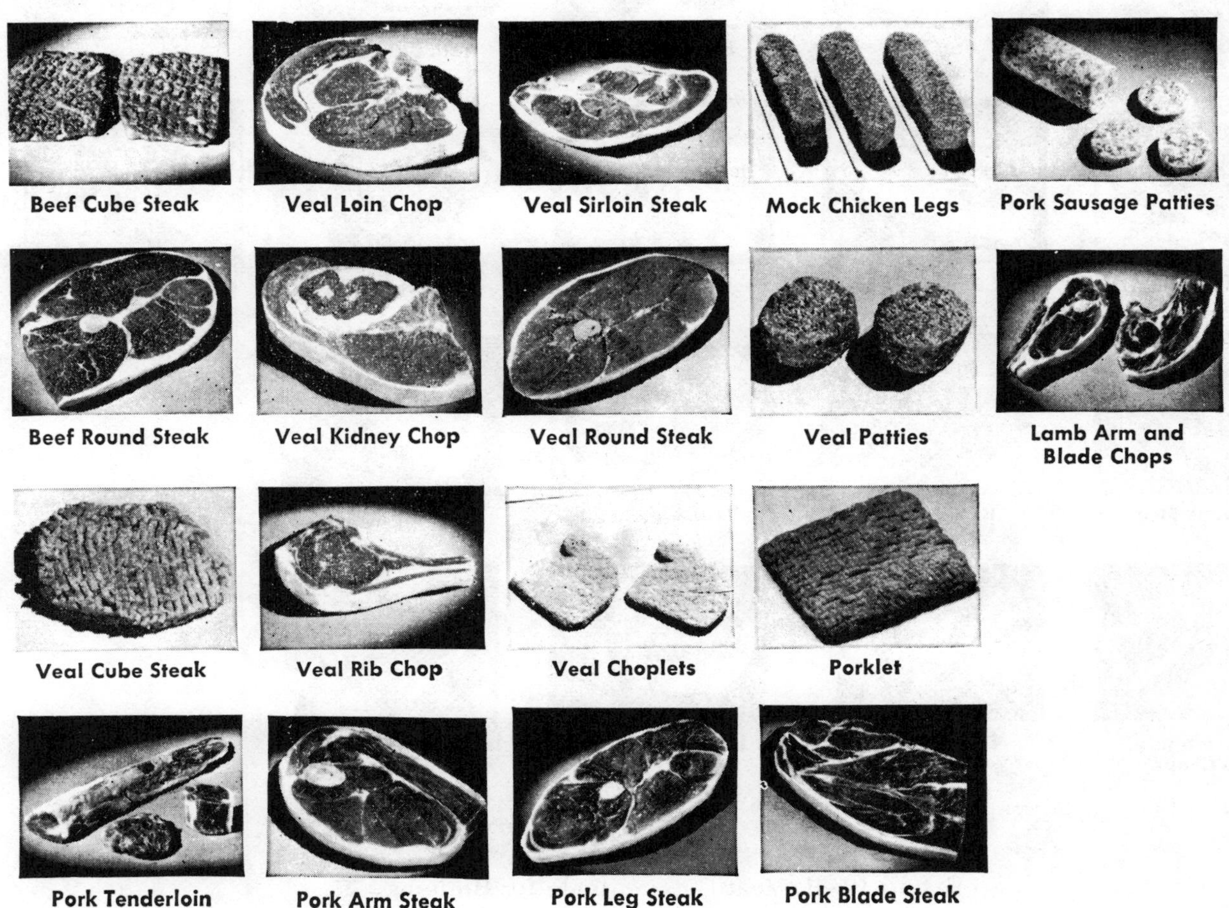

Figure 10-G. Meat Cuts Suitable for Panfrying.
(Courtesy National Meat and Live Stock Board, Chicago, Illinois.)

Deep Fat Frying. Cooking meat or other foods while completely covered with fat or oil is called deep fat frying. Most foods prepared in this manner are either breaded, or dipped in a batter, prior to immersion in the hot oil. The optimum temperature range for deep fat frying is 300° to 360° F. Higher temperatures cause a breakdown, and lower temperatures cause foods to absorb excessive amounts of the frying agent. Most all deep fat fryers use an automatic thermostat to control heat.

Braising. Although braising is most often used with the less tender cuts of meat, the more tender cuts are sometimes prepared by this method.

The standard procedure for braising meats is to brown the meat slowly on all sides. Season as desired and add enough liquid to cover about one-third of the meat. Cover the pan tightly, reduce the temperature and simmer until tender.

Braising may be done on top of a range or in an oven. Cooking large pieces of meat by braising is sometimes referred to as pot roasting. (See Figure 10-H.)

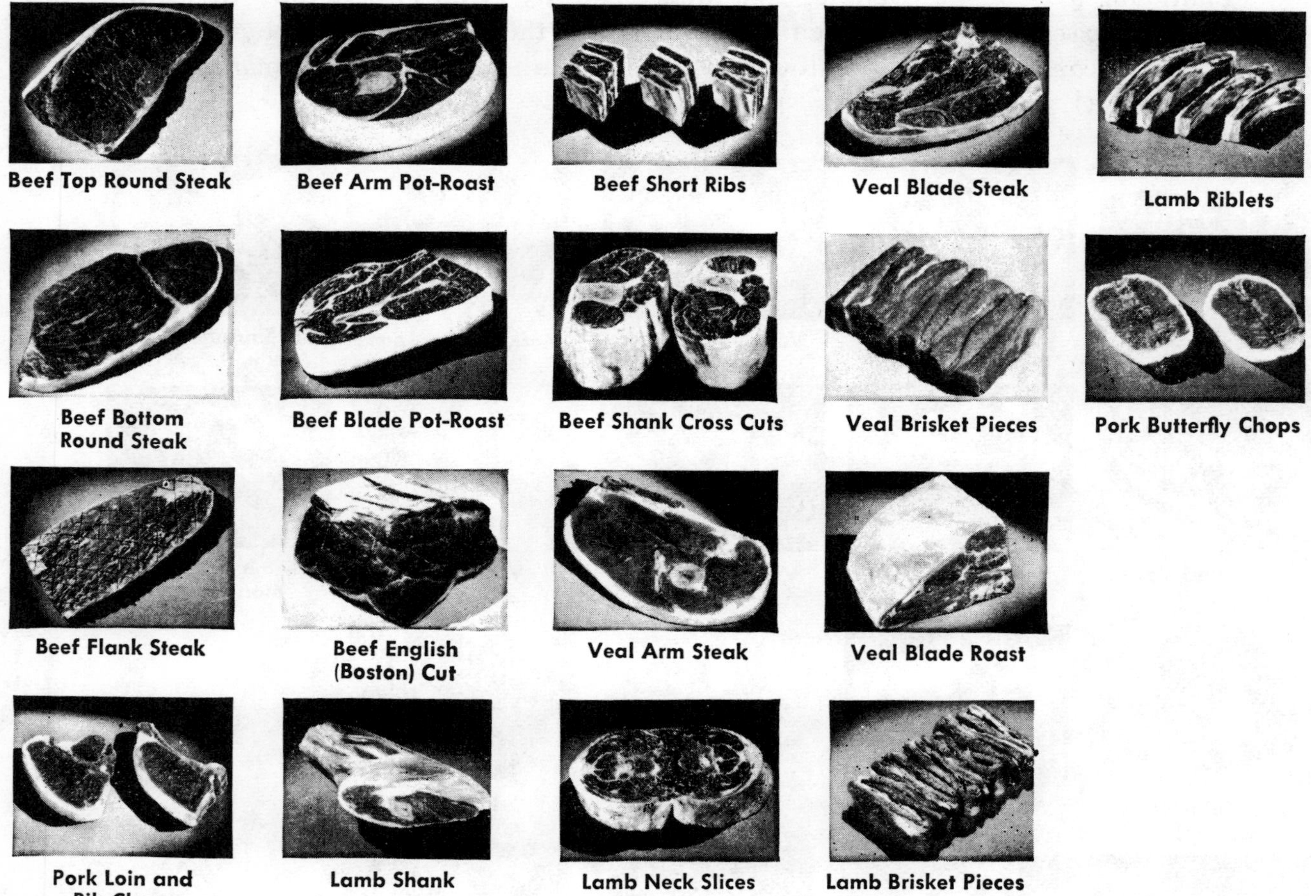

Figure 10-H. Meat Cuts Suitable for Braising.
(Courtesy National Live Stock and Meat Board, Chicago, Illinois.)

Cooking in Liquid. Less tender cuts of meat and stews are frequently prepared in a liquid; usually water.

When cooking large cuts:

1. Brown meat on all sides, if desired. The browning develops flavor and increases color. Exceptions to browning are corned beef and cured and smoked pork.
2. Cover the meat with water or stock. The liquid may be hot or cold. By entirely covering the meat with liquid, uniform cooking is assured without turning the meat.
3. Season with salt, pepper, herbs, spices and vegetables, if desired. (Cured and smoked meat and corned beef, of course, do not require salt.) Wisely used, seasonings add much to the variety and flavor.*

*Courtesy National Live Stock and Meat Board, Chicago, Illinois.

When preparing stews:

1. Cut meat in uniform pieces, usually 1 to 2 inch cubes. If preferred, the meat may be cut into rectangular pieces or into long narrow strips.
2. If a brown stew is desired, brown meat cubes on all sides. If meat is floured, fat must be added before browning. Dredging in flour often intensifies the browning. If a light stew is preferred, browning is omitted.
3. Add just enough water, vegetable juices or other liquid to cover the meat. The liquid may be added hot or cold. If it is hot, the meat starts cooking at once.
4. Season with salt, pepper, herbs and spices, if desired. (See Step 3 under large cuts on page 210.)
5. Cover kettle and simmer (do not boil) until meat is tender. It will require from one to three hours to cook the stew, depending upon the kind of meat and size of the pieces.
6. Add vegetables to the meat just long enough before serving to be cooked. The vegetables may be left whole, quartered or cut in small uniform pieces. Carrots, onions and potatoes are just one of many combinations that may be used.
7. When done, remove meat and vegetables to a pan, platter or casserole and keep hot. Peas or other bright green vegetables may be cooked separately for serving with the stew.
8. If desired, thicken the cooking liquid with flour for gravy. Allow 2 tablespoons flour for each cup of cooking liquid and just enough cold water to make a paste. Stir flour mixture into cooking liquid. Bring to a boil and boil 3 minutes or until thickened, stirring constantly.
9. Serve the hot gravy (or thickened liquid) over the meat and vegetables or serve separately in a sauce boat. The gravy is a desirable part of a stew but it does not necessarily have to be over the meat and vegetables when served.
10. Meat pies may be made from the stew. A meat pie is merely a stew with a top on it. (The top may be made of pastry, biscuit dough, mashed potatoes or cereal.)* (See Figure 10-I.)

*Courtesy National Live Stock and Meat Board, Chicago, Illinois.

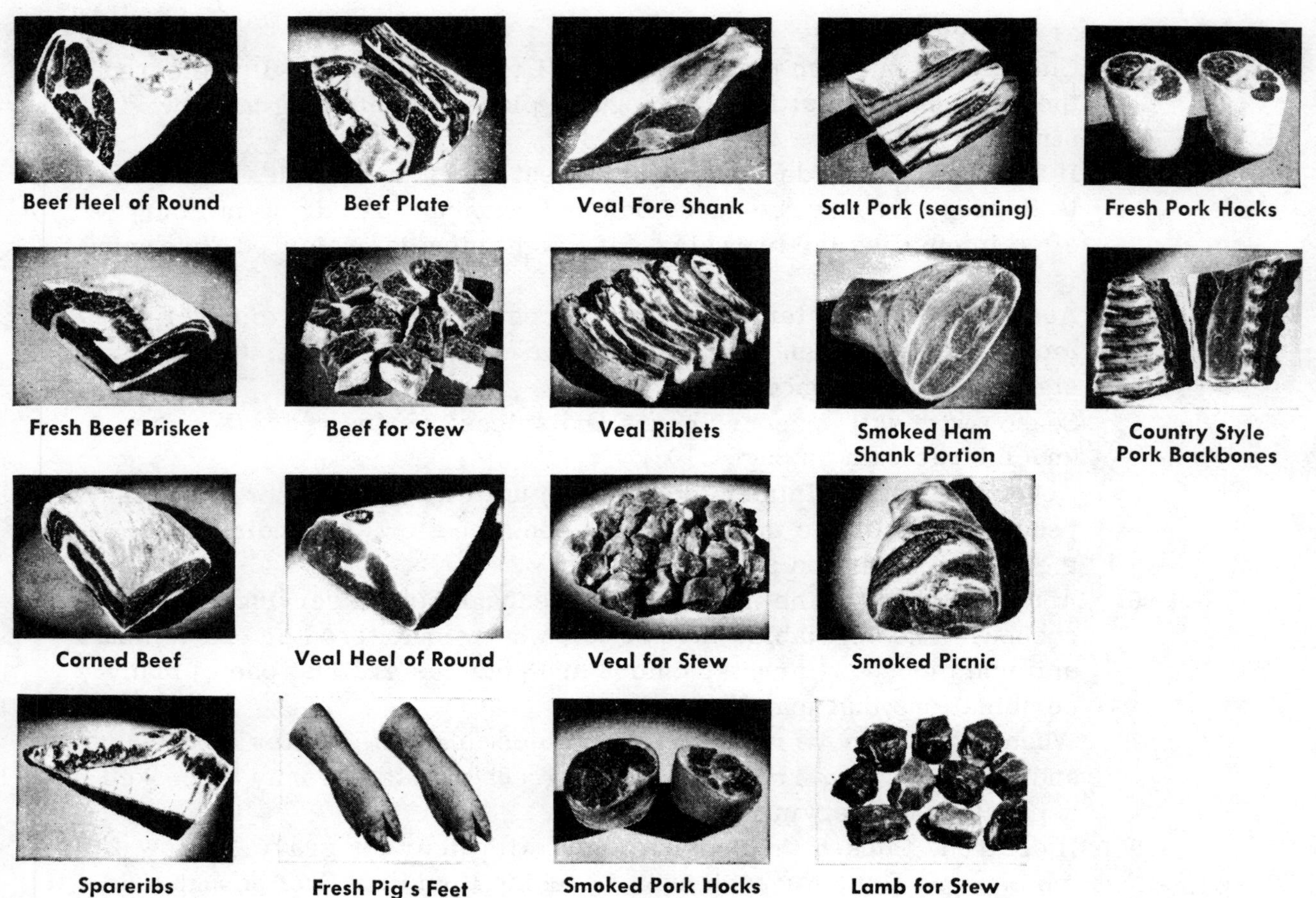

Figure 10-I. Meat Cuts Suitable for Cooking in Liquid.
(Courtesy National Live Stock and Meat Board, Chicago, Illinois.)

COOKING WITH MICROWAVE OVENS

Over the past several years the microwave oven has become a standard piece of equipment in modern manual food service and vending installations, and more than 10,000 microwave ovens are in use in cafeterias, hotels, hospitals, military installations, and commercial restaurants throughout the country. The microwave oven serves a unique purpose in providing fast food service with a minimum of food waste. With an ever-increasing number of microwave ovens in operation, it is appropriate to evaluate the safety of such devices, particularly in regard to fire hazards.

Microwave cooking principally employs the characteristics of high-frequency radio energy. Basically, it is no different from the energy which carries radio and television programs from broadcasting stations to receivers, except that the frequency of the oscillations is considerably higher. A standard broadcasting station transmits in the range of 550,000 to 1,400,000 oscillations per second, whereas microwave energy in a "Radarange" oven is transmitted at a frequency of

2,450,000,000 oscillations per second.

To understand how food can be heated or cooked by means of microwave energy, it is necessary to analyze its characteristics. Microwave energy can be reflected, transmitted, or absorbed. These properties are quite similar to those of, for instance, a light beam. A light beam can be reflected by a mirror, transmitted through a clear pane of glass, or absorbed by a semitransparent material. Microwave energy is reflected by metal, and transmitted through most ceramics, glass, and paper, but absorbed by food.

This means that when microwave energy is introduced into a Radarange oven it will be reflected by the metal walls, and transmitted through the glass, ceramic, or paper dish containing the food, but absorbed by the food itself, thereby causing the food to heat very rapidly. Since only absorption causes heating, the oven walls and the dish remain cool and only the food heats. The principal advantage of microwave cooking is the speed with which it cooks. A few examples illustrate this. In a Radarange a precooked hamburger is heated to serving temperature in 15 seconds, frozen pastry in 5 seconds; a potato bakes in minutes.

The ovens present no hazards other than those associated with electrical wiring. Present models are compact, constructed of rigid cold-rolled steel and stainless steel (or similar materials). The power source is alternating current, 120 and 240 volts, 3 wire, singlephase, 60-cycle, 30 and 50 amperes. Recommended line fuses are 30 and 50 amperes.

A microwave oven operates on a principle completely different from the standard heating appliance. This principle was pioneered by Raytheon Company, which markets its microwave oven under its trademark, Radarange.* Food in a microwave oven is heated by the molecular friction induced by absorbed microwave energy. The oven chamber is not heated and remains cool at all times. The food utensils are not heated by the microwave energy and remain at a lower temperature than the food. The only heat absorbed by the utensils or oven is from the conduction of the food.

In a microwave oven, the food product never exceeds a temperature of 212°F. This is quite unlike a standard food-cooking appliance, where it is necessary to have temperatures as high as 450°F. on the outside of the food product in order to reach an inside temperature of the food of 140°F. in a reasonable time.

In a microwave oven there is no open flame or hot heating element. Since there is no open flame or cooking surface where the temperature exceeds 300°F., the microwave oven should be considered a food warmer, similar to a steam table, which is often placed in the dining area and not vented. It is not necessary to vent these devices because the temperature never exceeds 212°F., which is not hot enough to produce smoke or grease vapors. In a steam table, water vapor may escape into the area surrounding the equipment; in a microwave oven, very little, if any, water vapor is noticeable.** (See Figure 10-J.)

*Litton Industries also produces an excellent Microwave Oven.

** Reproduced by permission from Fire Journal, copyright 1965 National Fire Protection Association, Boston, Massachusetts and Sten I. Persson, Engineering Manager, Raytheon Company, Waltham, Massachusetts.

Figure 10-J. Microwave Oven
(Courtesy Raytheon Company, Waltham, Mass.)

VEGETABLE PREPARATION

Depending on the specific type, vegetables may be baked, steamed, boiled or fried.

Canned vegetables have been pre-cooked in the container and should be brought to a boil just prior to serving. There is usually enough liquid in the can to preclude the necessity of adding water.

Dehydrated vegetables are normally reconstituted in lukewarm water prior to cooking. An exception to this rule is dehydrated onions which should be pre-soaked in cold water. After reconstitution, dehydrated vegetables are cooked the same as fresh vegetables.

Quick frozen vegetables frequently have the appearance and flavor of fresh vegetables. Because they are cleaned and trimmed prior to freezing, labor costs are reduced and handling time is decreased. Most frozen vegetables may be cooked without defrosting. For best results follow the cooking directions on containers.

Fresh vegetables are excellent in flavor and highly nutritious when properly prepared. When cooking fresh vegetables, the following rules should be observed:

a. Prepare small amounts as needed, rather than in large batches.
b. Use as little water as possible.
c. Add vegetables to boiling salted water.
d. Cook green vegetables in fast boiling water only until tender.
e. Use gently boiling water for root type vegetables.

f. Use a covered pan to speed cooking time and help retain nutrients.
g. Season and serve immediately after preparation, when possible.
h. Use the cooking liquid in soups, sauces and gravies to take advantage of the various nutrients in the water.

SALAD PREPARATION

The number and variety of salads are almost endless. There are thousands of salad recipes available to the interested chef. In addition to nutritional value, salads add "eye appeal" to the meal.

Most all salads should be mixed or tossed lightly together with a dressing just before serving.

COFFEE BREWING

Coffee is the most popular and widely consumed beverage in the United States. Americans drank over 450 billion cups of coffee in 1965, according to the Pan American Coffee Bureau. The average consumption in 1965 was 2.86 cups per person per day.

The importance of good coffee, then, is of such great significance that every possible step should be taken to produce the finest coffee beverage in every type of food service activity.

The Coffee. Use fresh coffee. Ground coffee ages rapidly losing flavor and aroma, the most important assets of good coffee. Coffee should be delivered at least once a week.

Storage. Store coffee in a cool, dry place. Heat and moisture cause it to stale rapidly. If possible, store in a refrigerator. Keep it away from other foods - coffee picks up outside odors very quickly.

Grind. Use the grind designed for your equipment. Too fine a grind for the equipment used produces bitter coffee and too much sediment. Too coarse a grind results in a weak, poorly flavored beverage. The grind determines the length of time coffee and water should be together. Water used for coffee brewing must be vigorously boiling, which means 212°F. When boiling water is poured over ground coffee at room temperature, and touches the equipment which is at room temperature, the water temperature reduces to 200° to 205°F., an ideal brewing temperature.

The following brewing times are for water at about 200°F. evenly distributed over ground coffee. The grind specifications quoted below are those described in Simplified Practice Recommendation R 231-48, U. S. Department of Commerce.

GRIND	TIME
Fine or Vacuum	1 to 3 minutes
Drip or Urn	4 to 6 minutes
Regular	6 to 8 minutes

The Water. Water should be free from any undesirable elements picked up in pipe lines, boilers, water tanks, etc. Never brew coffee with water you wouldn't drink. Never brew coffee with chemically softened water.

Whether coffee is brewed in an urn, a half-gallon type brewing device, or a vacuum coffee maker, the temperature of the water should be as near 200° F. as possible, as it comes in contact with the coffee grounds.

Brewing In An Urn. Never guess. Accurate measurement is the most important step in brewing good coffee. Use 2- never more than 2 1/2 gallons of water to 1 pound of coffee.

Spread fresh drip grind coffee evenly in the filter. To obtain good extraction, the layer of coffee should be spread evenly (1 to 2 inches in depth). If a new urn bag is used, rinse it thoroughly in hot water before placing it on the urn bag ring. If the urn is not equipped with a brewing basket, use a gridded riser to assure proper support of the urn bag.

Use fresh boiling water. The urn should be attached only to a cold water line. Be sure the water temperature is 212° F. before it comes in contact with the coffee. Pour the water in a slow, circular motion. This helps assure even extraction. Make sure you wet all the grounds evenly. Total contact time must be between 4 and 6 minutes Brewing time starts when the first water touches the coffee, and ends when the last water has passed through the grounds and the brewing device is removed. Replace the urn cover between pours to preserve the aroma.

Remove the filter device as soon as the water has dripped through. If the brewing device is left in the urn, steam from the coffee rises, condenses to water, and passes back through the grounds, releasing astringent and bitter materials. Rinse the cloth filter in clear hot water, then store in cold water until next use.

If all of the water cannot be passed through the grounds within the prescribed brewing time, it may be necessary to place some of the water (up to 40%) in the bottom of the urn before brewing. This practice is not ideal, but if necessary can be used. Of course in that case the brew must be made enough stronger to allow for the water dilution. This means that the amount of coffee used must be the same as if all the water were able to pass through.

Mix the brew. Draw off the heavy coffee from the bottom of the urn and pour it back into the brew to assure uniform mixing. Mix at least one gallon for each pound of coffee used.

Never repour brewed coffee back through spent grounds. It only makes the coffee weaker and bitter.*

*Courtesy of The Coffee Brewing Center, 120 Wall Street, New York.

LESSON 10 - BRAINTEASER

After you are certain you understand the material in this lesson, answer the questions below. When you have completed the brainteaser, check your answers in the text. Use the following scale to evaluate your comprehension of this lesson:

10 Correct - Outstanding
9 Correct - Excellent
8 Correct - Good
7 Correct - Fair
6 or Under
Correct - Restudy the Lesson

1) List the basic classifications of appetizers.

a.
b.
c.
d.
e.

2) Name the four basic stocks.

a.
b.
c.
d.

3) The normal cooking time for most stocks is:
a. 2 to 3 hours
b. 5 to 6 hours
c. 1 to 4 hours
d. 3 to 5 hours
e. 6 to 8 hours

4) The lesson points out seven factors that will have an effect on the amount of time required to cook meat. The first one is listed for you. Name the other six.

a. Cooking temperature
b.
c.
d.
e.
f.
g.

5) Name the advantages and disadvantages to SEARING meat.

6) The recommended thickness of steaks and chops to be used for broiling is:

a. 1/4 inch
b. 1/2 inch
c. 3/4 inch
d. 1 inch
e. 1 1/4 inches

7) The best temperature range for deep fat frying is _____ to _____ degrees F.

8) In a microwave oven, the food product never exceeds a temperature of ________ degrees F.

9) The lesson describes eight rules for cooking fresh vegetables. List four of the eight below.

a.

b.

c.

d.

10. How long is the recommended brewing time for DRIP or URN grind coffee?

__________ to __________ minutes.

LESSON 11

SERVING FOOD

LESSON 11 - PREVIEW

Lesson 11 acquaints the trainee with the basics of food service. Procedures and setup for American, French, Russian, Buffet and Cafeteria are explained. The duties and responsibilities of various service personnel such as the Maitre d'Hotel, captains, waiters, busboys, cashiers and checkers are also covered.

To a culinary student a knowledge of correct table service is extremely valuable. A chef can spend hours producing a gastronomic masterpiece only to have it ruined by poor or improper table service. In addition, a chef who knows table service realizes the method of cooking, degree of doneness and the carving and boning procedure required for various types of service.

Becoming familiar with the duties and responsibilities of service personnel provides the student with more insight into their problems, paving the way for better understanding and cooperation between departments. It is this cooperation and teamwork that results in higher production, lower cost, greater profit and higher pay for everyone.

In the food industry everyone is, or should be, working toward one common goal. All functions such as purchasing, receiving, pre-preparation, portioning, and preparation are designed and carried out with one main objective in mind. This objective is to present the paying customer with the best possible service, consistent with the decor, type, and price range of the establishment. The ornate, luxury operations will provide patrons with French, Russian or English service, while the more modest operations may use American, buffet, carry-out or other types of service.

AMERICAN TABLE SERVICE

The basic concept of serving food with American Service is to place the food on the plate in the kitchen. Side dishes normally consist of a bread and butter plate and a salad plate.

Solid foods are usually served from the LEFT, with the left hand and liquids from the RIGHT of the customer, with the right hand. Soiled dishes are removed from the guest's right.

The main advantages of American Service are:

a. Fast customer service
b. Economy because minimum dishes and silver are required
c. NOT complicated and easily taught to inexperienced waiters

Table Setup. The recommended setting for American Service is as follows:

a. Noise absorbing pad, or cloth
b. Clean tablecloth
c. Sugar bowl, salt and pepper shakers, and ashtray
d. Bread and butter plate, silverware, glass and napkin. (See Figures 11-A and 11-B following page.)

Figure 11–A. John M. Dodig, Table Service and Mixology Instructor, Culinary Institute of America shows students the correct way to set up for American table service.

Figure 11–B. American Table Service Arrangement.
Table setup by John M. Dodig, Table Service and Mixology Instructor, Culinary Institute of America.

Authorities differ as to the correct distance silverware should be from the edge of the table. While each operation will have its own specific rules, the most universally acceptable distance is from 1/4 inch to 1/2 inch.

General Procedures. Guests should be greeted at the door and escorted to their table. Any extra covers (settings) should be taken away. Provide the guest with a menu, fill the water glass, and suggest a cocktail. If a cocktail is ordered, it is served (and later removed), from the guest's right side.

The food order is taken and served. Bread and butter is served from the guest's left side. Soup (or appetizer) and salad is served from the left and removed from the right. The main course is served from the left.

If a guest prefers coffee with his meal, like all liquids, it is served from the right. After removing the main course dishes from the guest's right side, the water glass should be refilled and any crumbs brushed from the table. The next step is to determine if the customer desires dessert. If so, it is served from the left.

In general, the service rule stated earlier, "solids to the left and liquids to the right" of the patron is always followed. When serving to the left, it is obviously easier and better to use the left hand, and vice versa.

FRENCH TABLE SERVICE

One of the distinguishing features of French Table Service is that the food is often only partially prepared in the kitchen and then finished alongside the guest's table. Meats are boned, carved and placed on the guest's plate at tableside. Many foods (for example salads, salad dressing and some desserts) are almost completely prepared in full view of the guests.

With French Service two waiters work one station:

a. The Chef de Rang seats the guests, takes their orders, serves drinks, finishes food preparation at, or alongside the table, presents and collects the check.

b. The Commis de Rang assists the Chef de Rang in every way possible, such as orders food from the kitchen and brings it to the dining room cart, serves the guest after the Chef de Rang prepares and plates the food.

Table Setup. The recommended setting for French Table Service is as follows:

a. Pad, Tablecloth, Top

b. Hors d'oeuvre plate with folded napkin on top

c. To the right of the plate:

(1) Dinner Knife (cutting edge toward plate)

(2) Soup Spoon (providing it is known in advance exactly what type of soup the guest is having, if not, a soup spoon would be brought after the order was placed.)

d. To the left of the plate:

(1) Dinner fork

(2) Butter plate and butter knife

e. Above the hors d'oeuvre plate:

(1) Dessert fork and/or (Providing the dessert is known in advance as would be the case where only one dessert was offered. If a variety of desserts are offered, it is more sensible to omit the dessert silverware until after the guest has placed his dessert order. This way the proper silverware can be brought with the dessert.)

Coffee, if served at all, is always served after dessert. The coffee spoon is placed to the right of the cup.

General Procedure. Everything in French Service is served from the right and with the right hand. There are two exceptions to this rule; a) If the waiter is left handed, it is permissible to serve from the customer's left; b) Those dishes that are normally placed to the customer's left, are handled from the left. Final food preparation is always accomplished by the Chef de Rang and food is served by the Commis de Rang.

The table is never cleared until all guests have finished eating. In French Service a high seat turnover is not expected or required. The rule is always excellent cuisine, served and consumed in a leisurely manner. (See Figure 11-C.)

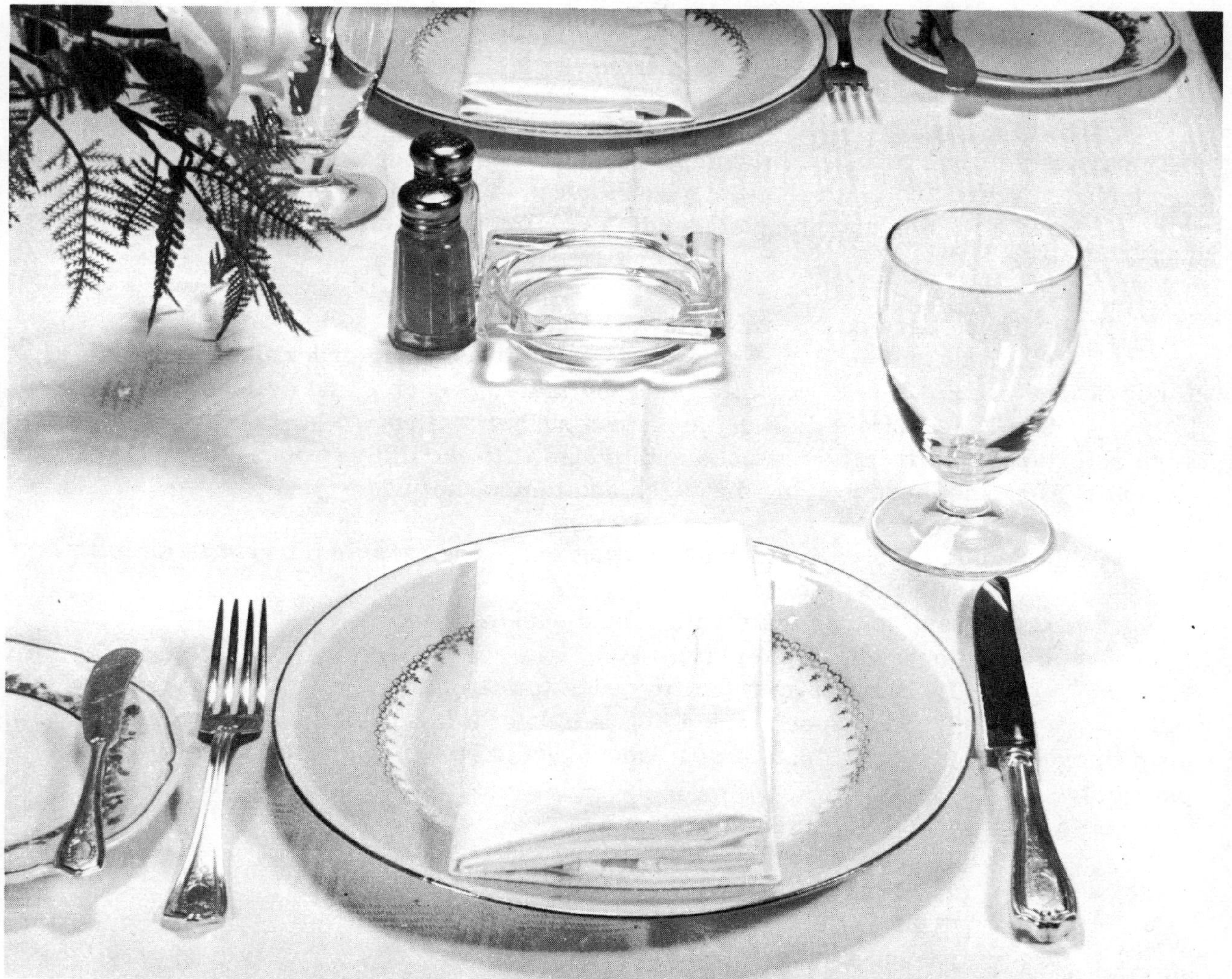

Figure 11–C. French Table Service Arrangement.
Table setup by John M. Dodig, Table Service and Mixology Instructor, Culinary Institute of America.

China, glassware and silverware should be partially scraped, stacked and/or separated as required, by personnel in the dining room, but never in front of the guest. A finger bowl accompanied by a clean napkin, is served with any food that the guest eats with his fingers. Finger bowls are normally filled only about one-third full of warm water to prevent splashing. A slice of lemon or rose petals are often allowed to float on the water.

Regardless of whether or not finger bowls were used during the meal, one is always served with a clean napkin, after a complete meal.

RUSSIAN TABLE SERVICE

The table arrangement for Russian Service varies and it may be set up exactly the same as for French Service, or it may be set up in accordance with a specific menu. For example, if we were serving a menu composed of: Melon with Proscuitto, French Onion Soup, Dover Sole Doria, Beef Wellington, Endive Salad, Baked Alaska, Rolls, Butter, Coffee, the table would be arranged as illustrated in figure 11-D.

Figure 11–D. Russian Table Service Arrangement.
Table setup by John M. Dodig, Table Service and Mixology Instructor, Culinary Institute of America.

Although Russian service is often confused with French service, there are some basic differences. For one thing the "guaridon" (cart), so prevalent in French service, is not used. All food is prepared and portioned in the kitchen, and attractively arranged on serving platters. Serving platters with the food, together with hot empty plates, are brought in to the dining room and placed on the sideboard. Plates are set in front of all guests, from the guest's right side, and using the right hand. After all guests have their plates, the waiter then serves each guest from the platter. To do this most efficiently and safely, the waiter must hold the platter on his left hand, and serve the food from the guest's left side, using his right hand.

In general, Russian service does not work out well with an a la carte type operation, where guests are apt to order different entrees. For one thing it is difficult to arrange several orders attractively on one tray. Another problem is keeping the food hot, after it has left the kitchen. When serving six or more customers, the last two or three orders on the tray are often cold, and unappetizing in appearance.

For banquets and other functions providing one common menu, Russian service has proven to be excellent. Sometimes the best points of Russian and French service are combined with outstanding results.

BUFFET SERVICE

With Buffet Service the guests help themselves to most of the selections. Foods should be attractively arranged on a table in trays, chafing dishes, platters, etc. (See Figure 11-E below, and 11-F and 11-G on following page.)

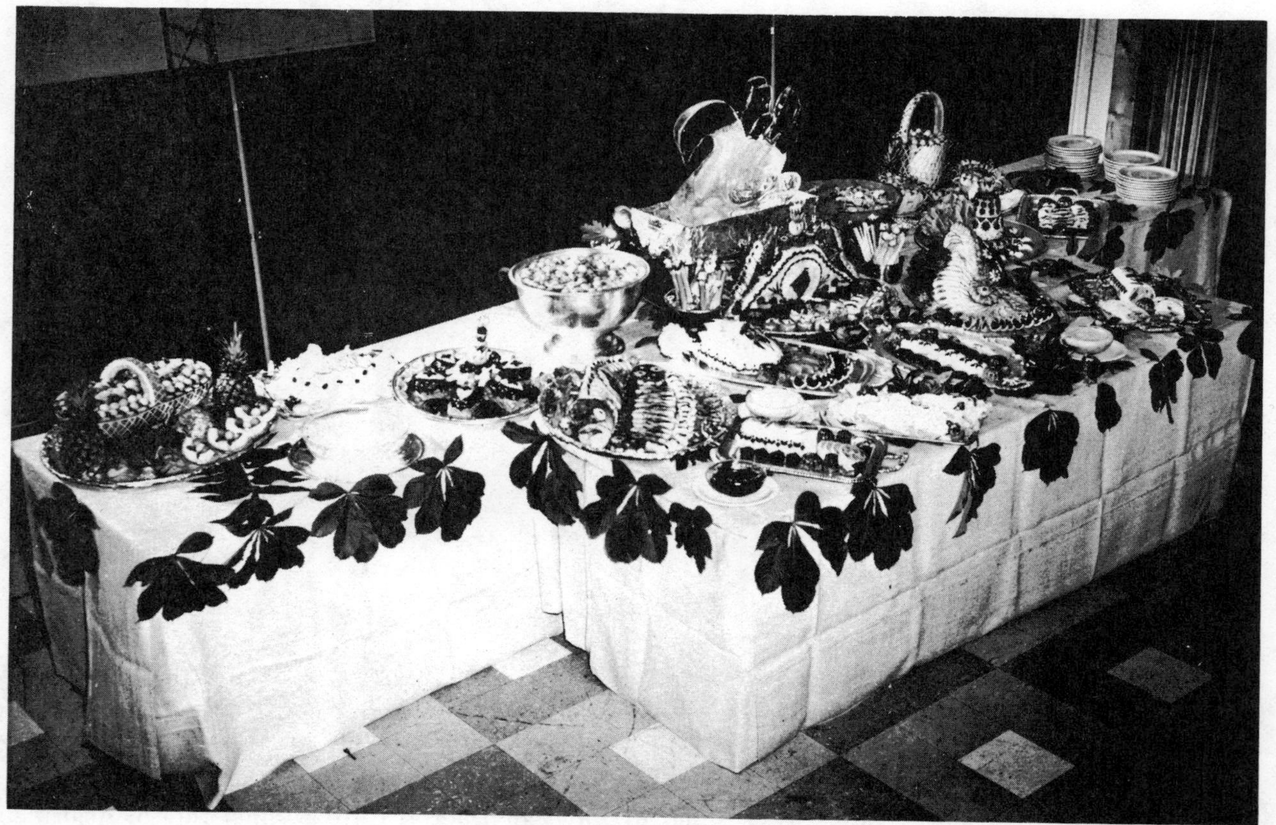

Figure 11–E. Buffet Line.
Created by Students at the Culinary Institute of America.

Figure 11–F. Prize-Winning Buffet Showpieces.
Created by Students at the Culinary Institute of America.

Figure 11–G. Prize-Winning Buffet Showpieces.
Created by Students at the Culinary Institute of America.

Plates are placed at the head of each line or table. Napkins and silverware are normally located at the end of the buffet line.

A qualified food service person should be available to handle any foods that must be boned, carved, or otherwise portioned out to guests. (See Figure 11-H.)

Buffet tables can and should be arranged to use various decorations and themes. Many times a particular holiday, such as Christmas or Thanksgiving, will suggest traditional colors, decorations and themes. (See Figure 11-I.)

Figure 11–H. These buffet foods should be carved and served. Created by Students at the Culinary Institute of America.

Figure 11–I. Pulled Sugar expert Charles Camerano illustrates various centerpieces made out of pulled sugar.

No buffet table is complete without a top quality centerpiece to highlight the display. Centerpieces can be made with flowers, company insignias or seals, etc. They can be done in cocoa paint, or decorated cakes, ice carvings, cornucopias, various food displays can be used. (See Figure 11-J below.)

Lighting a buffet table is an important feature and one that is often overlooked. Spotlights should be used whenever and wherever practical and are particularly effective when focused on the centerpiece.

Tables can be arranged in various shapes and designs such as U-shape, L-shape, or V-shape, to provide the required amount of food lines, consistent with the number of people to be served. Frequently hors d'oeuvre and/or beverage tables are set up separately, some distance from the regular buffet lines, to provide a faster traffic flow.

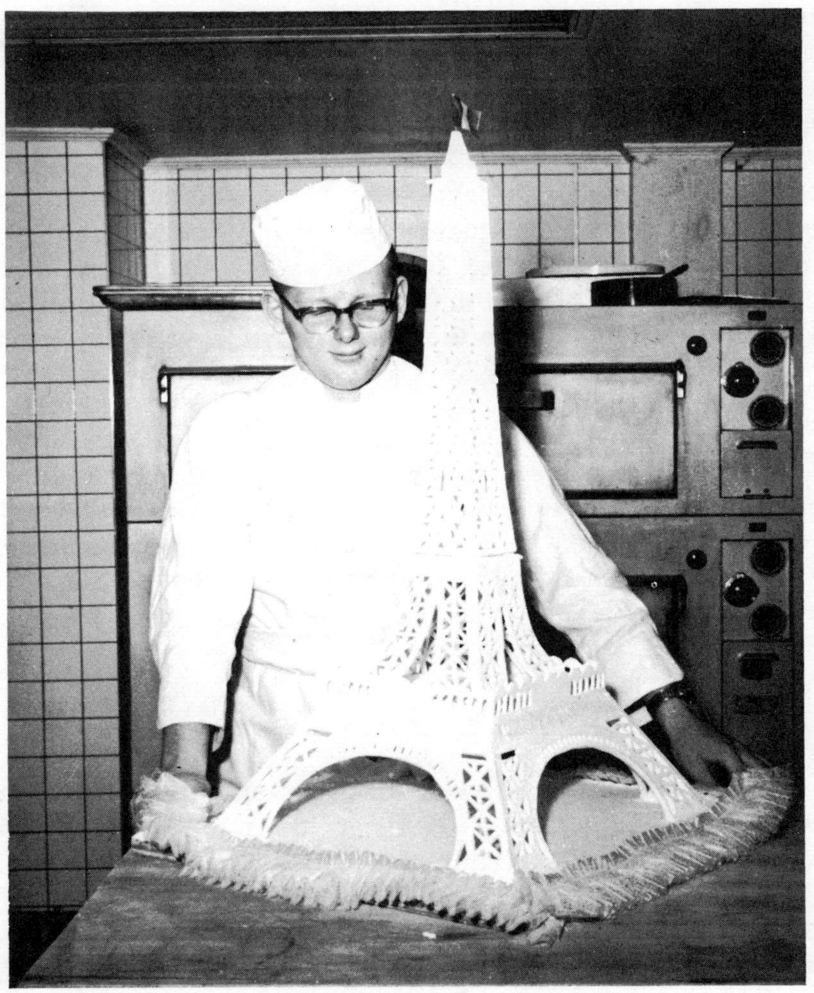

Figure 11–J. Eiffel Tower Centerpiece.
Created by a Student at the Culinary Institute of America.

CAFETERIA SERVICE

There are many different types of cafeteria service. Industrial plants, hospitals, institutions, and schools conduct all or part of their food service by this method.

The basic principles of cafeteria food service have remained relatively stable for many years. One or more counters, containing heated, refrigerated, and regular sections form a line on which food is displayed. Customers pick up a tray at one end and pass along the entire line selecting the items they desire. Napkins may be at either end of the line or on tables in the dining room.

Knives, forks and spoons are each placed in their own separate containers at the beginning or end of the food line, depending on the available space and physical set up of the unit.

Some cafeterias provide only minimum service to customers. Others may have someone at each station to restock foods and assist guests, as needed. Many cafeterias are equipped to provide short-order service such as breakfast, made-to-order sandwiches, etc.

Setting up a college cafeteria line. The order in which food should be placed on a cafeteria line is dependent upon the physical layout of the operation. For example, at a college where meals are sold on a contract basis,* lines are usually set up in the order of consumption. In other words, students starting down the line are offered soup, meat, gravy (or sauce), potato, vegetable, salad, dessert, and butter, in that order.

If possible, coffee urns, milk, cold drink and water dispensers should all be located in the dining room, rather than on the food lines, to avoid congestion and slowing down the service.

Setting up a regular cafeteria line. Regular cafeterias, where each dish is separately priced, arrange their food lines with a view towards merchandising, and subsequently, larger guest checks. This is usually done by presenting an attractive display of salads and other foods first. Customers entering the food line are naturally hungry and are more likely to select extra items (increasing check size) if these foods are made available before the main course.

AIRLINE FOOD SERVICE

Air travel in the United States is growing at a fantastic rate. The Civil Aeronautics' Board estimates that 330,000,000 people will engage in airline travel by 1975.

Airline catering companies are already concerned with the methods of feeding these large masses.

There are basically three methods of airline food handling. In the first system, the food is prepared just before flight time, held and put on the aircraft hot, and placed in warming ovens until service. The second system requires food be prepared and chilled up to 72 hours prior to departure. It is placed on the plane chilled and "heated in flight just before serving." The third method utilizes frozen food. Food is prepared wherever

*The student pays an advance fee, thereby contracting for 20 or 21 meals per week, for the entire semester.

and whenever practical, sent on board the airplane frozen, and heated in flight as needed. Many airline catering companies use a combination of methods with excellent results.

Each one of the above systems has its own particular advantages and disadvantages. Some experts believe chilled foods provide the best solution, while others favor the frozen food idea.

Some of the problems involved in airline feeding are common to any food operation. Other problems are peculiar only to airlines. For example, determining exactly how many meals will be needed on a given flight can develop into a major problem. In addition to reservation passengers, there are reduced fare standbys, missed plane connections, and last minute cancellations.

"Deadheading" equipment refers to food service equipment (trays, serving utensils, etc.) moved around to various locations to insure that each producing activity has sufficient equipment for its food service requirements.

Other problems concern dishwashing versus disposable dishware, too small preparation kitchens, high priced automation equipment, packaging serving utensils, and garbage and trash disposal.

EMERGENCY MASS FEEDING

Feeding for those whose lives have been disorganized by disaster and who are unable to provide for themselves is more than a means of relieving hunger and sustaining life. Food is a vital factor in raising and maintaining the morale of those forced from their homes by floods, explosions, hurricanes, tornadoes or other catastrophes; of those involved in rescue, evacuation and the protection of life and property; and of those under particular stress because of the effects of disaster.

Human beings react in much the same way to shock, tension and stress. Many become dependent. They want to talk, to be comforted, to be given something--a blanket, a cigarette, a cup of coffee --anything that conveys the feeling of being cared about and looked after. Food is a powerful social symbol as well as a symbol of security. There is something about eating that eases tensions and calms anxieties.

An alert and efficient team, on the spot with refreshment, fills an important psychological as well as physical need. Food in a disaster doesn't have to be fancy or be served with frills. It should be simple, suitable and speedily provided and there should be enough of it. Food service workers can help morale immeasurably by being good and sympathetic listeners.

Objectives of Disaster Feeding. Regardless of the specific disaster involved certain basic objectives remain constant. These are:

a. To keep people alive
b. To restore and maintain morale
c. To provide food that will keep people at work or get them back to work

Problems of Disaster Feeding. Basically the problems of disaster feeding include:

a. Feeding large numbers of people under adverse conditions.

b. Special problem feeding, such as infants, sick and injured personnel, aged people, etc.

c. Organizing, preparing and serving meals with limited supplies of food, fuel and water, as well as a lack of transportation and communication.

Adapting regular eating places to handle disaster feeding. In the event of a man made or natural disaster, food operations may be required to:

a. Feed continuously around the clock

b. Set up special sanitation measures

c. Serve foods requiring the simplest preparation and that are not suject to easy contamination

d. Feed infants and other special groups

e. Prepare food for service elsewhere

Methods of Disaster Feeding. Obviously the method to be used in disaster feeding will depend on the type of disaster, available facilities, amount of food, food preparation and serving personnel.

The three most common methods of disaster feeding are:

a. Indoor (Shelter) feeding utilizing an existing restaurant or other building.

b. Mobile feeding where trucks or other mobile units are dispatched to a specific area to handle a particular group..

c. Outdoor feeding when emergency conditions warrant, such as would occur following a natural disaster or atomic attack, eliminating feeding facilities in the area. If feeding facilities were obliterated during nuclear attack, outdoor feeding units would have to be in an area clear of fallout.

A special note about coffee is pertinent for "disaster feeding". Experience has proven that plenty of hot coffee is vitally important, especially in cold weather. It seems not only to provide warmth and comfort but is important to relieve and counter-act shock. Provision for disaster feeding therefore requires ample facilities for coffee. The same hot water can provide tea for the relatively few who prefer tea.

FOOD SERVICE PERSONNEL

The amount and type of service personnel will vary with the particular type of service utilized. Obviously, restaurants providing French or Butler Service will need more help than those using Russian or American Service. Listed below are many of the service positions found in a large, well staffed restaurant.

Maitre d'Hotel, Headwaiter, Hostess. Years ago the Maitre d' was in charge of all food and beverage service. Today it is more a title than a position. Regardless of what he or she is called, "Maitre d'", "Headwaiter", "Hostess", responsibilities now include supervision of service for one particular sales outlet, such as the main dining room. Within the scope of the position is the instruction, training and supervision of all personnel in the department. Additional responsibilities include work assignments. dining room setup, greeting and seating guests, and settling disputes or solving problems between employees, or employees and guests.

Captains. In the more luxurious restaurants the dining room may be divided into sections. Each section would have a captain in charge with responsibilities similar to that of the headwaiter. However, because he is in closer contact with each guest, the captain often assists with seating, orders and, if necessary, service. A captain is responsible to the headwaiter for all personnel assigned to him as well as for the cleanliness and over all condition of his station.

Waiters and Waitresses. The importance of personal appearance of a waiter or waitress cannot be overemphasized. When a guest enters a restaurant he makes a judgment of the sanitation standards by what he personally observes. This includes the appearance of the dining room, the menu, and the waiter. Waiters must always be clean shaven, with a short, neatly trimmed haircut. Waitresses should wear stockings without "runs", hairnets, and use make-up sparingly. Both waiters and waitresses must always have immaculate uniforms, clean hands, clean fingernails, and polished shoes. Obviously service personnel working in such close proximity to guests must always bathe daily and use a good deodorant.

Good guest relations must always be maintained. This includes being friendly, courteous, helpful, sincere, pleasant, and honest.

Busboys. The main responsibility of a busboy is to clear away soiled dishes and replace the tablecloth as quickly and quietly as possible. The large oval tray used in the past for this purpose is gradually being replaced by rolling carts. Additional responsibilities may include partial setting up of tables, various cleaning duties, etc. It is imperative for busboys to maintain an immaculate appearance at all times.

Checkers and Cashiers. Checkers have many important functions to perform. Their primary responsibilities are to insure that all foods are recorded on the guest check, portion sizes are correct, and each plate is attractively arranged and garnished. In addition, the checker may actually total the guest check for the waiter, thus reducing or eliminating costly arithmetical errors.

Cashiers, of course, collect money from customers (or the waiters) in payment of the guest check. The position of cashier requires someone who is friendly, courteous, neat and clean in appearance, and who has a quick responsive mind. Among other things, cashiers should be taught to place all bills received on the register shelf, (just above the drawer) in full view of the customer, until change is given. It is also wise to require cashiers to state the denomination of the bill upon receiving it such as, "Four ninety-five out of ten, Sir."

Bibliography:

Airline Feeding Service: Cornell Hotel and Restaurant Administration Quarterly, May 1967, Vol. 8, No. 1.

Emergency Mass Feeding: Basic Course in Emergency Mass Feeding. Handbook H-15, August 1966. Developed jointly by the Department of Defense, Office of Civil Defense, American National Red Cross, and Welfare Administration, Department of Health, Education and Welfare.

LESSON 11 - BRAINTEASER

After you are certain you understand the material in this lesson, answer the questions below. When you have completed the brainteaser, check your answers in the text. Use the following scale to evaluate your comprehension of this lesson:

10 Correct --- Outstanding
9 Correct --- Excellent
8 Correct --- Good
7 Correct --- Fair
6 or Under
Correct --- Restudy the Lesson

1) Name the three major advantages of American Table Service.

2) Describe the duties of the Commis de Rang.

3) In American Table Service, the general service rule regarding liquids and solids is:

4) Draw a table setup for French Service below.

5) Name two basic differences between Russian and French Service.

6) Describe how a waiter would correctly serve guests using Russian Service.

7) Draw a College Cafeteria Line setup below.

8) List the duties of the Maitre d'Hotel.

9) What is the main function of a checker? A cashier?

10) On a regular cafeteria line, where dishes are separately priced, how is food merchandised?

LESSON 12

FINANCIAL STATEMENTS AND RECORDS

LESSON 12 - PREVIEW

In the food industry, as in any other business, financial records fall into three categories, i.e.: MUST HAVE, SHOULD HAVE, and NICE TO HAVE. This lesson covers three forms belonging to the "must have" group. These three are: a) The Budget; b) The Balance Sheet; c) The Profit and Loss Statement.

The function of financial records is to present a graphic picture of the various transactions in order that management may make intelligent judgments, take appropriate corrective action, and otherwise plan, improve and perform in the best interests of the business.

A well constructed Budget presents a comprehensive estimate of what will happen to the business. The Balance Sheet provides the financial condition of the establishment as of a specific date. The Profit and Loss Statement yields a perceptive study of income, expenditures and, hopefully, profit, over a given interval of time. All three of these documents are tools of management. As with any tool, the end result depends on the skill of the user.

THE BUDGET

What is a budget? Websters' Dictionary defines a budget as, "A statement of financial position --- for a definite period of time based on estimates of expenditures during the period and proposals for financing them."

In the above definition, notice the phrase, " --- estimates of expenditures". A budget is nothing more than a listing of expected income, expenses, and profit, for a given period of time. It is a method of advance planning utilized by intelligent management to project income, expenses, and profit for the business.

There are various types of budgets available for management to choose from. The most common, and easiest to prepare, is the fixed budget. A fixed budget is based on one specific level of anticipated sales. Other types of budgets include "flexible" and "variable". They are used when different sales levels are expected throughout the year.

Annual Budget - New Operation. Setting up a budget for a new operation involves the same basics as with an established unit, but with a few modifications. In this section we will be concerned with planning a budget for a 12 seat luncheonette to be opened within six months. Using available surveys, the services of a good restaurant consultant, and by doing some personal checking, it was determined a reasonable estimate of sales would be $15.00 per seat, per day.[1.] A six-day week would then provide an estimated total annual sales of $56,160 (12 seats times $15.00 times 312 days). This figure is placed on line 1 of the budget. Because everything is based on sales, the sales figure always equals 100%. (See Figure 12-A.)

Utilizing the same sources of information (surveys, consultants, personal observations), a reasonable net profit[2] for this location is considered to be 10% of gross sales, or $5,616 annually. This figure is placed on Line 2 of the budget.

On the basis of $56,160 gross sales, and $5,616 net profit, a balance of 90% or $50,544 remains to cover all other operating expenses. The exact percentages or amounts to be used for operating expenses will vary with the type of restaurant, its size, location, and many other factors. Anyone interested in opening his or her own restaurant must be willing to spend months gathering the necessary data and percentages.

The primary purpose of this section is to acquaint the student with the mechanics of preparing and using a budget. However, students should also be aware of the many other factors involved in starting a new operation. For example, the cost of acquiring and of making alterations to a building, heating, lighting, air conditioning, decorating, parking facilities, and initial food inventory are but some of the many items involved in the investment necessary to start a business. Obviously, in our 12-seat example the projected value would hardly support very much of an investment.

In addition to the above, the owner will usually need to borrow money for the investment requirements and the interest he has to pay is, of course, a cost of doing

1. All figures and percentages used in this lesson are hypothetical and should not be construed as actually valid for business use.

2. Net Profit is the amount of money remaining after all expenses, except personal income tax and capital expenses, have been paid out. If the owner is drawing a salary it is computed and handled under Salaries and Expenses, just like any other employee's salary.

business, which must be considered in the budget. Even if the owner is fortunate enough to have all the capital he needs, he should figure the interest on his money as a cost to be budgeted because his money could earn that interest without his doing any work, if it were invested or deposited in a savings account.

For the purpose of our example, let us assume a thorough analysis indicates the following amounts and/or percentages to be applicable:

Line 3 Cost of Food Sold: 37%. Food Sold refers only to foods actually sold to guests. 37% times $56,160 (Food Sales) equals $20,779.

Line 4 Employees Meals: $1,685 divided by $56,160 equals 3%. This figure is derived by estimating the wholesale cost of feeding all employees.

Line 5 Cost of Food Consumed: 40%. Employees Meals 3% plus Food Sold 37% equals 40% times Food Sales of $56,160. Food Consumed is food used for any purpose such as sold to guests, given to employees as meals, sold to employees in the form of steward's sales, etc.

Line 6 Food Gross Profit: 63%. This figure is obtained by subtracting Cost of Food SOLD, (both the percentage and money figures) from Food Sales. To prove the accuracy of this figure Gross Profit ÷ Sales should equal 63%, or 63% times Sales dollars should equal $35,381*.

Line 7 Salaries and Wages: $17,690 ÷ $56,160 = 31.5%. This monetary figure is based on an estimate of the number of personnel required for each shift, times the hourly wages (and salaries), the type of menu, the service, etc.

Lines 8 to 18 are computed exactly the same way as Line 7. The monetary amount for each line is estimated separately and divided by the Food Sales Figure ($56,160) to determine the applicable percentage.

Line 19 Total Operating Expenses: 53%. Separately total up dollars and percentage columns. To prove these figures total Operating Expense ÷ Food Sales should equal 53%. (When rounding off to the nearest whole dollar the total Operating Expenses Percentage times Food Sales may NOT always equal total Operating Expenses DOLLARS.)

In order to be sure a budget is correctly calculated all the way through use the following formula as a verification:

Cost of Food Sold plus Total Operating Expenses plus Net Profit should equal Total Food Sales in dollars and also total 100 percent. Check the above lines in Figure 12-A to determine if they equal $56,160 and 100%.

*Rounded off to the nearest dollar.

ANNUAL FIXED BUDGET (New Operation)

Fiscal year: 1966 | Year ending: June 30, 1967

1.	Food Sales	$ 56,160	100%
5.	Cost of food consumed	$ 22,464	40%
4.	Less employees' meals	1,685	3%
3.	Cost of Food Sold	$ 20,779	37%
6.	Food Gross Profit	$ 35,381	63%

Operating Expenses:

7.	Salaries and Wages (Including Vacations)	$ 17,690	31.5%
8.	Employees' Meals	$ 1,685	3 %
9.	Payroll Taxes and Employee Relations	$ 1,685	3 %
10.	Rent	$ 2,527	4.5%
11.	Laundry and Linen	$ 562	1 %
12.	Utilities	$ 1,404	2.5%
13.	Cleaning Supplies	$ 1,123	2 %
14.	China, Glass, Silver, Utensils	$ 562	1 %
15.	Maintenance and Repairs	$ 842	1.5%
16.	Depreciation	$ 562	1 %
17.	Licenses, Taxes, Insurance	$ 842	1.5%
18.	Other Expenses	$ 281	.5%
19.	Total Operating Expenses	$ 29,765	53 %
2.	Net Profit (Before Income Taxes)	$ 5,616	10 %

Note: Figures are Rounded off to nearest whole dollar and for illustrations only. They should not be used in an actual budget.

Figure 12–A. Budget for New Luncheonette.

The preceding annual budget was designed for a new restaurant and based on an estimate of probabilities. In a new unit, lacking sales history data, the annual budget would probably be divided by twelve to break it down into months, and then adjusted as necessary each month.

Monthly Budget - Established Operation. Annual budgets have a place in efficient management but it is the monthly or quarterly budgets that provide the most information on the department level. To take a yearly budget figure in an established restaurant, where past records are available, and divide it by twelve is neither practical nor sensible. The best solution is to review all sales figures for the past year and determine what percentage of the annual sales is represented by each month. For example, suppose sales information over the past year was as follows:

MONTH		FOOD SALES*
July		$ 9,852
August		10,144
September		9,081
October		8,115
November		7,632
December		6,386
January		7,149
February		6,666
March		6,366
April		7,535
May		8,308
June		9,371
	TOTAL	$ 96,605

*Rounded off to nearest whole dollar.

By taking each monthly figure individually, and dividing it by the total annual sales, we are able to determine exactly what percentage of the year's total was sold each month.

MONTH	SALES		TOTAL SALES		PERCENTAGE
July	$ 9,852	divided by	$96,605	equals	10.2%
August	10,144	" "	"	"	10.5%
September	9,081	" "	"	"	9.4%
October	8,115	" "	"	"	8.4%
November	7,632	" "	"	"	7.9%
December	6,386	" "	"	"	6.6%
January	7,149	" "	"	"	7.4%
February	6,666	" "	"	"	6.9%
March	6,366	" "	"	"	6.6%
April	7,535	" "	"	"	7.8%
May	8,308	" "	"	"	8.6%
June	9,371	" "	"	"	9.7%
TOTAL	$96,605				100. %

Although the preceding percentages should remain fairly constant, it is still advisable to run spot checks at the end of each year to insure continued validity.

Once the annual budget is set up, it is merely a matter of multiplying by the appropriate percentage to change it to a budget for a specific month. For example, look over the following annual budget in Figure 12-B.

ANNUAL BUDGET

Fiscal year: 1967 — Year ending: June 30, 1967

1.	Food Sales	$ 101,000	100 %
5.	Cost of Food Consumed	$ 41,410	41 %
4.	Less Employees' Meals	$ 2,020	2 %
3.	Cost of Food Sold	$ 39,390	39 %
6.	Food Gross Profit	$ 61,610	61 %
	Operating Expenses:		
7.	Salaries and Wages (Including Vacations)	$ 29,492	29.2 %
8.	Employees' Meals	$ 2,020	2 %
9.	Payroll Taxes and Employee Relations	$ 2,626	2.6 %
10.	Rent	$ 5,050	5 %
11.	Laundry and Linen	$ 1,515	1.5 %
12.	Utilities	$ 2,727	2.7 %
13.	Cleaning Supplies	$ 1,313	1.3 %
14.	China, Glass, Silver, Utensils	$ 1,515	1.5 %
15.	Maintenance and Repair	$ 1,010	1 %
16.	Depreciation	$ 1,414	1.4 %
17.	Licenses, Taxes, Insurance	$ 1,515	1.5 %
18.	Other Expenses	$ 1,515	1.5 %
19.	Total Operating Expenses	$ 51,712	51.2 %
2.	Net Profit	$ 9,898	9.8 %

Note: Figures are rounded off to nearest whole dollar and for illustration only. They should not be used in an actual budget.

Figure 12–B. Annual Fixed Budget-Established Unit.

Suppose the Manager desired to compute a budget for the month of August. By referring back to the percentage chart it will be noted the August percentage is 10.5%. Multiplying 10.5% times each dollar amount on the annual budget (Figure 12-B) will simply and quickly provide the August Budget. Another acceptable method would be to take 10.5% times the annual estimated sales figure ($101,000), enter the answer ($10,605) and 100% on Line 1. Using the sales figure as the base figure, merely go down each line multiplying the figure times each percentage. (See Figure 12-C.)

BUDGET EXPENSL

Month of: August 1966 Fiscal Year: 1967

1.	Food Sales	$10,605	100 %
5.	Cost of Food Consumed	$ 4,348	41 %
4.	Less Employees' Meals	$ 212	2 %
3.	Cost of Food Sold	$ 4,136	39 %
6.	Food Gross Profit	$ 6,469	61 %
	Operating Expenses:		
7.	Salaries and Wages (Including Vacations)	$ 3,097	29.2 %
8.	Employees' Meals	$ 212	2 %
9.	Payroll Taxes and Employee Relations	$ 276	2.6 %
10.	Rent	$ 530	5 %
11.	Laundry and Linen	$ 159	1.5 %
12.	Utilities	$ 286	2.7 %
13.	Cleaning Supplies	$ 138	1.3 %
14.	China, Glass, Silver, Utensils	$ 159	1.5 %
15.	Maintenance and Repairs	$ 106	1 %
16.	Depreciation	$ 148	1.4 %
17.	Licenses, Taxes, Insurance	$ 159	1.5 %
18.	Other Expenses	$ 159	1.5 %
19.	Total Operating Expenses	$ 5,430	51.2 %
2.	Net Profit	$ 1,039	9.8 %

Note: Figures are rounded off to the nearest whole dollar and are for illustration only. They should not be used in an actual budget.

Figure 12–C. Monthly Budget-Established Unit.

Food and Beverage Budget. In an establishment serving both food and beverages the budget must be slightly modified. Prior to preparation a determination must be made as to the estimated (or actual) ratio of food to beverage sales. If research indicates 60% of the annual sales will probably be food, and 40% of the annual sales will probably be beverages, simply apply the following formula:

Total Sales:	$200, 000	
Estimated Food Sales:		X 60% ($120, 000)
Estimated Beverage Sales:		X 40% ($ 80, 000)

The estimated Food Sales of $120, 000 and 100% should be entered on Line 1. Estimated Beverage Sales of $80, 000 should be entered on Line 2, also as 100%. The combined total of Food and Beverage Sales, $200, 000, is entered on Line 3, again as 100%. (See Figure 12-D.)

To determine the Net Profit, multiply the expected percentage (in this case 12%) times Total Food and Beverage Sales ($200, 000). The resulting answer, $24, 000, is entered on Line 4.

We will assume a thorough study of conditions produced the following amounts and percentages:

Cost of Food Sold:	37% - Line 5
Less Employees' Meals:	$3, 840 - Line 6
Cost of Food Consumed:	40.2% - Line 7
Food Gross Profit:	63% - Line 8

(To determine dollar amounts, multiply the percentage times Food Sales, (Line 1.) (To determine percentages, divide dollar amount by Food Sales amount.)

The same study indicates the following beverage cost percentage:

Cost of Beverages Sold:	31% - Line 9
Beverage Gross Profit:	69% - Line 10

(To compute the dollar amounts, multiply the percentages times Beverage Sales, Line 2.)

The Cost of Food and Beverages Sold, Line 11, is calculated in the following manner:

Cost of Food Sold:	$44, 400
Cost of Beverages Sold:	$24, 800
Combined Cost	$69, 200 ÷ $200, 000 = 34.6%

To determine the Food and Beverage Gross Profit (Line 12) merely subtract the Cost of Food and Beverages Sold from the Total Food and Beverage Sales.

All operating expenses (Lines 13 through 24) are computed in the same manner as any budget. In this case the estimated dollar amount for each line is divided by $200, 000 (Total Food and Beverage Sales) to derive the correct percentage. Note the example given below:

Salaries and Wages (Line 13): $70, 000 ÷ $200, 000 = 35%

The more discerning student will note Employees' Meals on Line 6 is 3.2%, and only 1.9% on Line 14. This is because we are using two different base figures. The $3, 840 on Line 6 is 3.2% of the $120, 000 FOOD SALES, while the $3, 840 on Line 14 is only 1.9% of the $200, 000 FOOD AND BEVERAGE SALES. The employees' meal figure on Line 6 is useful because it provides a means of determining what percentage of Food Sales we are spending, and subsequently, the exact amount of Cost of Food SOLD. The employees' meal figure on Line 14 illustrates the percentage in relation to the overall sales. (See Figure 12-D.)

ANNUAL FIXED BUDGET

Fiscal Year: 1967 Year Ending: June 30, 1968

SECTION 1	1. Food Sales	$120,000	100 %
	7. Cost of Food Consumed	$ 48,240	40.2%
	6. Less Employees' Meals	$ 3,840	3.2%
	5. Cost of Food Sold	$ 44,400	37 %
	8. Food Gross Profit	$ 75,600	63 %
SECTION 2	2. Beverage Sales	$ 80,000	100 %
	9. Cost of Beverages Sold	$ 24,800	31 %
	10. Beverage Gross Profit	$ 55,200	69 %
SECTION 3	3. Total Food and Beverage Sales:	$200,000	100 %
	11. Cost of Food and Beverages Sold	$ 69,200	34.6%
	12. Food and Beverage Gross Profit	$130,800	65.4%
	Operating Expenses:		
	13. Salaries and Wages (Including Vacations)	$ 62,000	31 %
	14. Employees' Meals	$ 3,840	1.9%
	15. Payroll Taxes and Employee Relations	$ 9,000	4.5%
	16. Rent	$ 9,800	4.9%
	17. Laundry and Linen	$ 2,200	1.1%
	18. Utilities	$ 5,000	2.5%
	19. Cleaning Supplies	$ 2,600	1.3%
	20. China, Glass, Silver, Utensils	$ 2,380	1.2%
	21. Maintenance and Repair	$ 2,000	1 %
	22. Depreciation	$ 2,380	1.2%
	23. Licenses, Taxes, Insurance	$ 2,600	1.3%
	24. Other Expenses	$ 3,000	1.5%
	25. Total Operating Expenses	$106,800	53.4%
	4. Net Profit	$ 24,000	12 %

Note: Figures are rounded off to the nearest whole dollar and are for illustration only. They should not be used in an actual budget.

Figure 12–D. Food and Beverage Budget.

In summation, the student is reminded that budgets should always be considered flexible. A budget is never made up with the idea of jamming the business into it. On the contrary, just the opposite is true. The budget is made up and changed as business conditions warrant.

Students frequently have doubts about the value of a budget. They feel if it is so flexible, and can be changed, it has little or no value. Actually, changes are not as frequent or as large (from a monetary standpoint) as one might think. Barring an unexpected recession, or prosperity, sales remain fairly constant from one year to the next. After experience in budget preparation has been gained, the budgeter becomes more and more competent in his predictions. Needless to say, an accurate budget can be a tremendous asset to management.

In order to receive full value from a budget it is necessary to compare it with the Profit and Loss Statement each month, as well as annually. This vital comparison defines how well management anticipated expenditures in relation to what was actually spent. An operational analysis sheet, listing P & L figures, together with Budget figures and percentages, and showing the differences, will provide the desired information.

THE BALANCE SHEET

The Balance Sheet is one of the most valuable tools of management. Too often it is relegated to a "back seat" in favor of the more glamorous Profit and Loss Statement. The reasons for a lack of interest in the Balance Sheet are not clear. Perhaps many schools do not place the proper curriculum emphasis on it. Possibly food service supervisors may not understand, or know how correctly to interpret the Balance Sheet. Whatever the reason, the Balance Sheet can and will provide an exceptional amount of valuable information for the knowledgeable food operator.

Basically, a Balance Sheet is a written record of assets and liabilities of the business. The fundamental formula never changes: TOTAL ASSETS MUST EQUAL TOTAL LIABILITIES PLUS NET WORTH.

Proper understanding of the Balance Sheet will be much easier if the student first masters the definitions of the following words:

Assets. Items actually owned by the establishment. They are divided into two categories:

Current Assets include cash on hand for current use, cash on deposit, accounts receivable, food inventory, consumable supplies, deposits with public utilities companies, prepaid expenses*, and "other assets which may be sold, converted into cash, or consumed, by normal operations in the near future".

Fixed Assets are those items that will, or are expected to, last several years. This would include such things as real estate, buildings and improvements, equipment and furniture, small operating equipment such as china, glass, silver, utensils, etc.

Liabilities. Included are those amounts owed by the business. Like assets they are divided into two categories:

*Prepaid expenses are merchandise or services which have been purchased and will be used in the near future.

Current Liabilities are those debts normally due and payable within one year. Long-term liabilities could be included under current liabilities if the balance of the debt became due within one year of the Balance Sheet date. Also under current liabilities are taxes collected on sales.

Long-Term Liabilities are liabilities requiring one year or longer to reach maturity.

Net Worth. Refers to the owner's equity in the establishment. In a restaurant this account is frequently called "the proprieters' account." The important thing to remember is the basic principle cited earlier: TOTAL ASSETS MUST EQUAL TOTAL LIABILITIES PLUS NET WORTH. (See Figure 12-E.)

BALANCE SHEET

As of June 30, 1967

ASSETS

CURRENT ASSETS			
Cash on Hand	$ 721		
Cash on Deposit in Bank	10,000		
Total Cash		$10,721	
Accounts Receivable		419	
Deposits (Utilities)		75	
Inventories:			
Food	1,941		
Supplies	916		
Total Inventories		2,857	
Prepaid Expenses		1,243	
Total Current Assets			$15,315
FIXED ASSETS			
Land	20,000		
Building	35,900		
Operating Equipment	4,100		
Furniture & Equipment	18,000		
Sub-Total, Fixed Assets		78,000	
Less Depreciation		19,280	
Total Fixed Assets			58,720
TOTAL ASSETS			$74,035

LIABILITIES AND NET WORTH

CURRENT LIABILITIES			
Accounts Payable		$ 4,000	
Notes Payable		2,500	
Accrued Expenses		4,725	
Total Current Liabilities			$11,225
LONG-TERM LIABILITIES			
Equipment Contracts			6,972
Mortgage			12,130
TOTAL LIABILITIES			30,327
NET WORTH			
Owner's Capital		25,983	
Profit for Year		17,725	
Net Worth			43,708
TOTAL LIABILITIES AND NET WORTH			$74,035

Figure 12–E. Balance Sheet.

Analyzing the Balance Sheet. As with any type of management form, merely placing figures on a piece of paper, arriving at a balance and then filing the form is of little value. Each balance sheet contains certain relationships that should be analyzed. These financial ratios* materially aid the food manager in determining exactly how sound the business really is.

When discussing or writing ratios, care must be taken to word and write correctly. All ratios are computed by dividing the first item by the second one.

There are so many ratios available for calculation, (one authority lists 24), that managers and analysts are weighted down by sheer numbers. In most all instances, 9 or 10 ratios are sufficient to rate the liquidity, solvency and profitability of the establishment.

In an introductory course, such as this one, a thorough understanding of ratios is not considered necessary. The following two examples are cited to illustrate the mechanics of ratios:

Current Ratio. The ratio of current assets to current liabilities is valuable because it is indicative of financial strength. It clarifies the ability of the firm to meet short term debts. The formula for Current Ratio is Current Assets ÷ Current Liabilities. The Balance Sheet in this lesson (Figure 12-E) shows a Current Ratio of 1.36 Times,

$$\frac{\text{Current Assets}}{\text{Current Liabilities}} \quad \frac{\$15,315}{11,225} = 1.36 \text{ Times}$$

Not too many years ago, the accepted theory was that every business should operate on a 2-to-1 Current Ratio basis. In other words, a firm should have twice as many assets as liabilities. Today, modern analysts believe ratios vary with each type of business and, consequently, there is no perfect Current Ratio.

Quick Current Ratio. The quick Current Ratio (also called the "Acid Test Ratio" or "Quick Ratio") is used to determine whether the firm's "liquid assets"** are sufficient to meet current obligations. Businesses with a 1-to-1 ratio are considered to have good liquidity and be able to pay all current debts without further sales. Anything lower than a 1 - 1 ratio should be regarded as a "caution light".

The importance of this ratio lies in the fact that sometimes an emergency requires immediate payment of current liabilities. Unless the assets are liquid, which means that they are either cash or can be turned into cash at full value immediately, there could be both a delay and a substantial loss in turning the assets into cash.

The Quick Current Ratio for the Balance Sheet shown in Figure 12-E is 99.24%.

$$\frac{\text{Liquid Assets}}{\text{Current Liabilities}} \quad \frac{\$11,140}{11,225} = 99.24\%$$

"Limitations of Ratio Analysis. The use of financial and operating ratios is not a substitute for good management. They provide guides, not precise measurements, by which a food service operator can analyze his operation and compare the results with past periods, or with industry averages, for use in making decisions.

Ratios are general in nature. Like other statistical data, ratios merely represent a convenient means of calling attention to specific relationships which may require further analysis.

*A ratio is the relationship of one number to another number.

**Liquid assets include cash on hand (or deposit), and other things such as marketable bonds and securities that can rapidly be converted to cash.

Additional limitations of using ratios are as follows:

Ratios are computed from accounting records, and these records in themselves are not always precise statements. They are only interim reports.

Accounting practices differ among food service establishments. Personal judgment enters into the estimate on many items on the statements.

All items carried on the financial statements are based on recorded historical fact.

Recognizing these limitations, the use of financial statements and ratios, nonetheless, provides management with data for appraising intelligently the financial activity of the establishment and for making decisions. They adequately indicate overall profitability, conditions of the business, and significant trends in the operation of the establishment. When compared with standard ratios, they indicate weak spots and areas which may require further investigation and needed improvements."*

PROFIT AND LOSS STATEMENT

The Profit and Loss Statement is a resume of income, expenses, profit or loss, for a specified period of time.

"The difference between the data in the Balance Sheet and the Profit-and-Loss Statement is that the two statements offer two different views of the business. The Balance Sheet shows the status of the assets, liabilities, and net worth - the financial condition - at a given date. It shows how many dollars are available to continue with the business.

The Profit-and-Loss Statement shows or describes the financial activity over a stated period of time which leads to the present status of assets, liabilities, and net worth. The two statements are complementary and contain data of great importance to owners and managers.*

There is no "proper way" of laying out a Profit and Loss Statement. The format illustrated in Figure 12-F is most commonly accepted.

*Courtesy Food Management Program Leaflet 11 "Using Financial Statements in Food Service Establishments" by Robert F. Lukowski and Charles E. Eshbach, University of Massachusetts, Amherst.

PROFIT AND LOSS STATEMENT

Month of: August 1966 — Fiscal Year: 1967

	Amount	% of Sales
FOOD SALES	$11,230	100 %
Cost of Food Consumed	4,705	41.9%
Less Employees' Meals	393	3.5%
Cost of Food Sold	4,312	38.4%
GROSS PROFIT	$ 6,918	61.6%
OPERATING EXPENSES:		
Salaries and Wages (Including Vacations)	$ 3,201	28.5%
Employees' Meals	393	3.5%
Payroll Taxes and Employee Relations	281	2.5%
Rent	562	5 %
Laundry and Linen	124	1.1%
Utilities	270	2.4%
Cleaning Supplies	180	1.6%
China, Glass, Silver, Utensils	134	1.2%
Maintenance and Repair	90	.8%
Depreciation	156	1.4%
Licenses, Taxes, Insurance	168	1.5%
Other Expenses	101	.9%
Total Operating Expenses	$ 5,660	50.4%
NET PROFIT BEFORE TAXES	$ 1,258	11.2%

Figure 12–F. Profit and Loss Statement.

Compare the preceding Profit and Loss Statement with the August Budget, (Figure 12-C) to determine how well or poorly the establishment's funds were budgeted and spent.

COMPARISON OF FINANCIAL RECORDS

It is imperative that management make every possible comparison between records, accounting periods, past and present years, etc. Unless there is a comprehensive evaluation of one period of time to another, the full value of maintaining records is not utilized. In the food business, management must be constantly alert for changes and trends. Intelligent comparison will point out trends and changes easily and quickly.

Bibliography:

Establishing and Operating a Restaurant U.S. Department of Agriculture

Using Financial Statements in Food Service Establishments by Robert F. Lukowski and Charles E. Eshbach, University of Massachusetts Food Management Program Leaflet 11.

Starting and Managing a Small Restaurant by Paul Fairbrook, Small Business Administration, Washington, D.C.

LESSON 12 - BRAINTEASER

After you are certain you understand the material in this lesson, answer the questions below. When you have completed the brainteaser, check your answers in the text. Use the following scale to evaluate your comprehension of this lesson:

10 Correct --- Outstanding
9 Correct --- Excellent
8 Correct --- Good
7 Correct --- Fair
6 or Under
Correct --- Restudy the Lesson

1) Name the three types of budgets.

a.

b.

c.

2) When calculating a Budget why is Food Sales always shown as 100%?

3) To verify a Budget after it is calculated, add ______________________, plus ______________________, plus ______________________ should equal Total Food Sales in dollars and also Total 100%.

4) In the space below write the fundamental formula of the Balance Sheet.

5) Define the following terms:

a. Assets

b. Current Assets

c. Fixed Assets

d. Liabilities

e. Current Liabilities

f. Long-Term Liabilities

g. Net Worth

6) The relationship of one number to another number is called a _______________.

7) When discussing or writing ratios, why is it so important to word and write correctly?

8) Explain the difference between the Balance Sheet and the Profit and Loss Statement.

9) A business is considered to have good liquidity if the Quick Current (Acid Test) Ratio works out to be:

a. 1-to-1

b. 2-to-1

c. 3-to-1

d. 1-to-2

e. 1-to-3

10) Define NET PROFIT.

LESSON 13

WASHING AND SANITIZATION OF EQUIPMENT

LESSON 13 - PREVIEW

The washing and sanitization of dishes, utensils and equipment is one of the most important facets of professional food service. In this lesson the student has an opportunity to become familiar with various segments of dishroom operation, such as large dishroom organization, correct washing, rinsing and sanitization temperatures and the various types of equipment used. In addition, United States Public Health Service rules and regulations pertaining to dishroom operations are explained.

Personnel interested in the culinary profession will find this lesson to be a vital addition to their own knowledge, as well as invaluable to the welfare and profit of the food establishment where they are employed.

WASHING AND SANITIZATION OF EQUIPMENT

For some yet to be explained reason, the washing and sterilization of equipment has been relegated to an inferior position in the food service industry. Although we frequently pay "lip service" to this important function, it often seems as if many managers believe that ignoring the area will make the many problems disappear.

The fact that proper washing and sanitization of dishes is not given proper status in food service can be traced in part to these facts:

A. Dishwashing personnel are usually the lowest paid in the unit.

B. Personnel turnover in dishrooms is phenomenal.

C. Management often does not react to this department until after customers complain.

D. Most food service personnel are not familiar with health department regulations and correct procedures for cleaning and sterilizing equipment.

In the future, through the education of new personnel entering the culinary field and the re-education of experienced personnel, it is hoped that this extremely important department will obtain the attention it deserves.

UNITED STATES PUBLIC HEALTH SERVICE INSPECTIONS

Food service operations doing interstate business are usually subject to sanitary regulations specified by the United States Public Health Service, Food and Drug Administration. This federal governmental agency uses a form entitled, "Inspection Report - Food Service Establishments" (PHS-4006), when inspecting organizations under their jurisdiction.

It is interesting to note that of 118 possible violations listed, over 31 percent apply directly, or indirectly, to the washing and sanitization of food service equipment. (See Figure 13-A.)

When a health inspector conducts an inspection of a food service establishment, he is required to record his findings on form PHS-4006. After each inspection, the original of this form is presented to the permit holder of the establishment. Each violation on the form results in 1 to 6 demerits.

Demerits are totaled and a specific period of time is allowed for correcting deficiencies, subject to the following provisions:

A. When the demerit score of the establishment is 20 or less, all violations of 2- or 4- demerit points must be corrected by the time of the next routine inspection; or

B. When the demerit score of the establishment is more than 20, but not more than 40, all items of 2- or 4- demerit points must be corrected within a period of time not to exceed 30 days; or

C. When one or more 6-demerit point items are in violation, regardless of total demerit score, such items must be corrected within a period of time not to exceed 10 days.

PHS–4006
REV. 1–65

INSPECTION REPORT
FOOD SERVICE ESTABLISHMENTS

Permit No. ____________
Type ________ NSD ________

CITY, COUNTY OR DISTRICT	NAME OF ESTABLISHMENT	ADDRESS	OWNER OR OPERATOR

Sir: Based on an inspection this day, the items marked below identify the violation in operation or facilities which must be corrected by the next routine inspection or such shorter period of time as may be specified in writing by the health authority. Failure to comply with this notice may result in immediate suspension of your permit (or downgrading of the establishment).* An opportunity for an appeal will be provided if a written request for a hearing is filed with the health authority within the period of time established in this notice for the correction of violations.

SECTION B. Food

Item	1. FOOD SUPPLIES	Specify:	Bakery products	Poultry and poultry products	Meat and meat products	Frozen desserts	Shellfish	Milk and milk products	Demerit points
1	Approved source								6
2	Wholesome—not adulterated								6
3	Not misbranded								2
4	Original container; properly identified								2
5	Approved dispenser								
6	Fluid milk and fluid milk products pasteurized								6
7	Low-acid and non-acid foods commercially canned								6

Item	2. FOOD PROTECTION	Preparation	Storage	Display	Service	Transportation	Demerit points
8	Protected from contamination						4
9	Adequate facilities for maintaining food at hot or cold temperatures						2
10	Suitable thermometers properly located						2
11	Perishable food at proper temperature						2
12	Potentially hazardous food at 45° F. or below, or 140° F. or above as required						6
13	Frozen food kept frozen; properly thawed						2
14	Handling of food minimized by use of suitable utensils						4
15	Hollandaise sauce of fresh ingredients; discarded after three hours						6
16	Food cooked to proper temperature						6
17	Fruits and vegetables washed thoroughly						2
18	Containers of food stored off floor on clean surfaces						2

SECTION D. Food Equipment and Utensils (Continued)

Item	2. CLEANLINESS OF EQUIPMENT AND UTENSILS	Demerit points
37	Tableware clean to sight and touch	
38	Kitchenware and food-contact surfaces of equipment clean to sight and touch	4
39	Grills and similar cooking devices cleaned daily	
40	Non-food-contact surfaces of equipment kept clean	2
41	Detergents and abrasives rinsed off food-contact surfaces	2
42	Clean wiping cloths used; use properly restricted	2
43	Utensils and equipment pre-flushed, scraped or soaked	2
44	Tableware sanitized	
45	Kitchenware and food-contact surfaces of equipment used for potentially hazardous food sanitized	4
46	Facilities for washing and sanitizing equipment and utensils approved, adequate, properly constructed, maintained and operated	4
47	Wash and sanitizing water clean	2
48	Wash water at proper temperature	
49	Dish tables and drain boards provided, properly located and constructed	2
50	Adequate and suitable detergents used	2
51	Approved thermometers provided and used	
52	Suitable dish baskets provided	2
53	Proper gauge cocks provided	
54	Cleaned and cleaned and sanitized utensils and equipment properly stored and handled; utensils air-dried	2
55	Suitable facilities and areas provided for storing utensils and equipment	2
56	Single-service articles properly stored, dispensed and handled	2
57	Single-service articles used only once	

SECTION E. Sanitary Facilities and Controls (Continued)

Item	5. HAND-WASHING FACILITIES	Demerit points
79	Waste receptacles provided for disposable towels	2
80	Lavatory facilities clean and in good repair	2
	6. GARBAGE AND RUBBISH DISPOSAL	
81	Stored in approved containers; adequate in number	2
82	Containers cleaned when empty; brushes provided	2
83	When not in continuous use, covered with tight-fitting lids, or in protective storage inaccessible to vermin	2
84	Storage areas adequate; clean; no nuisances; proper facilities provided	2
85	Disposed of in an approved manner, at an approved frequency	2
86	Garbage rooms or enclosures properly constructed; outside storage at proper height above ground or on concrete slab	2
87	Food waste grinders and incinerators properly installed, constructed and operated; incinerators areas clean	2
	7. VERMIN CONTROL	
88	Presence of rodents, flies, roaches and vermin minimized	4
89	Outer openings protected against flying insects as required; rodent-proofed	2
90	Harborage and feeding of vermin prevented	2

SECTION F. Other Facilities

Item	1. FLOORS, WALLS AND CEILINGS	Demerit points
91	Floors kept clean; no sawdust used	2
92	Floors easily cleanable construction, in good repair, smooth, non-absorbent; carpeting in good repair	1

No.	Item	Weight
23	Unwrapped and potentially hazardous food not re-served	4
24	Poisonous and toxic materials properly identified, colored, stored and used; poisonous polishes not present	6
25	Bactericides, cleaning and other compounds properly stored and non-toxic in use dilutions	

SECTION C. Personnel

1. HEALTH AND DISEASE CONTROL

No.	Item	Weight
26	Persons with boils, infected wounds, respiratory infections or other communicable disease properly restricted	6
27	Known or suspected communicable disease cases reported to health authority	6

2. CLEANLINESS

No.	Item	Weight
28	Hands washed and clean	6
29	Clean outer garments; proper hair restraints used	2
30	Good hygienic practices	4

SECTION D. Food Equipment and Utensils

1. SANITARY DESIGN, CONSTRUCTION AND INSTALLATION OF EQUIPMENT AND UTENSILS

No.	Item	Good repair; no cracks	No chips, pits or open seams	Cleanable; smooth	Approved material	No corrosion	Proper construction	Accessible for cleaning and inspection	Weight
31	Food-contact surfaces of equipment								2
32	Utensils								2
33	Non-food-contact surfaces of equipment								2
34	Single-service articles of non-toxic materials								2
35	Equipment properly installed								2
36	Existing equipment capable of being cleaned, non-toxic, properly installed, and in good repair								2

No.	Item	Weight
59	From approved source; adequate; safe quality	6
60	Hot and cold running water provided	4
61	Transported water handled, stored; dispensed in a sanitary manner	6
62	Ice from approved source; made from potable water	6
63	Ice machines and facilities properly located, installed and maintained	2
64	Ice and ice handling utensils properly handled and stored; block ice rinsed.	2
65	Ice-contact surfaces approved; proper material and construction	

2. SEWAGE DISPOSAL

No.	Item	Weight
66.	Into public sewer, or approved private facilities	6

3. PLUMBING

No.	Item	Weight
67	Properly sized, installed and maintained	2
68	Non-potable water piping identified	1
69	No cross connections	6
70	No back siphonage possible	
71	Equipment properly drained	2

4. TOILET FACILITIES

No.	Item	Weight
72	Adequate, conveniently located, and accessible; properly designed and installed	6
73	Toilet rooms completely enclosed, and equipped with self-closing, tight-fitting doors; doors kept closed	2
74	Toilet rooms, fixtures and vestibules kept clean, in good repair, and free from odors	2
75	Toilet tissue and proper waste receptacles provided; waste receptacles emptied as necessary	2

5. HAND-WASHING FACILITIES

No.	Item	Weight
76	Lavatories provided, adequate, properly located and installed	6
77	Provided with hot and cold or tempered running water through proper fixtures	4
78	Suitable hand cleanser and sanitary towels or approved hand-drying devices provided	2

No.	Item	Weight
97	Floors and wall junctures properly constructed	2
98	Walls, ceilings and attached equipment clean	2
99	Walls and ceilings properly constructed and in good repair; coverings properly attached	1
100	Walls of light color; washable to level of splash	2

2. LIGHTING

No.	Item	Weight
101	20 foot-candles of light on working surfaces	2
102	10 foot-candles of light on food equipment, utensil-washing, hand-washing areas and toilet rooms	
103	5 foot-candles of light 30" from floor in all other areas	
104	Artificial light sources as required	2

3. VENTILATION

No.	Item	Weight
105	Rooms reasonably free from steam, condensation, smoke, etc.	2
106	Rooms and equipment vented to outside as required	2
107	Hoods properly designed; filters removable	2
108	Intake air ducts properly designed and maintained	1
109	Systems comply with fire prevention requirements; no nuisance created	2

4. DRESSING ROOMS AND LOCKERS

No.	Item	Weight
110	Dressing rooms or areas as required; properly located	1
111	Adequate lockers or other suitable facilities	1
112	Dressing rooms, areas and lockers kept clean	2

5. HOUSEKEEPING

No.	Item	Weight
113	Establishment and property clean, and free of litter	2
114	No operations in living or sleeping quarters	2
115	Floors and walls cleaned after closing or between meals by dustless methods	2
116	Laundered clothes and napkins stored in clean place	2
117	Soiled linen and clothing stored in proper containers	1
118	No live birds or animals other than guide dogs	2

*Applicable only where grading form of ordinance is in effect.

DEMERIT SCORE OF THE ESTABLISHMENT ______ Date ______ Health Authority ______

REMARKS: (Use Reverse Side)

For sale by the Superintendent of Documents, U.S. Government Printing Office Washington, D.C., 20402

Figure 13–A. U.S. Public Health Service Inspection Report.

D. When the demerit score of the establishment is more than 40, the operating permit is immediately suspended.

E. In the case of temporary food service establishments, violations must be corrected within a specified period of time not to exceed 24 hours. Failure to comply with such notice shall result in immediate suspension of the operating permit.

Any establishment doing business under this system that receives 21 to 40 demerits is placed on "provisional" status. Provisional status means re-inspection is scheduled within 24 hours to 30 days at the discretion of the inspector. If, at the time of re-inspection, demerit deficiencies have not been reduced to 20 or below, the operation is placed on a "use prohibited" status and can no longer produce food or serve customers. A "use prohibited" status is also given to any establishment receiving 41 or more demerit points during an initial inspection.

OTHER HEALTH DEPARTMENTS

Food establishments under the regulation of the United States Public Health Service may also be under the jurisdiction of state, county or city health departments. For this reason it is prudent to become familiar with all health laws applicable to the particular locale of the operation.

Some cities have actually started publishing in the local newspaper the name of food service establishments failing to pass a health inspection. It does not take much imagination to visualize the effect this type of publicity can have on prospective and regular customers.

Although the regulations of the U.S. Public Health Service and all state, county and city health departments are established for the protection of the consumer, the method of attaining that objective may vary from one location to another. For this reason we will explore only those standards and regulations for cleaning and sanitizing equipment that are set forth by the U.S. Public Health Service, Food and Drug Administration. Any food service establishment maintaining these standards should have few or no problems with local state, city or county health departments.

CLEANLINESS OF EQUIPMENT AND UTENSILS

Existing Equipment. Any equipment that was installed in a food service establishment prior to the effective date of the United States Public Health Service Food Service Sanitation Ordinance and Code (1962) shall be considered acceptable, even if it does not fully meet design and construction standards, provided it is in good repair, can be kept sanitary and has non-toxic food contact surfaces.*

* Toxic food contact surfaces are those surfaces which could result in chemical food poisoning to humans, such as cadmium, antimony, lead, etc. (Also see Chapter 3.)

Cleaning of Equipment and Utensils. The Food Service Sanitation Ordinance and Code requires that all tableware such as eating utensils, dishes, glasses, cups, etc., be cleaned and sanitized after each use. This rule also applies to all kitchenware and food contact surfaces used in the preparation, serving, display or storage of food. An exception to this rule is that the cooking surfaces of grills, griddles and similar cooking devices need not be cleaned after each use but must be cleaned at least once a day.

Non-food contact surfaces of all other equipment including tables, counters, mixers, grinders, dishwashing machines, etc., shall be cleaned as frequently as necessary in order to prevent accumulations of dust, dirt, food particles and other soil or debris.

All detergents and abrasive cleansers must be rinsed off food contact surfaces.

Cloths used by waiters, chefs and other personnel must always be clean. Any cloths used for wiping food contact surfaces may not be used for any other purpose.

Methods and Facilities for Washing and Sanitizing. The USPH Sanitation Ordinance and Code further states that "prior to washing, all equipment and utensils shall be pre-flushed or prescraped and, when necessary, presoaked to remove food particles and soil."

Detergents must be used when washing by hand or machine. The amount of detergent used must be concentrated enough to remove grease, stains and soil. Under normal conditions an effective concentration will be obtained by following the detergent manufacturers' instructions.

Manual Washing. In the manual washing of equipment and utensils, it is important to use a good quality detergent. It is equally important that both water and detergents be changed at frequent intervals to assure items are actually washed clean.

It is difficult to define "frequent intervals," because it depends largely on the amount of soil, and the number of items requiring washing. As a general rule of thumb, detergent and rinse water should be changed at least every 4 hours. Management must take an active interest in this matter to assure that water is in fact changed and clean.

There are three approved methods for hand-sanitizing eating and drinking utensils and, where required, food contact surfaces after washing:

1. Completely immerse for at least 30 seconds in clean, hot water at a temperature of at least 170°F.

2. Completely immerse at least 1 minute in a sanitizing solution of:

   A. Not less than 50 PPM (parts per million) of available* chlorine at a temperature of at least 75°F.; or

   B. Not less than 12 1/2 PPM of available iodine in a solution with a pH** factor not higher than 5 and a temperature of a least 75°F.

* The word "available" in this context means, "floating free." In other words, the chlorine or iodine is available (floating free) in the rinse water.

** The pH factor is used to express both acidity and alkalinity in liquids. The scale runs from 0 to 14 with 7 equaling neutrality. Numbers less than 7 represent increasing acidity. Numbers greater than 7 indicate increasing alkalinity.

3. Large equipment that cannot be sanitized by methods 1 or 2 may be handled as follows:

   A. Use live steam from a hose for equipment where steam can be confined; or
   B. Rinse with boiling water; or
   C. Spray or wash down with a chemical sanitizing solution at least double the strength of solutions described in 2-A or 2-B.

When hand washing of eating and drinking ware and utensils is necessary, USPH rules dictate that a three-compartment sink will be used. (See Figure 13-B.) The first compartment is for washing, the second for rinsing, and the third for sanitizing, using methods 1 or 2 described earlier.

Sinks must be of sufficient length, width and depth to permit complete immersion of equipment and utensils in each compartment. Hot and cold running water must also be available to all three compartments.

For cleaning equipment other than eating and drinking utensils, the USPH will allow a two compartment sink or in some cases, a one-compartment sink.

Dishtables and drainboards must be of adequate size to allow for the proper handling of soiled utensils prior to washing, and for air drying of cleaned utensils following rinsing and sanitizing. If air drying can be accomplished by some other approved method, such as a pot and pan rack (See Figure 13-C.), the drainboard or table on the clean end of the machine need not be too large.

Sinks and drainboards must be constructed of galvanized or better quality metal (for example stainless steel), suitably reinforced and thick enough to resist denting and/or buckling. Metal surfaces on drainboards and sink bottoms must be sloped, to provide self draining.

Machine Washing. Machines must be designed and constructed in such a manner that they can be easily cleaned. They must also have the capacity to clean and sanitize all surfaces of equipment and utensils. Needless to say, dishwashing machine manufacturers are aware of these requirements and all reputable companies build machines conforming to standards.

Most machines manufactured today are the "spray type", providing a water spray from the top and the bottom. The Public Health Code states spray type machines shall meet the following criteria:

1. Water shall be kept reasonably clean. (Although "reasonably clean" is not defined, under normal operating conditions, in a large volume establishment, it would probably be necessary to change the machine water every 4 to 8 hours.)
2. Rinse water tanks must be protected by baffles, dividers, or some other effective method, in order to keep wash water from mixing with rinse water.
3. Water flow pressure on the line must be from 15 pounds PSI, (per square inch) to 25 pounds PSI. Rinse nozzle pressure shall not be less than 10 pounds PSI. A pressure gauge immediately upstream from the final rinse spray nozzles must be provided to permit flow pressure checks.

Figure 13–B. Three-compartment Sink.
(Courtesy Sky Chefs, Inc.)

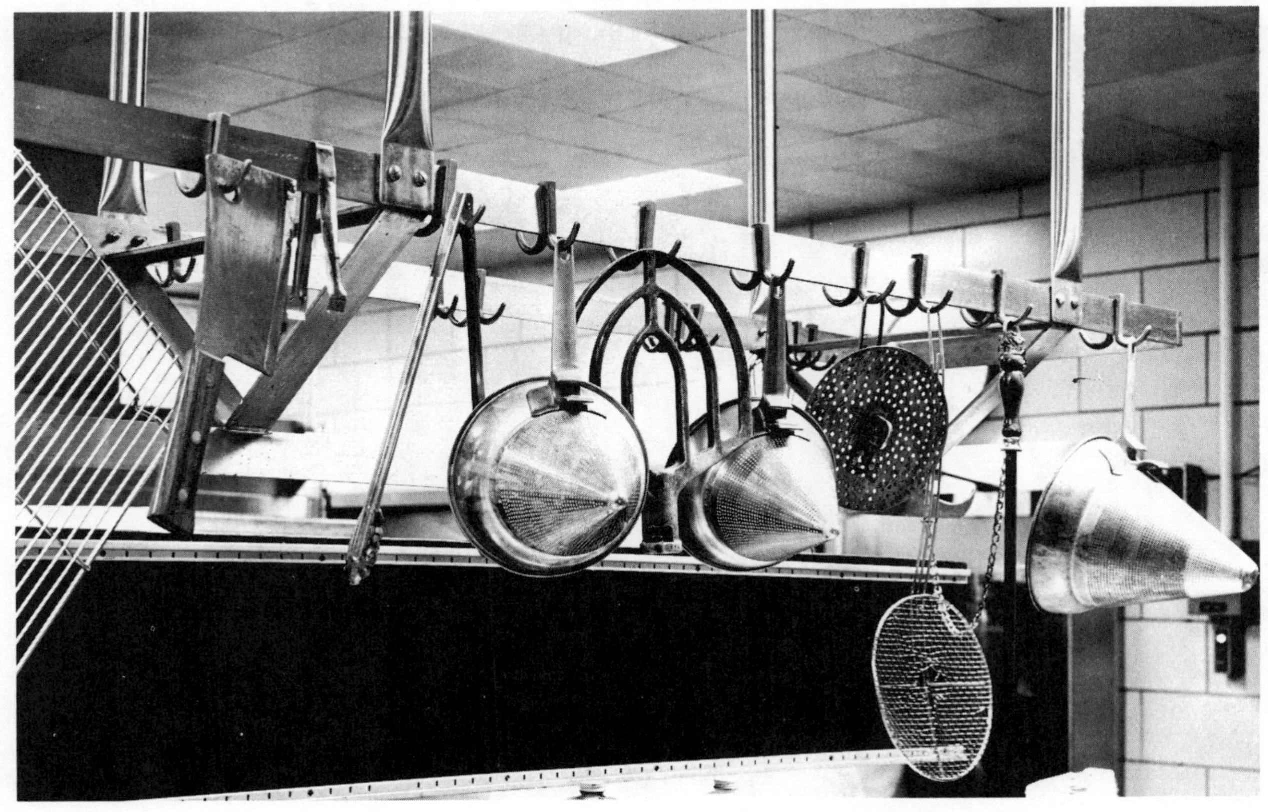

Figure 13–C. Pot and Pan Rack for Air Drying and Storage.
(Courtesy Sky Chefs, Inc.)

4. Wash water temperature in multiple tank machines shall be at least 140°F. Single tank machine wash water temperature must be at least 160°F. (See Figure 13-D.)
5. When using only hot water to sanitize equipment the final rinse must be clean, fresh water with a temperature of not less than 180°F. If the machine provides a pumped final rinse, a temperature of at least 170°F. is acceptable.

Chemical sanitizing is permitted provided that the chemicals are approved by the health authority. In addition, they must be provided in a concentration and used for a length of time to assure effective bactericidal treatment.

6. Conveyors in dishwashing machines must be accurately timed to assure that each wash and rinse cycle is effective.
7. Easily readable thermometers, with an accuracy of plus or minus 2°F. must be installed for each tank. (See Figure 13-E.) In addition, an equally accurate thermometer must be installed to be used in checking the temperature of the final rinse water as it enters the manifold.*
8. All parts of dishmachines such as jets, nozzles, etc., shall be kept free of chemical deposits, debris, and other soil. The most common chemical deposit is alkaline which can build up on the inside of pipes and significantly reduce water pressure and flow. In many cities alkalinity is so high that special alkaline reducing chemicals must be added to the water to prevent build-up. Debris in the form of chipped pieces of plastic, glass, bits of paper, or other items, frequently works its way past the strainer baskets and ends up in the manifold or spray arm nozzles. This obviously reduces the effectiveness of the nozzle and prevents proper cleaning and sanitizing. (See Figure 13-F.) Spray arms and nozzles should be taken apart and thoroughly cleaned <u>at least</u> once a day.

* The manifold is the piece to which spray arms are attached.

Figure 13–D. Single Tank Dishwasher.
(Courtesy Hobart Manufacturing Company, Troy, Ohio)

Figure 13–E. Dishmachine Temperature Gauges.
This machine was shut down a few minutes prior to taking the photo.
(Courtesy Sky Chefs, Inc.)

Figure 13–F. Clogged Manifold Spray Arm.
Note piece of plastic protruding from nozzle to left.

STORAGE AND HANDLING OF CLEANED EQUIPMENT

After cleaning and sanitizing, all equipment and utensils must be handled in a manner that will insure their protection from contamination. Fingers and thumbs must not touch inside surfaces or lip contact surfaces of clean cups, glasses, bowls or plates. If knives, forks and spoons must be handled, only the handles must be touched.

A more sanitary method of handling clean silverware is through the use of plastic or metal cylinders. For machine washing, eating utensils are placed in cylinders with the handles down. After washing, a clean, empty cylinder is placed on top of the cylinder containing the sanitized utensils. The cylinders are inverted, allowing the food contact end of the eating utensils to drop into the clean cylinder. This places the handles up, ready for customer use. (See Figures 13-G, 13-H, 13-I.)

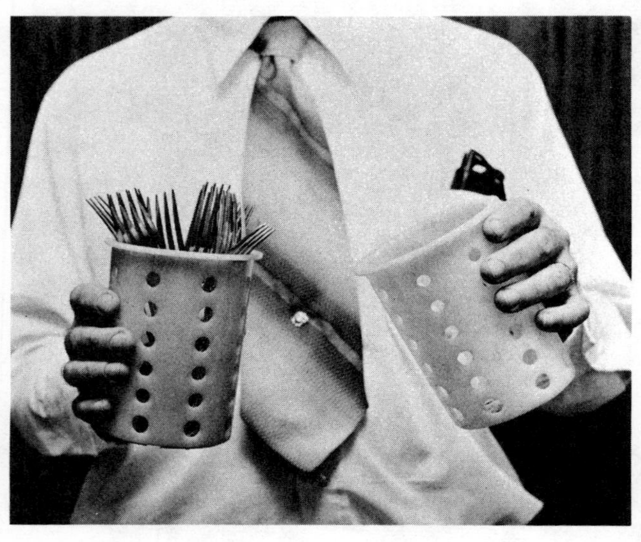

Figure 13–G.
Clean flatware should be inverted without touching the eating end, as at left.

Figure 13–H.
Transfer flatware into clean cylinder, left below.

Figure 13–I.
Flatware handles are now ready for pick up by customers, below.

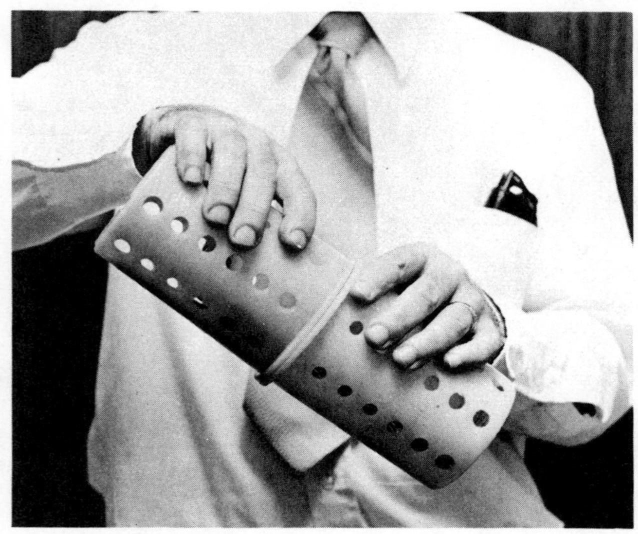

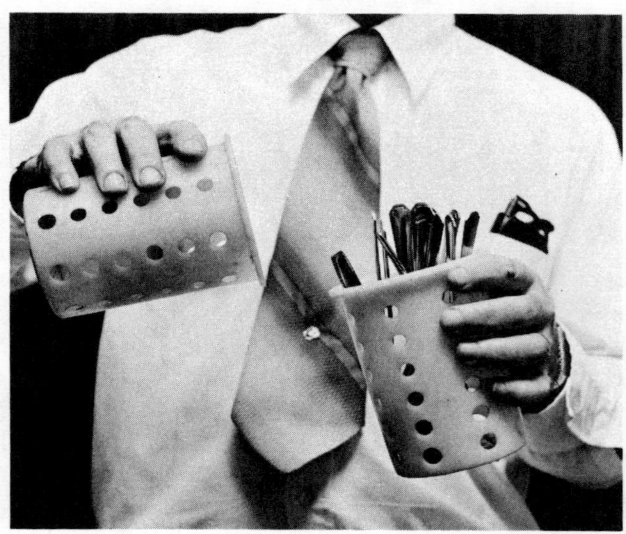

Portable equipment and utensils must always be stored above the floor in a clean, dry location.

Food contact surfaces of all clean and sanitized equipment must be protected from splashing of foods, liquids, dust and other contamination.

Utensils must be air-dried prior to storing or stored in such a manner as to provide self draining and air drying. This can be accomplished on hooks or racks, providing the hooks or racks are constructed of a corrosion-resistant material, such as stainless steel. (See Figure 13-C. at the bottom of page 271.) Whenever possible stored containers must be covered or turned upside down. All silverware shall be stored to provide only the handles for customer and employee pick up.

SINGLE SERVICE ARTICLES

Today, many food service establishments use a large quantity of single service or so-called "throw-a-way" items. Most of these items are of paper or plastic. The United States Public Health Service has some specific rules regarding these items, such as:

1. Single service items must be stored in closed cartons or containers which will protect them from contamination.
2. All such articles shall be handled and dispensed to customers in such a way as to prevent contamination of those surfaces which will come in contact with the mouth of the user. This would include such safe practices as presenting only handles of plastic eating utensils or the base of cups to patrons.
3. Single service items must be used only once and thrown away.
4. Establishments without adequate, approved, cleaning and sanitizing facilities shall use only single service items.

ORGANIZATION OF DISHWASHING DEPARTMENTS

As with any department, the specific organization of dishwashing departments will depend on the size of the washing area, the volume of business and the amount of equipment. In a large operation receiving soiled dishes and other equipment required to prepare and serve 5,000 meals per day, such as an in-flight catering kitchen, (See Figure 13-J.), the following organization could be used:

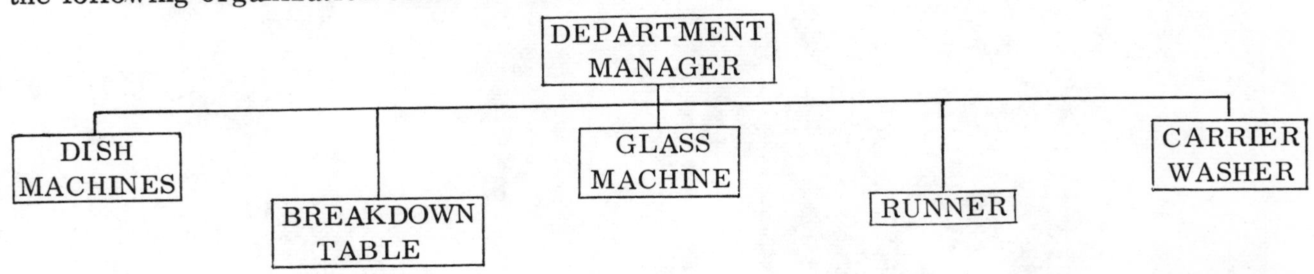

A dishwashing department of this size would normally operate 3 shifts per day with approximately 11 employees per shift.

Two (2) large machines, similar to the one shown in Chapter 2 (See Figure 2-O, page 40), would be required. Each machine would require one man feeding in soiled dishes and one man removing clean dishes.

Because of the large volume, glasses are washed in a separate machine, requiring the services of 1 employee. (See Figure 13-K.) Tray Carriers, Entree Carriers and

Figure 13–J. A Large In-flight Catering Kitchen Dishroom.
(Courtesy Sky Chefs, Inc.)

Figure 13–K. Hobart Double Tank Dishmachine.
In this flight kitchen, this machine is used only for washing glasses.
(Courtesy Sky Chefs, Inc.)

miscellaneous items are washed in the "Carrier Washer." (See Figure 13-L.)

Depending on size and volume at least three employees are required for each shift to break down and sort incoming soiled equipment.

A runner is assigned to move clean equipment to various departments for packing and use on outbound flights.

Large operations normally require one man per shift for pot washing. This employee may be assigned to the dishwashing department or the food department, depending on the size of the kitchen and the physical location of the pot washing area. Even though an automatic pot and pan washing machine is used, (See Figure 13-M.), burned food or stubborn stains require installation of large soaking sinks.

Smaller establishments using a single tank machine may have one or more dishroom employees.

When planning dishwashing areas for new food operations, the following points should be considered:

1. Type of dishes and utensils to be washed.
2. Anticipated work load: Estimate the maximum number of soiled dishes, eating utensils and cooking equipment that will require washing on the busiest days.
3. Proximity of dishwashing area to waitresses, kitchen personnel, and/or incoming equipment: The ideal situation, of course, is to locate dishwashing areas where they are convenient to all personnel. Since it is rarely possible to develop ideal situations, it may be necessary to sacrifice one group for another. In a large restaurant this usually means locating the dishroom where it will be most convenient to the waitresses. In a flight kitchen the most practical location is near the unloading dock.
4. Noise factor to customers: Because dishrooms are not noted for quietness, some thought must be given to customer comfort. Breaking dishes, dishmachine operating noises, etc. are hardly conducive to pleasurable dining.
5. Waste removal: Dishrooms obviously generate a large amount of trash and waste. This factor must be considered prior to building, in order to avoid removing trash and garbage within customer view, through clean food preparation areas, etc.

Figure 13–L. This machine has an extra long belt to handle airline meal tray and entree carriers, plus a variety of miscellaneous items.
(Courtesy Sky Chefs, Inc.)

Figure 13–M. Pot and Pan Washer.
(Courtesy Sky Chefs, Inc.)

LESSON 13 - BRAINTEASER

When you are certain you understand the material in this lesson, answer the questions below. After you have completed the brainteaser, check your answers in the text. Use the following scale to evaluate your comprehension of this lesson:

10 Correct---Outstanding
9 Correct---Excellent
8 Correct---Good
7 Correct---Fair
6 or Under
Correct---Restudy the Lesson

1) Each violation on the "Inspection Report-Food Service Establishments" (PHS-4006) results in:

A. 1 to 4 demerit points
B. 1 to 5 demerit points
C. 1 to 6 demerit points
D. 1 to 7 demerit points
E. 1 to 8 demerit points

2) A "provisional" status exists if a food service establishment receives ________ to ______ demerits.

3) A "use prohibited" status is placed on any food service operation receiving how many demerits?

A. 21 or more
B. 31 or more
C. 41 or more
D. 51 or more
E. 61 or more

4) Regardless of the total demerit score, any item of _______ demerit points must be corrected within a period of time not to exceed 10 days.

5) List at least four (4) items that must be cleaned after each use:

A.
B.
C.
D.

6) Answer the following questions about the pH factor?

A. The scale runs from ___________ to ______________, with _____________ equaling neutrality.

B. Numbers less than __________ represent increasing_________________.

C. Numbers greater than________ indicate increasing__________________.

7) USPH rules require a ____________compartment sink for handwashing eating and drinking utensils.

8) Wash water temperature in <u>multiple</u> tank machines shall be at least:

A. 140°F.
B. 150°F.
C. 160°F.
D. 170°F.
E. 180°F.

9) When using only hot water to sanitize equipment, the final machine rinse must be clean, fresh water with a temperature of not less than:

A. 140°F.
B. 150°F.
C. 160°F.
D. 170°F.
E. 180°F.

10) The most common chemical that builds up on the inside of pipes, reducing water pressure and flow, is called____________________________.

glossary

Aging: A term applied to meat held at a temperature of 34 to 36 degrees F. to improve its tenderness.

Agneau: (an-yo') Lamb.

a la: (ah-lah) According to the style of a standard in vogue such as: a la Francaise or according to the French way.

a la Bourgeoise: (ah-lah-boor-jwahz') Family style. See Bourgeoise.

a la Broche: (ah-lah-brosh') Cooked on a skewer. See Brochette.

a la Carte: (ah-lah-cart') Foods prepared to order: each dish priced separately.

a la King: Foods served in a white cream sauce which contains mushrooms, green peppers and often pimientos.

a la Mode: (ah-lah-mod') Usually refers to ice cream on top of pie, but may be other dishes served in a special way. See Beef a la Mode.

a la Provencale: (ah-lah-pro-vahn-sal') Dishes with garlic and olive oil. See Provencale.

a la Russe: The Russian way.

Allemande Sauce: (Ahi-mahnd) White, reduced veloute, egg yolks.

Allumette Potatoes: (all-eu-met') Cut like matches, similar to Shoestring Potatoes and Pommes Paille.

Andalouse, a l': (ahn-dah-loose') Consommé and Potage: Tomatoes and rice. Garnish: Tomatoes, rice, eggplant, red peppers. Sauce: Mayonnaise with tomatoes and red peppers. Spanish onions, cucumbers, tomatoes, eggs, oil-vinegar.

Anglaise: (ahn-glayz') In English style.

Appareil: Mixture of different elements for preparation for a dish.

Appetizer: A small portion of food or drink designed to stimulate the appetite.

Argenteuil, a la': (ahr-zhahn-toy') Consommé: With asparagus. Poached or scrambled eggs with asparagus tips. Garnish: Asparagus points with Hollandaise.

Aspic: (as'pick). (English) Clear meat or poultry jelly.

au Gratin: (ah-grah-tan') Food covered with a sauce, sprinkled with crumbs and baked.

au Jus (oh-zhue') Served with natural juices or gravy.

au Lait: (oh-lay') with milk.

au Naturel: (oh-nah-tue-rel') Plainly cooked. See Nature.

aux Croutons: Bread cut in small dices and fried in butter. (See Croutons.)

Avocado, also Avocat: Alligator pear. Brownish or purple berry filled with pulp-like marrow, from Southern California, tropical America and West Indies.

Bain Marie: Double boiler or steam table.

Baking: To cook by dry heat, usually in an oven.

Barbecue: To broil over hot coals. Also to cook foods in a barbecue sauce.

Bar le duc: (bahr-le-duek') Famous jam made of red currants.

Bard: To wrap poultry, game or fish with thin slices of fat or salt pork.

Baste: To moisten a food product with stock, drippings, or fat while cooking.

Barley Pearl: Polished barley.

Batter: Mixture of flour and liquid of a consistency that can be stirred.

Bean Sprouts: Mung beans from China. Sprouts are tiny and green when used.

Bearnaise: (bay-ahr-nayz) Name of sauce: Contains egg yolks, butter, tarragon, and seasoning.

Beating: Regular lifting motion to bring mixture to smooth texture.

Bechamel: (bay-shah-mel') A rich cream sauce or white sauce.

Beef a la Stroganoff: Tenderloin of beef sautéed in sauces and sour cream.

Beef, Dried: Soaked in brine and then smoked and dried.

Beurre: (ber) Butter.

Beurre noir: (ber-nahr') Browned butter.

Bind: To cause to cohere, unite, or hold together, such as bind a croquette mixture.

Bisque: (bisk) Thick soup, usually of shellfish.

Bisque Ice Cream: High butter-fat content ice cream with dried macaroons or sponge cake crumbs.

Blanc: (blahn) White.

Blanch: To pour boiling water over an item, drain and rinse with cold water. Used to whiten or remove skins of almonds.

Blanquette d'Agneau: (blahn-ket-dahn-yo') Stewed lamb with white sauce. Usually shoulder and breast.

Blending: Thoroughly mixing two or more ingredients.

Blue: Cheese like Roquefort; but made from cow's milk.

Blinis: Russian pancakes. Usually served with caviar.

Boeuf: (buff) Beef.

Boil: To cook submerged in a liquid at 212° F. (at sea level).

Boiled Dressing: Cooked dressing for salads.

Bonne Femme, a la: (bon-fem') Consommé with potage: With potatoes, leeks, carrots, onions. Fish: With onions, shallots, mushrooms.

Bordure: (bohr-dur') With a border, used in garnishing.

Borscht: (bohrsht) Russian: A Russian or Polish soup made with beets or duck. Sour cream is often added.

Bouchee: (boo-shay') Small meat pattie or pastry shell filled with meat, poultry or lobster.

Bouillabaisse: (boo-yah-bays') Fish soup.

Bouquet garni: (boo-kay-garnee') A bouquet of fresh herbs tied together, immersed in a liquid, and removed before the dish is served.

Bouquetiere, a la: (boo-k-tyair') With a variety of vegetables in season.

Bourgeoise: (boor-jwahz') Plain, family style.

Bourgignonne: (boor-guee-nyohng) Pertaining to Burgundy.

Braise: Brown thoroughly on all sides and finish cooking in a small amount of liquid.

Brazier: Heavy duty stewing pan with tightly fitting cover.

Breading: To roll in bread crumbs or other breading agent before cooking.

Brine: Liquid of salt and vinegar for pickling.

Brioche: (bree-osh') French, a sweet dough roll of French origin.

Broccoli: (bro'-ko-lee) Italian cabbage, resembling green cauliflower.

Broche: Metal skewer. (See brochette).

Brochette: (bro-shet'L Meat broiled and served on a skewer. A metal pin to hold meat in place. See a la Broche.

Broil: To cook food by exposing it directly to heat.

Brunoise: (brun-wahz) Cut in fine dice.

Buffet: Display of ready to eat foods. Often self service from table of assorted foods.

Café: (kah-fay) Coffee.

Calories: Fuel value in food.

Calavo: Trade name for California Avocados.

Canadian Bacon: Trimmed, pressed, smoked loin of pork. Lean.

Candying: Cooking fruit in heavy syrup until transparent. Then drain and dry.

Canape: (kah-nay-pay') An appetizer. Always prepared on a base, such as bread, toast or crackers.

Canard: (kah-nahr) Duck.

Cannelon: (kan-ay-lohn) Meat stuffed, rolled up and roasted or braised.

Capon: (kah-pohn') Castrated poultry noted for its tenderness and delicate flavor.

Cardinal Sauce: Bechamel with shrimp or lobster roe and lemon juice.

Casaba Melon: Lemon yellow skin, white meat, large oval shape, season September to April.

Caviar: (ka-vee-are') Eggs or roe of fish, usually sturgeon. Seasoned.

Cayenne Pepper: Hot seasoning. Red.

Celestine Consommé: (say-less-teen) Consommé with sliced unsweetened pancakes.

Cepes: (sep) Species of mushrooms.

Champignons: (shahm-pee-neeon') Mushrooms.

Chantilly Cream: (shahn-tee-yee') Vanilla whipped cream.

Chantilly Sauce: (shahn-tee-yee') Hot hollandaise with whipped cream.

Chasseur: (shah-seur') Hunter style.

Chateaubriand: (shah-toh-bree-ahn') Thick tenderloin Steak. Sauce: Brown sauce. Fat, lemon juice, parsley, Spanish Sauce.

Chaud: (show) Hot.

Chaud-Froids: (show-fro-ah') Decorated poultry jelly.

Cheese, Blue: Looks same as Roquefort but made of cow's milk instead of sheep's milk.

Chef: (shef) Chief of kitchen.

Chemise: Potatoes boiled with their skins on.

Chiffonade: (shee-fohn-ahd') French: shredded vegetables or meats used on soups or salads, or as garnishings. Also dressing: Shredded and chopped vegetables in French Dressing base.

China Cap: A cone shaped strainer or sieve.

Chop: Cut into small pieces.

Cisler: To cut, to make an incision in the skin of fish, so that it will not crack during cooking.

Cloche, sous: Under bell, usually glass.

Cobbler: (Drink) Liquor, sugar, sliced fruit and mint. Fruit dessert.

Cocotte: Small earthen cooking ware.

Coddling: Cooking below boiling point.

Colbert Sauce: Shallots, butter, claret, brown gravy, butter, lemon.

Compote: (kom-pot') A stew or combination of fruit, sometimes applied to a stew of birds.

Concasser: To chop roughly.

Condiments: Seasonings.

Consommé: (kan-so-may') A strong, clear, sparkling soup.

Coppel: Metal cooking unit, stationary, heated with steam jacket.

Court Bouillon: A preparation of vinegar or wine, water and savory herbs in which fish is cooked.

Cover Charge: Fixed fee for table service independent of the charge for food.

Cream Sauce; A white sauce originally made with cream.

Crepe: (krayp) Pancakes (French).

Crepes Suzette: Thin french pancake served with rich brandy sauce.

Cresson: (kray-sohn) Watercress.

Croquette: (kro-ket) A food product or combination of food products, usually breaded and deep fried.

Croutons: (kroo-tohn') Small pieces of fried or toasted bread used in soups.

Cuisine: (kwee-seen') Art of cookery, cookery, kitchen.

Cumberland Sauce: Orange and lemon peel and juice, currant jelly, port wine.

Curry: East Indian dish. Was originally a stew. Now referred to with mixing of pungent curry seasoning.

Custard: A baked or cooked mixture consisting mainly of eggs and milk.

Dejeuner: (day'zhoe'nay). or Dejeuner a la Fourchette—Lunch—mid-day meal. Petite Dejeuner—breakfast.

Demi: (de-mee) Half.

Diced: Cut in small squares.

Dindonneau: (dan-doh-noh) Young turkey.

Dough: A mixture of various ingredients that are stiff enough to be handled.

Drawn butter: Melted butter.

Dredging: Coating with dry ingredients (as flour).

Drippings: The fat and juice which drops from roasting meat.

Dry: As applied to a beverage, meaning a low percentage of sugar.

Duchessé Potatoes: Mashed with eggs and squeezed through a pastry tube.

Dugleré a la: (du'-glay-ray). With onions, shallots and tomatoes.

Dusting: Sprinkling with flour or sugar.

Ecossaise: Scottish style.

Eggplant: Large purple pear-shaped vegetable.

Eggs a la Goldenrod: White sauce with chopped whites of eggs poured over toast. Hard cooked yolks pressed through sieve and sprinkled on top.

Eggs Benedict: (bay-nay-dick'). Poached and served with ham or tongue with hollandaise sauce on toast or a muffin.

Emincé: (ay-man-say') Cut fine.

Emincé of Beef: (ay-man-say') Thin slices of meat.

en Brochette: (ahn-broh-shet). On a skewer. See a la Broche.

en Casserole: (ahn-kahs-rol'). Food served in the same dish in which it was baked.

Enchiladas: Mexican. Tortillas covered with sauce of grated cheese, spices, etc.

en Chemise: With their skins. Usually potatoes.

en Coquille: (ahn-koh-keell') In the shell.

Entree: The main dish, or dishes of a meal.

Epigramme: (ay-pee-gram') Boned breast of lamb.

Escoffier: (ays'koh-fee-ay). Trade name for bottled sauce. Also name of famous French chef.

Farce: (fahrs) Stuffing.

Farci: Stuffed.

Farina: The coarsely ground inner portion of hard wheat.

Farinaceous: Consisting of or made of meal or flour.

Fermiere, a la: (fair-mee-air') with discs of carrots, turnips, onions, potatoes, celery, cabbage.

Filet: (fee-lay) May be tenderloin of beef, mutton, veal or pork without the bone. Boned fish are also called filets.

Finnan Haddie: Smoked haddock.

Florentine, a la: (floor-ahn-teen). With spinach.

Foie gras: Foie d'ole: (fwah grah) (fwah dwah). Fatted goose liver.

Fold In: Combining a mixture of liquid and solid ingredients gently, by lifting the liquid from the bottom and through the rest of the mixture.

Fondant: A sugar and water mixture cooked to the soft ball stage (235° F.), then cooled and kneaded.

Fondantes Potatoes: Oval shaped, partially cooked by boiling, reshaped in towel and finished in oven.

Fondue: (fohn-du') Cheese dish. See Welsh Rabbit.

Forcemeat: Chopped meats and seasoning used for stuffing.

French Lamb Chops: Made by scraping the meat and fat from the bones of rib chops a little distance from the end. Broiled over high heat.

Fritter: Vegetable, fruit, or other food item mixed in a batter and deep fat fried.

Frizzling: Cooking in small amount of fat until crisp.

Froid: (frwa) Cold.

Fromage: (froh-mahzh') Cheese.

Frosting: A cooked or uncooked mixture of any type of sugar. Used to cover and/or decorate cakes and other desserts.

Fry: To cook in fat.

Garbanzo: (gar-ban-tho) Chick peas. Spanish national dish.

Garde Manger: (guard-mon-zhay). Cold meat dept. or person in charge of it.

Garnish: To embellish foods; to decorate. Also a noun, referring to food stuff being used to garnish.

Garniture. (gar-nee-tur). French for garnish.

Gastric: (gas-treek'). Cooking term for a mixture of white wine or vinegar, crushed pepper, shallots and spices.

Gateau: (gah-toh). Cake

Gaufres: (goh-fr) Wafers.

Gaufrette Potatoes: (goh-fret). French fried potatoes in waffle form.

Gefulte Fish: Jewish favorite. Stuffed fish. Today, in dumpling form.

Gelatin: Purified protein from animal bones and tissues.

Gherkins: Small cucumbers (a few days old). Usually pickled.

Giblets: Liver, heart and trimmings from poultry.

Glaze: A semi-transparent or glossy coating. To cover with same.

Gnocchi: Light dumplings.

Gourmet: (goor-may) Connoisseur of food and drinks.

Grate: To reduce anything into small pieces by rubbing against a rough perforated object called a "grater"

Gratin, au (grah-tan) Sprinkled with cheese or buttered crumbs and baked brown.

Gruyere (grue-yair'). Swiss type of cheese made in France and in Switzerland.

Guava: Tropical fruit: Apple or pear shaped, acid sweet flavor.

Gumbo: (Soup) Chicken, onions, okra, green peppers and tomatoes.

Harché: (hah-shay). Hashed; minced.

Haricots Verts: (ah-ree-coh-vair') Small green string beans.

Hasenpfeffer: German rabbit stew.

Heifer: A young female cow that has not had a calf.

Herb Bouquet: Mixed herbs used for seasoning.

Hollandaise: A sauce made of eggs, butter, and other ingredients. Served hot with, or over, vegetables and other foods.

Hongroise, a la (ohn-grwahs') Prepared in Hungarian way. Onions, sour cream and paprika. Garnish: With red and green peppers, cabbage and leeks.

Hors d'oeuvres: (ohr-doe'vr). Small relishes or appetizers. Served as first course of the meal. See Antipasto, Assiette Parisienne.

Hush Puppies: Southern deep fat fried dish of corn meal, baking powder, milk, onion, seasoning.

Hydrogenated Fat: Fat treated with hydrogen to maintain stable consistency.

Indian Pudding: Slow baked dessert of corn meal, milk, brown sugar, eggs, raisins and seasoning.

Infusion: Liquid obtained from steeping a food.

Italian Minestrone: (mee-nay-stroh-nay). Vegetable soup with a macaroni product and cheese.

Johnny Cake: Bread from yellow corn meal, eggs, milk.

Julienne: (zhu-lee-en'). Potatoes: cut in long slices thinner than for French fries and served very crisp. Soup: Clear soup with chopped vegetables. Vegetables: Cut in long slices.

Junket: Brand name of dessert of flavored curdled milk and rennet.

Jus: (zhue). Usually refers to drippings from meat. See au Jus.

Karo: Corn syrup, light or dark.

Kasha: Buckwheat groats.

Kippered Herring: Dried or smoked herring.

Kitchen Bouquet: Trade name for bottled gravy coloring and flavoring.

Kosher: (meat) Meat sold within 48 hours after butchering in accordance with prescribed Hebrew religious laws. Or, style of cooking with dietary restrictions.

Kumquats: Gold-orange color; small oval citrus fruit.

Lait: (lay) Milk

Lamb Fries: Lamb testicles.

Langouste: (lahn'goost). Crawfish.

Larding: Strips of salt pork inserted into meat.

Leaven: To add a leavening agent such as baking powder, in order to cause a baked food item to rise.

Leek: Small onion-like plant. Seasoning.

Legumes: (lay-guem). Vegetables. Also refers to such dried foods as beans, peas and lentils.

Lentil: Flat seed somewhat like peas. Used for soups and garnishes.

Lichi Nut: Chinese. Small hard shell dried nut.

Lyonnaise Potatoes: Sautéed with slices of onions.

Mace (seasoning): Outer shell of nutmeg.

Macedoine: (mah-say-dwan) Mixture usually of fruit or vegetables. Macedoine de fruits: Fruit salad.

Madrilene Soup: (mah-dree-lain') Clear consommé with tomato, highly seasoned, served jellied or hot.

Maggi: Brand name for Swiss liquid seasoning.

Maitre d'Hotel: (mai-tre-doh-tel') Head of catering department; head of food service.

Maitre d'Hotel, a la: (mai-tre-doh-tel') Sauce: Yellow sauce. Butter Sauce, lemon juice parsley, salt, pepper. Butter: Mixture of lemon juice, butter, parsley, salt, pepper.

Manhattan Clam Chowder: With tomatoes

Maraschino: (mah-rahs-kee'nah). Italian cherry cordial. Also cherries.

Margeno, a la: Sautéed chicken with mushrooms, tomatoes, olives and olive oil.

Marinade: A mixture (usually of high acid content) in which a food, especially meat, is allowed to stand (or marinate) for flavor and/or tenderizing.

Marrow: Soft tissue from the inside or cavity of bones.

Marsala: Pale golden semi-dry Italian Sherry from Sicily.

Masking: To cover completely (usually with a sauce).

Mate: (mah-tay). South American Paraguay tea.

Matelots: (mah-te-lot). Fish stewed with wine, onions and seasoning.

Melba: Vanilla ice cream, raspberry jelly or sauce and whipped cream served with peach or pear. See Peach Melba.

Melba Toast: Very thin white bread baked in oven until brown.

Menthe, Creme de: (Kraim-de-mahnt'). Peppermint cordial.

Melting: Making liquid by application of heat.

Menu: (men'u) or (may-nu). Bill of fare.

Meringue: (may'rang) Paste made of egg whites and sugar.

Meuniere, a la: (me-nee-air) Fish: Dipped in flour, sautéed in butter, served with brown butter and lemon, sprinkled with parsley.

Mignon Filets: Small tender filets usually from beef tenderloin.

Minced: Chopped fine.

Mincing: Chopping in less regular parts similar to grinding.

Minestrone: Thick Italian vegetable soup.

Mirepoix: (Mere'eh-Pwah) Mixture of onions, carrots, celery.

Mixing: Uniting two or more ingredients.

Mongol Soup: Tomatoes, split peas, Julienne vegetables.

Mortadella: Italian pork and beef sausage.

Mousse: (moose) Frozen dessert of whipped cream, flavoring and sweetening. May also be hot or cold buffet food.

Mouton: (moo-tahn) Mutton

Mozzarella: Soft Italian cheese made of milk, shaped in rounds.

Muffin: A quick bread made from a batter and baked in small individual pans.

Mushroom Sauce: Brown sauce, fat, flour, stock, sliced mushrooms, seasoning.

Navarin: (nah-vah-ran') Stew of mutton with carrots and turnips.

Noir: (nwar). Black

Nouilles: (noo'ee) (German: Nudeln). Noodles: Narrow strips of dried dough, resembling macaroni, used in soups and garnishes.

Oeuf: (uff) Egg. See eggs.

Okra: Vegetable pods. Used in soups, gumbos. Also served as a vegetable.

Ovaltine: Brand name for a flavored malt and milk powder for milk drinks.

Over-Run: Increased volume produced by whipping in air as in ice cream.

Oysters, Blue Points: Name of oysters from certain Atlantic Coast waters.

Pain: (pan) Bread

Pan Broiling: Cooking uncovered in a hot skillet. Fat is poured off in cooking.

Palm Hearts: Hearts of young palms. A canned product.

Panache: (pah-nash') Several kinds of mixed birds, fruits, vegetables, usually with contrasting colors.

Papaya: Tropical fruit, the juice of which yields an enzyme used as a meat tenderizer.

Papillote, Cotelette en: Cutlet cooked in paper.

Paprika: Dried and powdered or ground ripe fruit of various kinds of peppers. Used as seasoning and for color.

Parboiling: Partial boiling.

Pare: To remove the outer skins.

Parisienne Potatoes: Small round scoop. Browned.

Parmentier, a la (parmahn-tee-ay) Soup: Potato Soup.

Parmesan: Hard, sharp cheese grated for soups and toppings.

Parsley: An herb used largely for garnishing.

Pasteurized Milk: Milk held 140 degrees F. for 30 minutes to check fermentation.

Pastry Bag: Cone bag with metal tip at small end. Used to decorate cakes.

Paté: (paht) Paste: Meat paste.

Pauplette (pooh-pee-et'). Stuffed rolled thin slices of meat braised.

Peche: (paish) Peach

Petit: (pe-tee) f. (pe-teet) Small.

Petite Marmite: (pe-teet-mahr-meet'). A strong consommé with beef, chicken and vegetables.

Petit Dejeuner: (pe-tee'-day-shoe-nay') Breakfast.

Petits Fours: (pe-tee-foor') Small cakes.

Petits Pois: Small green peas.

Picnic Ham: Lower end of hog shoulder.

Piece de Resistance: (pee-es-de-resee-stahns') Main Dish.

Pilau: (pee-loh') Rice boiled with meat, poultry or fish and spices. Also pilaf.

Pimiento: Red sweet Spanish pepper pod.

Piquant: (pee-kahn') (pee-kahnt'). Flavored, highly seasoned.

Pistachio Nuts: Small, pale green. Thin hard shell. Tropical.

Plank: A board made of hard wood. Also to cook and serve on a board or plank, usually with an elaborate garnish of vegetables.

Poaching: Cooking in water that bubbles lightly.

Poisson: (pwah-sohn). Fish.

Poivrade (Sauce): (pwav-rahd'). Pepper sauce.

Polonaise, a la: (poh-loh-nayz). With rasped bread, beurre noir, hashed hard boiled eggs.

Pommes de Terre: (pom-de-tair) Potatoes. Literal translation—apples of the earth.

Popovers: Quick puffed-up hot bread of milk and eggs.

Postum: Cereal coffee substitute.

Potage: (pot-tahzh') Soup—usually thickened.

Pot-au-feu: (pot-oh-fe'). Meat broth with vegetables.

Potiron: (poh-tee-rohn'). Pumpkin.

Potpourri: (pot-poo-ree') Mixture.

Poulet: (poo-lay). Chicken.

Portion Control: Control of size and weight of individual portions.

Poulette Sauce: Allemande with sliced mushrooms and chives or parsley.

Prefabricated: Refers to meat, and associated products trimmed and cut; often to specification of purchaser.

Pullman Bread: Sandwich bread.

Puree: (pu-ray) Pulp or paste of vegetable or fruit. Thick soup.

Quahog: (kwah-hawg). Atlantic Coast round clam.

Quenelles: (kay-nel') Dumplings.

Ragout: (rah'goo) Thick savory stew.

Raisins: (ray-san). Dried grapes.

Ramekins: Food baked in shallow baking china or shallow baking dish itself.

Rasher of Bacon: Side portion of back: 3-4 slices.

Reduce: To reduce volume by cooking or simmering.

Rendering: Freeing fat from connective tissues by heat.

Rice, Brown. Rice with hulls on. Before polishing.

Rissole': (ree-soh-lay') Browned.

Rissole' Potatoes: (Pommes rissolees). Cut into shape of large nut (with scoop) and browned.

Riz: (ree) Rice

Roasting: Cooking in the oven and very little moisture.

Robert Sauce: (sauce ro-bair') Brown sauce. Onions, flour, stock, lemon juice, French mustard, white wine.

Roe: Mass of fish eggs. Roe-corn: single fish egg.

Romaine: (ro-main'). Long, narrow crisp-leaved Roman lettuce, inner leaves are light in color.

Roti: (ro-tee) Roast

Rouge: (roozh). Red

Roulade: Rolled (Meat)

Roux: (roo) Equal parts of fat and flour used to thicken sauces and gravies.

Rusks: Light bread or biscuit, sometimes twice baked.

Russian Dressing: Mayonnaise, lemon juice, chili sauce and Worcestershire sauce and chopped pimientos.

Sabayon: (sah-bah-yohn). Dessert. Egg dish served in glasses. Egg yolks, vanilla, sugar, sherry, white wines.

Saffron: Seasoning. Deep orange dried part of purple crocus. To color foods.

Sage: Leaves of an herb. For seasoning.

Salamander: A broiler-like stove with heat from above and a shelf below. Open front so that dishes can be put on lower shelf for glazing.

Salami: (sah-lah'-mee). Sausage of pork, beef, red wine, highly seasoned.

Salmagundi: Mixture, usually refers to meat, fish, onions and seasoning.

Saute: To fry in a small amount of fat.

Scald: To heat liquid just below the boiling point.

Score: To cut lines about 1/8 in. to 1/4 in. deep. Usually done on meat to give a nice appearance. Also applied to marking of cakes for cutting.

Searing: Browning surface by intense heat.

Sec: (sek) Dry

Semolina: High gluten flour from durum wheat.

Serviette: Napkin.

Shad: Fish of the herring family.

Shallots: Vegetables of the onion family (Eschalotes-pl.)

Shaslik of Lamb: (Brochette of Lamb) Lamb seasoned and broiled on a skewer.

Sherbet: A frozen dessert mixture of sugar, egg white, fruit juice, milk or water.

Shirred Eggs: (Oeufs sur le plat). Baked in cooking china with butter.

Shoestring Potatoes: Like french fried, but cut very thin. (See Allumette, Paille)

Simmering: Slow cooking at just below boiling point.

Sizzling Steak: Steak served on aluminum platter which has been heated so that the steak and juices sizzle.

Skewering: To fasten meat or poultry on long pin during cooking.

Smorgasbord: (smur-goes-board). Swedish tidbits or appetizers usually arranged on large table.

Smother: To cook in covered kettle until tender.

Soiree: Evening party.

Sole: (sohl) Flat white fish, common to Europe. Also flat fish from the Pacific coast of the United States.

Sommeller: (soh-meh-lyay') Wine waiter.

Souffle: (soo-flay) Light puffed baked custard.

Souffle Potatoes: (soo-flay) Potato slices puffed up like little pillows.

Sous Cloche: Under bell, usually glass.

Soy Sauce: Made from soy beans. Brown. For flavoring Chinese foods.

Spanish Rice: With onions, tomatoes, green peppers.

Sparkling Burgundy: Bright ruby sparkling wine.

Spit: A pointed rod to hold meat or poultry for roasting in front of fire.

Split: 6 oz. size bottle.

Spumoni: (spoo-mah-nee). Fancy Italian ice cream.

Squab: Young pigeon.

Steaming: Cooking in steam in enclosed vessal.

Steeping: To soak in liquid below boiling point to extract flavor or color.

Steer: A young castrated beef animal.

Sterilizing: Destroying bacteria and microorganisms by boiling water, heat or steam.

Stew: Cooking in water on top of stove.

Stirring: Mixing food in circular motion.

Stock. The liquid in which meat, poultry, fish or vegetables have been cooked.

Sub Gum (Chinese): Base of many Chinese dishes. Bamboo shoots, water chestnuts, french mushrooms.

Suet: Hard fat in beef, veal, mutton and lamb.

Sweetbreads: Thymus gland of calf or lamb.

Swiss Chard: Green tender leaf vegetable prepared like spinach.

Tabasco: Brand name for liquid hot red pepper sauce.

Table d'Hote: (tahbl-dhot') Fixed price meal.

Tartare Steak: Raw hamburger steak heavily seasoned.

Suisse, a la: (sweess) Swiss style.

Tasse: (tahss). Cup

Tea, Black: India, Java, Ceylon—Leaves are fermented.

Tea, Green: Mostly from Japan, unfermented.

Tea, Oolong: Formosa—Semi-fermented.

Tea, Orange Pekoe: Pekoe refers to downy appearance of underside and ends of leaf buds.

Terrine: (tay-reen') Forcemeat and stuffing molded in earthenware jar. Served cold.

Tete: (tait). Head.

Thyme: An herb for flavoring.

Timbale: (tan-bahl') Baked mold.

Tortillas: Mexican flapjack or griddle cake made from corn.

Tripe: Beef stomach.

Truffles: Fungus like mushrooms grown underground; a seasoning and garnish.

Try Out: To cook fat until oil is out (as in making lard). Render.

Turkish Coffee: (Cafe turque). Strong, sweet coffee, made of equal amounts of pulverized coffee and sugar.

Tutti Frutti: (too-tee'-froo-tee'). Mixture of fruit as in ice cream.

Veal Birds: Thin slice of veal rolled around seasoned stuffing. May be stewed or cooked in covered casserole.

Vermicelli: Long thin threads of pasta. Like spaghetti.

Vert: (vair) (vairt). Green

Viande: (vee-ahnd') Meat.

Vin: (van). Wine

Vol-au-vent: (vahl-oh-vahn'). Case made of puff pastry in which meat or poultry is served, usually covered with a crust lid.

Vitamins: Growth producing, health protective elements of food.

Waldorf Salad: Celery, apples, nuts, whipped cream and mayonnaise.

Washington Pie: Cake with raspberry or loganberry jam between layers.

Waterless Cooker: Cooking utensils of heavy metal in which foods are cooked in their own juices.

Welsh Rabbit: Cooked cheese, butter, beer, eggs flavored with Worcestershire sauce and spices. (French—Fondue a l'Anglaise).

Whipping: Rapid beating to increase volume of mixing air.

Wild Rice: Northern watergrass seed—served with game, not a true rice.

Wan Tan: Stuffed noodle paste with Chinese soup. Chicken or pork.

Yams: Much like sweet potatoes. From the Southern United States and West Indies.

Yorkshire Pudding: Paste of flour, milk and salt, baked and served with roast beef.

Zucchini: (tsoo-kee-nee). Italian squash.

Zwieback: (tsvee-bahk). Hard crispy German biscuit. Twice toasted.

TABLE OF APPROXIMATE WEIGHTS AND MEASURES OF COMMON FOODS

Item	1 Tablespoon	1 Cup (Standard)	1 Pint		1 Quart	
	Ounces	Ounces	Lb.	Oz.	Lb.	Oz.
Allspice	¼	4				
Apples, fresh diced					1	
Applesauce		8	1			
Bacon, diced, raw			1			
Bacon, diced, cooked					1	8
Baking Powder	½	6		12	1	8
Baking Soda	½	6	1		2	
Barley, pearl		8	1		2	
Bread Crumbs, dry		4		8	1	
Bread Crumbs, moist		2		4		8
Butter		8	1		2	
Cabbage, shredded or chopped						12
Carrots, diced, raw					1	3
Celery, chopped, raw				8	1	
Celery Seed	⅙	2⅔				
Cheese, American, ground		5		10	1	4
Cheese, shredded		4		8		
Cheese, cottage		8	1			
Chocolate, grated	¼	4		8	1	
Chocolate, melted		8	1		2	
Cinnamon, ground	¼	3½				
Cloves, ground	¼	4				
Cloves, whole	⅙	2⅔				
Cocoa	¼	3½		6½		
Coconut, shredded		2¾		5½		
Coconut, grated		2½		5		
Cornflakes						4
Cornmeal				10½	1	5
Cornstarch	⅓	5⅓			1	5
Cracker Crumbs						10½
Cranberries, raw				8	1	
Currants, dried		5⅓			1	5
Curry Powder	¼	3½				
Egg, whites (approx.)		8	1		2	
Eggs, whole (without shells)		8	1		2	
Egg, yolks		8	1		2	
Extracts (variable)	½					
Farina		6¼		12½	1	9
Flour, bread (sifted)		4¼		8½	1	1
Flour, cake (sifted)		3⅞		7¾		15½
Gelatin, flavored		5¾		11½	1	6
Gelatin, unflavored		5½		11	1	5
Ginger	½	3¾				

TABLE OF APPROXIMATE WEIGHTS AND MEASURES OF COMMON FOODS

Item	1 Tablespoon	1 Cup (Standard)	1 Pint		1 Quart	
	Ounces	Ounces	Lb.	Oz.	Lb.	Oz.
Hominy Grits		6		12	1	8
Honey		11	1	6	2	12
Legumes:						
Beans, kidney, dry				12½	1	9
Beans, lima, dry				13	1	10
Beans, white, dry				14	1	12
Lettuce, broken or shredded						8
Mace	¼					
Mayonnaise		8	1		2	
Milk, liquid, whole		8½	1	1	2	2
Molasses		12	1	8	3	
Mustard, ground	¼	3¼				
Nuts, ground		4¼		9½	1	3
Nuts, pieces		4		8	1	
Nutmeg, ground	¼	4¼				
Oats, rolled		3		6		12
Oils, cooking or salad		8		16	2	
Onions, dehydrated, flakes		2½		5		10
Onions, chopped		4		8	1	
Paprika	¼	4				
Parsley, chopped		3		6		
Peanut Butter		9	1	2	2	4
Pepper, ground	¼					
Peppers, green, chopped		4		8	1	
Pimientos, drained, chopped		7		14		
Potatoes, cooked, diced (approx.)				12½	1	9
Prunes, dry		5¼		10½	1	5
Raisins, seedless		5½		11	1	6
Rice, raw		8	1		2	
Sage	⅛					
Salt	½	8				
Seasoning, poultry	¼					
Sugar:						
Brown (firmly packed)		7		14	1	12
Confectioners		4¾				
Granulated		8	1		2	
Syrup, corn		11	1	6	2	12
Tapioca, granules		6¼		12½	1	9
Tapioca, pearl		5¼		10½	1	6
Tea		2¾		5½		
Vinegar		8¼	1	½	2	1
Water		8	1		2	

MEAT AND POULTRY TIME TABLES

TIMETABLE FOR ROASTING VEAL

Cut	Approx. weight of single roast (pounds)	Oven temper-ature	Interior temper-ature of roast when removed from oven	Minutes per pound based on one roast	Approx. total time
Leg	16	300°F.	170°F.	22	6 hrs.
Leg	23	300°F.	170°F.	18 to 20	7 to 7½ hrs.
Loin	4½ to 5	300°F.	170°F.	30 to 35	2½ to 3 hrs.
Rack (4 to 6 ribs)	2½ to 3	300°F.	170°F.	30 to 35	1½ hrs.
Shoulder	7	300°F.	170°F.	25	3 hrs.
Shoulder	12 to 13	300°F.	170°F.	25	5 to 5½ hrs.
Rolled shoulder	5	300°F.		40 to 45	3½ to 4 hrs.

TIMETABLE FOR ROASTING CURED PORK*

	Approx. weight of single roast (pounds)	Oven temper-ature	Interior temper-ature when removed from oven	Minutes per pound based on one roast	Approxi-mate total time
Whole ham	10 to 14	300°F.	160°F.	15 to 18	3 to 3½ hours
Shoulder butt	2 to 4	300°F.	170°F.	30 to 35	1 to 2 hours
Picnic	3 to 10	300°F.	170°F.	30 to 35	2 to 5 hours
Canadian style bacon (casing on)	7	350°F.	160°F.	10 to 12	1 to 1½ hours

TIMETABLE FOR COOKING FRESH ROAST PORK*

Cut	Approx. weight of single roast (pounds)	Oven temper-ature	Interior temper-ature of roast when removed from oven	Minutes per pound based on one roast	Approxi-mate total time
Loin (bone in)	11 to 15	350°F.	185°F.	15 to 18	3 to 3½ hours
Rolled loin (two halves tied together)		350°F.	185°F.		4 hours
Half loin (bone in)		350°F.	185°F.		4½ hours
Center Cut loin	3 to 4	350°F.	185°F.	35 to 40	2 to 2½ hours
End cut loin	3 to 4	350°F.	185°F.	45 to 50	2½ to 3 hours
Shoulder	12 to 14	350°F.	185°F.	30 to 35	6½ hours
Cushion shoulder (with stuffing)	4 to 6	350°F.	185°F.	35 to 40	3 to 3½ hours
Rolled shoulder	4 to 6	350°F.	185°F.	35 to 40	3 to 3½ hours
Boston butt	4 to 6	350°F.	185°F.	45 to 50	3½ to 4½ hours
Ham (leg)	10 to 12	350°F.	185°F.	30 to 35	6 hours
Ham (leg)	15	350°F.	185°F.	30	8 hours
Ham (leg) boned, split, and tied in two rolls	10	350°F.	185°F.	20 to 25	4 to 5 hours

*Courtesy of the National Live Stock and Meat Board

TURKEY—Stuffed ready-to-cook weight**

Ready to Cook Weight Pounds	Oven Temperature	Total Roasting Time—Approximate Hours—Stuffed Bird	Internal Temperature
Whole Birds			
4 to 6	325°F.	3 to 3¾	190—195°F.
6 to 8	325°F.	3¾ to 4½	190—195°F.
8 to 10	325°F.	4 to 4½	190—195°F.
10 to 12	325°F.	4½ to 5	190—195°F.
12 to 14	325°F.	5 to 5¼	190—195°F.
14 to 16	325°F.	5¼ to 6	190—195°F.
16 to 18	325°F.	6 to 6½	190—195°F.
18 to 20	325°F.	6½ to 7½	190—195°F.
20 to 24	325°F.	7½ to 9	190—195°F.
Half and Quarter Turkey			
3½ to 5	325°F.	3 to 3½	190—195°F.
5 to 8	325°F.	3½ to 4	190—195°F.
8 to 12	325°F.	4 to 5	190—195°F.

It is advisable to plan work schedules so that turkeys are out of the oven 20 to 30 minutes before serving time. This gives the meat a chance to absorb the juices. It will carve more easily.

CHICKEN**

Ready to cook Weight	Oven Temperature	Approx. Time Stuffed Bird	Approx. Time Unstuffed Bird
1½ to 2½ lb.	325°F.	1¼ to 1¾ hr.	1 to 1¾ hr.
2½ to 3½ lb.	325°F.	2 to 3 hr.	1¾ to 2¾ hr.
3½ to 4¾ lb.	325°F.	3 to 3½ hr.	2¾ to 2½ hr.
4¾ to 6 lb.	325°F.	3½ to 4 hr.	3¼ to 3¾ hr.

DUCK**

2½ to 3 lb.	325°F.	1¾ to 2 hr.	1½ to 1¾ hr.
3 to 3½ lb.	325°F.	2 to 2½ hr.	1¾ to 2¼ hr.
3½ to 4 lb.	325°F.	2½ to 3 hr.	2¼ to 2¾ hr.

GOOSE**

Ready to cook Weight	Oven Temperature	Approx. Time Stuffed Bird	Approx. Time Unstuffed Bird
6 to 8 lb.	325°F.	3 to 3½ hr.	2¾ to 3¼ hr.
8 to 10 lb.	325°F.	3½ to 3¾ hr.	3¼ to 3½ hr.
10 to 12 lb.	325°F.	3¾ to 4¼ hr.	3½ to 4 hr.

Internal Temperatures of Large Beef Roasts for Different Degrees of Doneness*

Degree of Doneness	Oven Temperature	Color of Inside Roast	Meat Thermometer Reading When Roast Comes From Oven
Rare	300°F.	Bright Pink	120° to 125°F.
Medium	300°F.	Pinkish Brown	135° to 145°F.
Well Done	300°F.	Greyish or Light Brown	150° to 160°F.

The temperatures at which color changes takes place in beef as it cooks are considerably higher than the temperatures above indicate; however, large roasts continue cooking for some time after they are removed from the oven. Therefore, to prevent overcooking, roasts should be removed from the oven when the meat thermometer shows several degrees lower than the temperature at which the actual color change takes place.

Timetable for Roasting Beef*

Cut	Approx. wt. of single roast lb.	Oven temper-ature	Interior temp. of roast removed from oven	Minutes per lb. based on one roast	Approx. total time
Standing rib (7 rib)	23	300° F.	125°F. (rare)	11	4 hr.
			140°F. (medium)	12	4½ hr.
			150°F. (well)	13	5 hr.
Rolled Rib (7 rib)	17	300° F.	150°F. (well)	24	6 hr.
Chuck rib	5 to 8	300° F.	150°F. to 170°F.	25 to 30	2½ to 4 hr.
Rump	5 to 7	300° F.	150°F. to 170°F.	25 to 30	2½ to 3½ hr.

**Courtesy of Poultry and Egg National Board

SPICES AND HERBS*

Name	Description and Source	Uses
Allspice	Dried berry of pimento (not pimiento) tree, grown in West Indies. Flavor resembles blend of cinnamon, nutmeg and cloves, hence the name.	Used whole in pickling, stews, soups, preserved fruit, boiling fish, spicing meat and gravy. The ground is used to season pot roasts, baked goods, apple butter, conserves, catchup, mincemeat.
Anise	Dried seed of plant belonging to celery family. Grows in Southern Europe, Tunis, India, Chile and Mexico.	Sprinkled on coffee cake, sweet rolls, cookies; in sweet pickles; flavoring cough syrups, licorice products, some candies, and in chocolate cake icing.
Balm	A lemon-scented herb. Cultivated in Europe, grows wild in U. S. Also cultivated for bees.	Pleasant seasoning for broiled fish, meats, salads, soups, sauces. Few bruised leaves in cold tea and punch add nice touch.
Basil, Sweet	Belongs to mint family; one of the best known of herbs. Grown in Europe and U. S.	Famous in tomato dishes; bean, mock turtle and potato soups; good in potato, spaghetti, egg dishes, steaks, venison, wild duck.
Bay Leaf	Dried leaves of laurel. Grows in many parts of world. Leaves from shrubs of Eastern Mediterranean considered best.	Famous in pickled beets, stews, gravies, relishes, spiced vinegar or marinade, in meats, as sauerbraten, etc.
Borage	A rough, hairy, blue-flowered European plant, cucumber odor.	Used to season cucumber salad, green beans and green salads.
Burnet	Belongs to the rose family.	Flavoring green salads, vinegar.
Caraway Seed	Dried pungent seeds from herb of the carrot family. Grows in Holland, Russia, Poland.	In rye bread, baked goods, kraut, cabbage, potatoes, roast pork, goose, cheese, cake, cookies.
Capers	Low growing shrub of the Mediterranean. Green flower buds and young berries of shrub are pickled.	In fish, chicken, potato, green salad. Sauces for fish, lamb, mutton, heart, cold tongue, and as garnish.
Cardamon	Belongs to ginger family. Seeds enclosed in small pod. Grows in Malaya, India, Ceylon. Seed and pod may be ground together, or only seeds are ground. Put seeds between folds of muslin and pound to powder.	Seeds in pod used in pickling; ground adds delectable flavor to danish pastry, coffee cake, fancy rolls. Bruised seeds in coffee is delicious.
Cassia Bark	From cassia tree. Grown in Malaya, China. Resembles cinnamon flavor. Called Chinese cinnamon.	For pickling, preserving. Ground in combination with allspice, nutmeg, clove. Used in mincemeat.
Cassia Buds	Dry unripe fruit of cassia tree.	Pleasing, sweet pickling spice.
Cayenne	Smallest, hottest member of red pepper family. Grown in Africa.	Used sparingly to season meats, fish, sauces, egg dishes, mayonnaise.
Celery Salt	Made by grinding celery seed and fine salt together.	In soups, cream sauces, salads, dressings; on roast poultry, meats.
Celery Seed	Pungent seed from plant similar to garden celery. Comes from India.	Croquette mixtures, stews, slaw, potato salad, salad dressing, pickles, cheese, fish, meat spreads.
Chervil	Aromatic herb of carrot family, like parsley but more delicate.	Used fresh or dry in salads, soups, egg and cheese dishes.
Chile Peppers	A fine satiny surfaced red pepper. Grown in Mexico and Southwest U. S.	Used to make chili powders for chili con carne, tamales, pickles, cooking dried beans. Both green and ripe peppers pickled and used to make hot sauces.

Adapted from "Spices—and How to Use Them," published by American Spice Trade Association, New York City.

Name	Description and Source	Uses
Chile Tepines	Very, very hot tiny red peppers. Grown in Mexico.	Used in preparing hot Mexican foods such as meat and egg dishes.
Chili Powder	A blend of chili, red peppers, cumin seed, oregano, garlic powder, salt, etc.	Most widely used in chili con carne. Also used in cocktail sauces, gravies, stews, appetizers.
Chives	Grows indoors or outdoors from clumps of small onion-like bulbs. Has mild, onion-like flavor.	Adds color and flavor to cottage and cream cheese, egg and potato dishes, soup and vegetable garnish.
Cinnamon	Bark of true cinnamon tree that grows in Ceylon. Milder in flavor and thinner than cassia bark.	To flavor pickles, preserves, fruits, hot drinks and as "spoons" for after-dinner coffee. Ground in baked goods, puddings, cake, mincemeat.
Cloves	Nail-shaped dried flower bud of the clove tree. Rich and pungent in flavor.	Whole in baked ham, pickling and beverages. Ground in cakes, cookies, conserves, desserts.
Coriander	Biblical aromatic herb of carrot family. Grows in India, Morocco. Flavor like lemon peel and sage.	Spicy seeds used in curry powder, oriental candy, pickles, meat products and frankfurters.
Cumin or Comino	Native of Palestine, of carrot family. Esteemed by Jews. An Italian and Mexican favorite. Aromatic seeds with bitter warm flavor.	In curry powder; cookies, egg and cheese dishes, sauerkraut, soup, meat, rice, pickles, sausage, chili con carne, hot tamales.
Curry Powder	Blend of spices from India. By varying proportions of 16 spices, different flavored curries are produced. Contains turmeric, ginger, red pepper, cumin, coriander, etc.	Used to make curries of meat, fish, eggs, chicken; curry sauce and flavoring gravies. Adds Oriental touch to rice, veal, shrimp, chicken dishes.
Dill	Herb of carrot family with aromatic leaves, seeds and stem. Grows widely in Europe and U. S.	Fresh leaves in sauces for potatoes, beans, fish, lamb, veal; fresh seed heads make lovely garnish. Dried or green heads and stems in pickles.
Dill 'Seed'	Dried tiny fruit of dill plant. Pleasant pungent flavor.	Good in pickles and to garnish split pea and lentil soup.
Fennel Seed	From plant of carrot family. Aromatic, resembles anise and dill, but has distinct flavor of its own.	Popular with Italians and Scandinavians. For rolls, rye bread, other baked goods, bean and lentil soup.
File	A powder made from dried tender sassafras leaves and other herbs. It thickens and flavors.	Used in Creole cookery in place of okra to thicken gumbos.
Garlic	Potent flavored bulb of onion family. Flavor either very popular or unpopular. Enjoyable if used with discretion.	Used either fresh or dried to enrich flavor of salad dressing, meat, many cooked vegetables.
Ginger	Dried root of subtropical plant grown in China, Japan, India, British West Indies. Warm in flavor.	Cracked root used in pickles, preserves, chutney. Ground root in cake, gingerbread, cookies, puddings, soups, pot roasts.
Juniper Berries	Dried berries of evergreen shrub, with warm, pungent flavor.	Used sparingly for epicure's touch to roast venison, lamb, duck, goose and some stews.
Lovage	European herb of carrot family. Pronounced, rich celery flavor.	Used to flavor tomato juice, soups, stews and gravies.
Mace	Lacy covering on inner shell holding nutmeg. Nutmeg tree grows in East and West Indies. Flavor more delicate than nutmeg.	Ground mace good with chocolate. Used in pound and other yellow cakes, oyster stew, spinach. Whole in pickling, preserving and fish sauces.

Name	Description and Source	Uses
Marjoram	One of best known herbs; belongs to mint family. Grown mostly in Europe. Potent in flavor.	Dried, good pounded into veal, used in meat, potato, spinach, cheese, egg and fish dishes; chicken or green vegetable salads. Season poultry stuffings, sausage, stews, soups. Use sparingly. Often used with other herbs.
Mint	A widely grown herb with a delightfully cool, pungent flavor. Obtainable in dried form.	Popular in sauce or jelly with roast lamb. Used chopped as edible garnish on carrots, beets. Delicious in iced tea and fruit beverages.
Mono Sodium Glutamate (Not a spice)	Neutral salt of glutamic acid which is one of twenty odd amino acids—the building blocks of all proteins. Is extracted from wheat protein and sugar beets.	Used to heighten flavor in meat, poultry, fish and vegetable dishes.
Mustard Seed	Seed of mustard plant grown in England, Europe and the U. S. Prepared mustard is ground seed blended with other spices and vinegar.	Whole seed in pickles, boiled with beets, cabbage, sauerkraut. Smart salad garnish. Ground mustard flavors sauces, gravies. Prepared mustard in salad dressing, on ham, frankfurters, cheese.
Nasturtium	Leaves and seeds of the common nasturtium flower.	Leaves in salads and sandwiches. Seeds used to flavor vinegar.
Nutmeg	Kernel of fruit of the nutmeg tree. Grown in Dutch East Indies and British West Indies. One of the oldest known spices.	Traditional flavoring for baked custard and other desserts. Also used in cream soups, sauces, stews, vegetables such as spinach.
Oregano	Is wild marjoram. Has a pleasing, pungent fragrance.	Widely used in Mexican and Italian dishes; in meat stews, dried beans, lentils, pizza.
Paprika	A red pepper grown in Hungary or Spain. Rich fiery flavor. Method of grinding determines ultimate flavor. Spanish milder than Hungarian.	Used for color and mild flavor. In fish, shellfish, vegetable and egg dishes and in salad dressing.
Parsley	Widely grown useful herb. Rich in Vitamin A. Good source of vitamin when eaten in salad-like portions. Obtainable dried.	Chopped to season and garnish soups, stews, salads, potatoes, stuffings. Sprigs as salad ingredient and edible garnish.
Pepper, Black and White	Black pepper is dried small, immature berries of climbing vine grown in India and Dutch East Indies. White pepper is mature berries with hulls removed.	Used whole in pickling, soups, gravies and meats. Used ground in most meat, vegetable, fish and egg dishes.
Pimiento	Ripe fleshy fruit of a sweet pepper plant. Packed in small cans in its own viscous juice.	Used for spots of brilliant color, mild flavor in soups, stews, salads; as garnish for green vegetables like asparagus, green beans.
Poppy Seed	Tiny seeds of poppy plant—about 900,000 seeds to the pound. Imported from Holland.	Used whole as topping for breads and cookies; as filling for kolachy; in cookies and cake. Garnish for noodles.
Poultry Seasoning	A mixture of several spices as sage, pepper, marjoram, savory, thyme, onion powder and celery salt.	Used in poultry, pork, veal and fish stuffings; to season meat loaf, dumplings, biscuit crusts for meat and poultry pies.
Rosemary	Belongs to mint family. Grown in Southern Europe and Western Asia. Dry, needle-like leaves. Used for flavoring.	Delicious in tomato and egg dishes; soups, fish, roast lamb, pork, beef and duck. Improves stuffings, vegetable and cheese dishes when combined with sage. In biscuit and muffin mixtures.
Rue	A strong scented perennial herb that is woody and bitter in flavor.	A few fresh leaves are an interesting addition to green salads.

Name	Description and Source	Uses
Saffron	Dried stigmas of a species of purple crocus. Grown in Mediterranean region.	Used primarily in Scandinavian and Spanish foods for yellow color as well as flavor in yellow rice, breads and pea soup.
Sage	The most familiar of herbs. Dried leaf of shrub belonging to the mint family. Grown in U. S., Yugoslavia and Greece.	Powerful in flavor. Used to season stuffings, sausage, veal and pork dishes, beans, tomatoes and fresh cheese.
Sausage Seasoning	White pepper is chief ingredient. For pork sausage, sage added; for frankfurters, coriander and nutmeg. Other seasonings added for liver sausage and bologna.	Used in seasoning home produced sausages.
Savory	Grown principally in Southern France. Flavor is at its best in early summer, so term, "Summer Savory" denotes top quality. Has a clean balsam fragrance.	Good in boiled fish. Known as the "bean herb." Fine flavor for peas, beans, lentils, fresh or dried; in stuffing, meat balls, croquettes, meat sauces, gravies, egg dishes.
Seasoning Salt	Includes celery, garlic, onion salt, etc. Made by grinding dried, fresh seeds or dried, fresh vegetable flakes with pure salt.	Used as an alternate for part or all of the salt. Added to meat, poultry and egg dishes and in stuffings and sauces.
Sesame or Benne Seed	From pods within blossoms of a plant grown in India, China and Turkey. Hulled seeds are pearly white with toasted almond flavor.	Baked on rolls, breads and buns to give rich, nutty flavor to crusts. Used in Jewish candy, Halvah. Sesame oil is used in commercial flour mixtures.
Shallots	Small type onion producing large clusters of small bulbs.	Used like garlic to flavor meats, poultry, sausage, head cheese.
Smoke Salt	A synthetic smoke flavoring ground into salt.	Home-curing meat and seasoning bean, lentil or split pea soups.
Sorrell	Belongs to dock family. Long slender leaves used fresh have pleasant acid flavor.	Shredded and added to lettuce, makes lemon juice or vinegar unnecessary. Also in some soups.
Soy Sauce	Made from soy beans by a long curing process.	Used in many Chinese and Japanese dishes.
Tabasco (Hot Liquid Pepper Sauce)	Made by macerating fresh picked, small hot Mexican peppers, salting and curing 3 years, blending with vinegar, straining, bottling. Produced in Avery Islands.	Used to season egg dishes, gravies, marinades, salad dressings, sauces, sea foods, poultry and soups.
Tarragon	Related to wormwood family. Has aromatic leaves of a slightly bitter flavor.	Fresh prized for flavoring vinegar and to shred with lettuce for salad. Fresh or dried adds excitement to fish, egg and chicken dishes, lobster thermidor, fish sauces, beets, spinach, aspics.
Thyme	Grown principally in Southern France. The No. 2 of American favorite herbs.	An essential in the famous New Orleans Cuisine. Present in the French Bouquet Garni. Excellent seasoning for Manhattan Clam Chowder, lamb, meat soups, stews. Good on vegetables such as carrots, peas, egg plant, escalloped onions, also in stuffings.
Turmeric	Root of plant belonging to ginger family. Bright yellow with rich appetizing aroma, and a rather sharp, mustardy flavor.	Often combined with mustard for pickling and used in meat and egg dishes. An ingredient of curry powder.

**Adapted from "Spices—and How to Use Them," published by American Spice Trade Association, New York City.*

FOOD	Size of Serving		Calories	Protein gm.	Fat gm.	Carbo-hydrate gm.	Calcium mg.	Phosphorus mg.	Iron mg.	Vitamin A I. U.	Thiamine (Vit. B_1) mg.	Riboflavin (Vit. B_2) mg.	Niacin mg.	Ascorbic Acid (Vit. C) mg.
	Weight gm.	Approximate measure												
FRUITS														
Apple sauce, unsweetened	115	½ cup	47	.2	.2	12.5	5	10	.5	40	.03	.03	—	1
Apple sauce, sweetened	120	½ cup	88	.3	.2	23.6	5	10	.5	40	.03	.04	—	1
Apricots, syrup	120	4 med. size halves & 2T syrup	95	.7	.1	25.7	12	18	.4	2,600	.02	.03	.4	5
Blackberries, syrup	115	½ cup	86	.8	.2	22.8	20	22	.8	210	.02	.02	.2	7
Blueberries, syrup	120	½ cup	113	.5	.5	30.0	13	7	.6	40	.02	.02	.2	15
Cherries, red, sour, pitted (water pack)	115	½ cup	55	.9	.4	13.7	13	14	.4	830	.03	.02	.2	6
Cherries, sweet, syrup	120	½ cup	114	.7	.2	30.5	13	14	.4	40	.02	—	—	4
Cranberry sauce, sweetened	60	¼ cup	115	.1	.2	31.3	4	4	.2	20	.02	.02	.1	2
Figs, syrup	120	3 figs & 2T syrup	136	.9	.3	36.0	42	25	.5	60	.03	.04	.4	1
Fruit cocktail, syrup	115	½ cup	81	.4	.3	21.4	11	13	.4	180	.01	.01	.4	3
Grapefruit sections, syrup	115	½ cup	80	.6	.2	21.3	15	16	.4	10	.04	.03	.3	35
Olives, ripe*	15	3 large	24	.2	2.6	.4	12	2	.2	30	—	.03	—	—
Peaches, cling, syrup	115	2 med. size halves & 2T syrup	84	.6	.1	22.3	4	13	.4	520	.01	.02	.7	5
Peaches, freestone, syrup	115	2 med. size halves & 2T syrup	88	.6	.1	23.9	5	14	.4	380	.01	.02	.6	4
Pears, syrup	115	2 med. size halves & 2T syrup	78	.2	.1	21.1	9	12	.2	—	.01	.02	.2	2
Pineapple, sliced, syrup	120	2 small or 1 large slice & 2T syrup	93	.5	.1	25.3	30	9	.7	100	.09	.02	.2	11
Purple plums, syrup*	120	3 plums & 2T syrup	91	.5	.1	24.5	10	16	1.2	1,440	.03	.03	.4	2
JUICES AND NECTARS														
Apple juice	185	5 fl. oz.	92	.2	—	25.4	11	19	.9	70	.04	.06	—	2
Apricot nectar	185	6 fl. oz.	101	.6	.1	27.2	13	21	.6	2,200	.01	.03	.4	2
Grape juice	180	6 fl. oz.	120	.7	—	32.7	18	18	.5	—	.07	.09	.4	—
Grapefruit juice	185	6 fl. oz.	78	.9	.2	20.5	15	24	.6	20	.06	.03	.3	65
Grapefruit & Orange juice	190	6 fl. oz.	92	.9	.2	24.2	18	28	.6	80	.09	.03	.4	73
Lemon juice	15 120	1 T 4 fl. oz.	5 36	.1 .5	— .2	1.2 9.2	2 17	2 13	— .1	— —	— .05	— —	— .1	6 50

Nutritive Values of Average Size Servings of Canned Foods
(Courtesy National Canners Association, 1133 20th St., N.W., Washington, D.C. 20036)

NUTRITIVE VALUES OF AVERAGE SIZE SERVINGS OF CANNED FOODS (Continued)

Orange juice	190	6 fl. oz.	85	1.5	.4	21.1	18	33	.5	180	.15	.04	.4	80
Peach nectar	185	6 fl. oz.	93	.6	—	25.2	7	12	.6	600	.01	.02	.6	2
Pear nectar	185	6 fl. oz.	83	.2	.1	22.5	10	14	.7	—	.01	.02	.2	1
Pineapple juice	190	6 fl. oz.	92	.6	.2	24.5	28	15	.9	150	.09	.03	.3	17
Prune juice	180	6 fl. oz.	128	.8	—	34.8	45	72	3.2	—	.06	.15	.7	2
Tangerine juice	185	6 fl. oz.	73	1.7	.6	17.0	35	30	.4	780	.12	.05	.5	48
Tomato juice	180	6 fl. oz.	37	1.8	.4	7.7	12	27	.7	1,890	.09	.06	1.4	29
Vegetable juice cocktail	180	6 fl. oz.	31	1.6	.2	5.6	22	40	.9	2,040	.09	.05	1.4	32
SOUPS (as served)														
Beef broth, bouillon and consomme	200	¾ cup	26	4.2	—	2.1	—	26	.4	—	—	.02	1.0	—
Bean with bacon or pork	200	¾ cup	134	6.4	4.6	16.0	50	101	1.8	550	.11	.06	.8	2
Chicken noodle	200	¾ cup	53	2.8	1.6	6.5	7	30	.4	30	.01	.02	.7	—
Mushroom, cream of	200	¾ cup	111	1.9	8.0	8.2	34	43	.3	60	.01	.10	.6	—
Tomato	200	¾ cup	72	1.6	2.1	12.3	11	27	.6	810	.05	.03	.9	10
Vegetable	200	¾ cup	63	2.6	1.3	10.3	14	34	.9	2,520	.03	.02	1.0	—
Vegetable beef	200	¾ cup	65	4.2	1.8	7.5	10	39	.6	2,200	.03	.04	.8	—
VEGETABLES														
Asparagus, green	115	6 med. size spears	20	2.2	.4	3.4	21	49	1.9	690	.09	.11	1.0	17
Asparagus, white	115	6 med. size spears	21	1.8	.4	3.8	17	38	1.0	50	.07	.08	.9	17
Beans, baked, pork & molasses	125	½ cup	154	7.2	3.8	24.1	70	141	2.6	40	.06	.05	.7	3
Beans, pork and beans—tomato sauce	125	½ cup	140	7.2	2.6	23.1	51	141	2.2	110	.06	.05	.6	3
Beans, red kidney	120	½ cup	108	6.8	.5	19.7	48	149	2.3	—	.06	.06	1.0	—
Beans, green	110	½ cup	20	1.1	.1	4.6	29	21	1.6	450	.04	.05	.4	5
Beans, wax	110	½ cup	20	1.1	.1	4.6	29	21	1.6	110	.04	.05	.4	5
Beans, lima, green	115	½ cup	81	4.3	.4	15.5	31	84	1.9	150	.05	.05	.6	10
Beets	115	½ cup	38	1.0	.1	9.1	17	34	.7	20	.01	.03	.1	6
Carrots	115	½ cup	29	.7	.3	7.0	25	28	.7	15,000	.03	.03	.4	3
Corn, cream style, white	115	½ cup	91	2.5	.7	21.9	3	63	.7	20	.03	.05	1.3	6
Corn, cream style, yellow	115	½ cup	92	2.4	.7	22.5	4	66	.7	130	.04	.06	1.1	6
Corn, whole kernel, white	115	½ cup	70	2.2	.7	16.4	5	52	.5	40	.03	.05	1.1	5
Corn, whole kernel, yellow	115	½ cup	75	2.2	.7	18.0	4	57	.4	150	.03	.05	1.0	5
Mushrooms	90	⅓ cup	17	1.1	.2	3.3	7	81	.7	—	.02	.22	1.8	—
Peas, Alaska	115	½ cup	69	4.0	.4	12.8	23	76	1.9	520	.12	.06	1.0	11
Peas, sweet	115	½ cup	60	4.0	.5	10.4	22	67	1.7	510	.14	.06	1.2	11
Peppers, sweet	40 115	1 med. size 3 med. size	11 32	.3 1.0	.2 .5	2.4 7.0	3 9	7 21	.7 2.0	1,400 3,900	.01 .04	.03 .09	.3 .8	47 136
Pimientos	40 115	1 med. size 3 med. size	8 24	.3 1.0	.1 .3	1.9 5.5	3 7	6 17	.5 1.5	810 2,300	.01 .03	.03 .07	.2 .4	45 130

Nutritive Values of Average Size Servings of Canned Foods

FOOD	Size of Serving		Calories	Protein gm.	Fat gm.	Carbo-hydrate gm.	Calcium mg.	Phosphorus mg.	Iron mg.	Vitamin A I. U.	Thiamine (Vit. B_1) mg.	Riboflavin (Vit. B_2) mg.	Niacin mg.	Ascorbic Acid (Vit. C) mg.
	Weight gm.	Approximate measure												
Potatoes, white	115	3-4 very small	96	2.3	.1	22.0	13	60	1.0	30	.09	.05	1.1	15
Pumpkin	115	½ cup	34	1.4	.6	7.1	22	41	.8	13,000	.03	.06	.6	--
Sauerkraut	110	½ cup	21	1.2	.3	4.2	39	20	.6	50	.04	.07	.1	18
Spinach	110	½ cup	22	2.6	.5	3.3	99	36	2.2	7,500	.02	.11	.4	16
Sweetpotatoes	125	½ cup	123	1.9	.1	32.1	26	63	.8	10,000	.06	.05	.5	20
Tomatoes	115	½ cup	21	1.1	.3	4.5	40	31	.7	1,200	.07	.04	.8	19
Turnip greens	110	½ cup	16	1.6	.3	2.7	110	33	5.0	4,800	.02	.09	.7	22
FISH AND SEAFOOD														
Clams**	85	½ cup	37	6.6	.9	—	73	105	5.3	70	.04	.08	.9	—
Crab meat**	85	½ cup	83	14.2	2.5	—	38	153	.8	—	.04	.05	2.1	—
Lobster**	85	½ cup	75	15.4	1.1	—	55	161	.7	—	.03	.06	1.9	—
Mackerel	105	½ cup	192	20.2	11.7	—	194	287	2.2	460	.06	.22	6.0	—
Salmon, pink	115	½ cup	188	22.7	10.1	—	177	333	1.0	80	.03	.16	8.3	—
Salmon, red	115	½ cup	188	22.7	10.1	—	177	333	1.0	350	.03	.16	8.3	—
Sardines in oil**	60	5 med. or 7 small	168	11.8	13.0	—	212	260	2.1	140	.01	.08	3.0	—
Sardines in tomato sauce (Pilchards)	105	1½ large	227	18.7	15.6	1.6	400	176	4.4	—	.01	.27	5.3	—
Shrimp**	65	10-12 med.	46	9.8	.5	—	36	97	1.4	40	.01	.02	.9	—
Tuna in oil**	100	½ cup	280	29.0	17.3	—	8	350	1.2	50	.04	.12	12.8	—
MEAT, POULTRY, MISC. PREPARED FOODS														
Beef, corned	90	3 oz.	192	22.7	10	—	18	95	3.9	—	.02	.22	3.0	—
Beef, corned, hash	115	½ cup	163	15.8	7.0	8.2	29	168	1.5	—	.03	.16	3.4	—
Beef, gravy	61	¼ cup	30	1.9	1.2	3.0	—	20	.4	—	—	.02	.9	—
Beef, roast	90	3 oz.	202	23	11	—	15	105	2.2	—	.02	.21	3.8	—
Beef stew with carrots	200	¾ cup	158	11.6	6.2	13.6	24	90	1.8	2,000	.06	.10	2.0	6
Chicken, boned	85	3 oz.	151	17.3	8.5	.2	12	126	1.5	—	—	.09	4.7	—
Chicken stew with carrots	200	¾ cup	162	10.2	6.8	15.0	64	62	.8	2,000	.04	.10	4.2	—
Chili con carne	115	½ cup	167	7.5	10.9	9.8	44	175	1.6	—	.04	.09	1.8	—
Luncheon meat, pork	90	2 slices (1¾"x⅜"x3½")	260	13.4	21.9	1.4	8	144	2.0	—	.29	.20	2.5	—
Macaroni/cheese sauce	188	⅔ cup	179	7.3	7.5	20.0	156	143	7.5	207	.09	.19	.8	—
Spaghetti/tomato sauce	188	⅔ cup	143	4.1	1.1	28.6	30	66	2.1	695	.26	.21	3.4	7
Vienna sausage	60	4-5	127	9.5	9.6	—	5	102	1.4	—	.02	.09	1.6	—

OTHER FOODS .... In addition to the foods individually listed in this chart many canned foods make major nutritional contributions to infant, youth and adult diets.

Values for the canned products listed here have been taken from the results of research work sponsored jointly by the National Canners Association and the Can Manufacturers' Institute, and from U.S.D.A. Agriculture Handbook No. 8. Other recent sources have been used in some instances. Values are based on total content of can except where noted. Size servings are based on commonly served portions, representing equal divisions of common can sizes.

*Edible portion **Drained

• CANNED FOODS: SERVINGS PER CAN OR JAR

Product	Content—Can or Jar (approximate)			Size of each Serving (approximate)
	Net weight or volume	Cups or Pieces	Servings	
FRUITS				
Apples; Apple sauce; Berries; Cherries; Grapes; Grapefruit and Orange Sections; Fruit cocktail; Fruits for Salad; Sliced Peaches; Pears; Pineapple Chunks, Crushed, Tidbits	8½—8¾ oz. 16—17 oz. 1 lb. 4 oz. 1 lb. 13 oz. 6 lb. 2 oz. to 6 lb. 12 oz.	1 cup 1¾—2 cups 2¼—2½ cups 3¼—3½ cups 12—13 cups	2 3—4 5 5—7 25	½ cup ½ cup ½ cup ½ cup ½ cup
Apricots, Whole (Medium Size)	16—17 oz. 1 lb. 13 oz. 6 lb. 10 oz.	8—14 15—18 50—60	3—4 5—7 25	2—3 apricots 2—3 apricots 2—3 apricots
Apricots, Halves (Medium Size)	8¾ oz. 16—17 oz. 1 lb. 13 oz. 6 lb. 10 oz.	6—12 12—20 26—35 95—130	2 3—4 5—7 25	3—5 halves 3—5 halves 3—5 halves 3—5 halves
Peaches, Halves Pears, Halves	16—17 oz. 1 lb. 13 oz. 6 lb. 10 oz.	6—10 7—12 45—65	3—4 5—7 25	2 medium halves 1 large half 2 medium halves
Pineapple, Sliced	9 oz. 1 lb. 4 oz. 1 lb. 14 oz. 6 lb. 12 oz.	4 10 8 28—50	2 5 8 25	2 slices 2 slices 1 large slice 1 large or 2 small slices
Plums; Prunes	8¾ oz. 16—17 oz. 1 lb. 14 oz. 6 lb. 10 oz.	7—9 10—14 12—20 40—60	2 3—4 5—7 25	2—3 plums 2—3 plums 2—3 plums 2—3 plums
Figs	8—9 oz. 16—17 oz. 1 lb. 14 oz. 7 lb.	6—12 12—20 18—24 70—90	2 3—4 5—7 25	3—4 figs 3—4 figs 3—4 figs 3—4 figs
Cranberry Sauce	6—8 oz. 1 lb. 7 lb. 5 oz.	¾—1 cup 2 cups 12—13 cups	4 8 50	¼ cup ¼ cup ¼ cup
*Olives, Ripe	4½ oz. 9 oz. 1 lb. 2 oz. 4 lb. 2 oz.	....	....	3 olives 3 olives 3 olives 3 olives
VEGETABLES				
Asparagus Cuts; Beans, Green and Wax, Kidney, Lima; Beets; Carrots; Corn; Hominy; Okra; Onions; Peas; Peas and Carrots; Black Eye Peas; Pumpkin; Sauerkraut; Spinach and other Greens; Squash; Succotash; **Sweetpotatoes; Tomatoes; Mixed Vegetables; Potatoes, White, Cut, Sliced	8—8½ oz. 12 oz. 16—17 oz. 1 lb. 4 oz. 1 lb. 13 oz. 6 lb. 2 oz. to 6 lb. 12 oz.	1 cup 1½—1¾ cups 2 cups 2¼—2½ cups 3¼—3½ cups 12—13 cups	2 3—4 3—4 5 5—7 25	½ cup ½ cup ½ cup ½ cup ½ cup ½ cup

Canned Foods: Servings Per Can or Jar
(Courtesy National Canners Association, 1133 20th St., N.W., Washington, D.C. 20036)

Product	Content—Can or Jar (approximate)			Size of each Serving (approximate)
	Net weight or volume	Cups or Pieces	Servings	
Asparagus Spears (Medium Size)	10½ oz. 14½—16 oz. 1 lb. 3 oz. 4 lb. 4 oz.	9—12 spears 16—28 spears 20—30 spears 115—145 spears	2 3 5 25	4—6 spears 4—6 spears 4—6 spears 4—6 spears
Potatoes, White, Peeled, Whole, Small	16—17 oz. 6 lb. 6 oz.	8—12 55—65	3—4 25	2—3 potatoes 2—3 potatoes
Beans: Baked; with Pork; in Sauce	8¾ oz. 1 lb. 1 lb. 10 oz. 6 lb. 14 oz.	1 cup 1¾ cups 3 cups 12—13 cups	1—2 3—4 4—6 16—25	½—¾ cup ½—¾ cup ½—¾ cup ½—¾ cup
* Mushrooms	2 oz. 4 oz. 8 oz. 4 lb. 4 oz.	⅓ cup ⅔ cup 1½ cups 12—13 cups	1 2 4 36	⅓ cup ⅓ cup ⅓ cup ⅓ cup
Pimientos; Peppers, Red Sweet	2 oz. 4 oz. 7 oz. 6 lb. 13 oz.	¼ cup ½ cup 1 cup 12—13 cups	....	....
JUICES				
Apple; Cherry; Cranberry; Grape; Grapefruit; Grapefruit-Orange; Loganberry; Nectars; Orange; Pineapple; Prune; Tangerine; Carrot; Sauerkraut; Tomato; Vegetable; Vegetable Cocktail	6—8 oz. 12 fl. oz. 1 pint 1 pt. 2 fl. oz. 1 pt. 7 fl. oz. 1 quart 1 qt. 14 fl. oz. 3 quarts	¾—1 cup 1½ cups 2 cups 2¼—2½ cups 3 cups 4 cups 5¾ cups 12 cups	1—2 3 2 4 3 5 3 6 4 8 5 12 8 24 16	4—6 oz. 4 oz. 6 oz. 4 oz. 6 oz. 4 oz. 6 oz. 4 oz. 6 oz. 4 oz. 6 oz. 4 oz. 6 oz. 4 oz. 6 oz.
Lemon; Lime	5½—6 oz.	¾ cup	......	....
SOUPS				
Condensed	10½—12 oz. 3 lb. 2 oz.	1¼ cups (2½ cups prepared soup) 5¾ cups (11½ cups prepared soup)	3 12—16	¾ cup ¾ cup
Ready-to-serve	8 fl. oz. indv. 12 fl. oz. 15 fl. oz. 1 pt. 5 fl. oz. to 1 pt. 9 fl. oz. 3 qt.	1 cup 1½ cups 2 cups 2½—3 cups 12 cups	1 2 3 4 20	1 cup ¾ cup ¾ cup ¾ cup ¾ cup
MEATS & POULTRY				
Chili Con Carne; Chili Con Carne with Beans	15—16 oz. 1½ lb. 6 lb. 12 oz.	2 cups 3 cups 12—13 cups	3—4 4—5 18—24	½—⅔ cup ½—⅔ cup ½—⅔ cup
Corned Beef	12 oz. 6 lb.	....	4 30	3 oz. 3 oz.
Corned Beef Hash	8 oz. 1 lb. 1½ lb. 5 lb. 8 oz. to 5 lb. 14 oz.	1 cup 2 cups 3 cups 12—13 cups	1—2 3—4 5—6 18—24	½—⅔ cup ½—⅔ cup ½—⅔ cup ½—⅔ cup

Canned Foods: Servings Per Can or Jar
(Courtesy National Canners Association, 1133 20th St., N.W., Washington, D.C. 20036)

Product	Content—Can or Jar (approximate)			Size of each Serving (approximate)
	Net weight or volume	Cups or Pieces	Servings	
Deviled Ham	2¼—3 oz. 4½ oz.	⅓ cup ½ cup	3—4 5—6	1½ tablespoons 1½ tablespoons
Deviled Meat; Potted Meat; Meat Spreads	2—3¼ oz. 5½ oz.	⅓ cup ¾ cup	3—4 8	1½ tablespoons 1½ tablespoons
Luncheon Meat	12 oz. 6 lb.	....	4 32	2 slices (3½" x 1 ¾" x ⅜")
Tongue: Beef; Lamb; Pork	6 oz. 12 oz. 1—2 lb.	....	2 4 5—10	3 oz. 3 oz. 3 oz.
Hams, Whole (Small) (Medium) (Large)	1½—4 lb. 6—8 lb. 9—14 lb.	....	3—4 per pound	2 slices (4"x3"x⅛")
Poultry, Boned: Chicken; Turkey	5—6 oz. 12 oz. 1 lb. 14 oz. 2 lb. 3 oz.	....	2 4 10 12	3 oz. 3 oz. 3 oz. 3 oz.
Sausage, Pork; Frankfurters	8 oz. 12 oz.	11—12 8—9 large	3—4 4	3 sausages 2 sausages
Stew: Beef: Lamb	1 lb. 1 lb. 4 oz. 1½ lb.	2 cups 2½ cups 3 cups	2 3 4	¾ cup ¾ cup ¾ cup
Vienna Sausage	4 oz. 9 oz.	8—10 16—20	2 4	4—5 sausages 4—5 sausages
FISH AND SEAFOOD				
Clams	7½ oz.	1 cup	2	½ cup
Crab Meat	5½—7½ oz.	¾—1 cup	2—3	⅓—½ cup
Mackerel	1 lb.	2 cups	4	½ cup
Oysters	8 oz.	1 cup	2	½ cup
Salmon	7¾ oz. 1 lb.	1 cup 2 cups	2 4	½ cup ½ cup
Sardines Sardines, Pilchards	3¼—4 oz. 15 oz.	6—10 6—7 large	1½ 4	5—7 sardines 1½ sardines
*Shrimp	4½—6½ oz.	25—35	3—4	10—12 medium size 6—8 jumbo size
Tuna in Oil	6—7 oz. 13 oz.	1 cup 1¾ cups	2 4	½ cup ½ cup
INFANT FOODS				
VEGETABLES AND FRUITS Infant: Strained; Homogenized Junior: Chopped	4¾ oz. 6½ oz. 8 oz.	½ cup ¾ cup ⅞ cup	....	....
MEATS Infant: Strained Junior: Chopped	3½ oz. 3½ oz.	7 tablespoons 7 tablespoons	....	....
SOUPS Infant Junior	4¾ oz. 8 oz.	½ cup ⅞ cup	....	....

*Declared as drained weight. The number of olives per container varies as to size of the olives.
**Sweetpotatoes also come in 1 lb. 2 oz. to 1 lb. 7 oz. cans.
NOTE: The net weight of various foods in the same size can or glass jar will vary with the density of the food. For the most part only minimum weights are shown in the table.
Cups or pieces and servings in the table have been given in approximates; and sizes of servings are given in rounded numbers in order to furnish a practical guide.

Canned Foods: Servings Per Can or Jar
(Courtesy National Canners Association, 1133 20th St., N.W., Washington, D.C. 20036)

INDEX

A

B

C

C (Continued) | Page Number

D

D (Continued) **Page Number**

E

F

F (Continued) Page Number

G

L

Page Number

M

S (Continued) Page Number

T

T (Continued) Page Number

U

V

W

Y

T (Continued) Page Number

U

V

W

Y

TX 911.5 .C63 1974

Coffman, James P

Introduction to profes sional food service